The Seven Wisdoms of Life

a journey into the chakras

Shai Tubali

scientifically edited by Nir Brosh, M.D.

For information, contact:

MSI Press
1760-F Airline Highway, 203
Hollister, CA 95023
Orders@MSIPress.com
Telephone/Fax: 831-886-2486

Library of Congress Control Number 2012952358

ISBN 9781933455686

Cover design by Carl Leaver

I dedicate this book to the divine intelligence that wove our miraculous subtle structures, thus enabling us to know God and to become ourselves manifestations of divine awareness.

I also dedicate this book to Gabriel Cousens, a kundalini expert and a true Yogi, who served in this play of life as my own gateway, through which I realized the dormant potential of these subtle structures. The love, patience and wholesome knowledge of the true teacher are undoubtedly vital nourishment for every yearning aspirant.

Table of Contents

Shai Tubali

Part One:
The World of the Chakras

Shai Tubali

Introduction

Man is not just flesh and bone. By saying that, I do not mean to support abstract and romantic ideas such as *the soul*. On the contrary, I mean to stress a whole realm of *physiological* dynamics, that may be invisible to our outer eyes but nonetheless are active all the time. Invisible is not irrelevant, just like atoms are a necessity in the total understanding of matter.

There is another anatomy for man, a subtler one, which envelops the visible plain of the physical body like invisible sheaths. This anatomy is extraordinarily important both for the complete understanding of our psyche and for the realization of the further evolution of our consciousness. In-depth inquiries into the nature of this anatomy have taken place in many cultures throughout human history—from the *ancient Egyptians* to the *Mayans*, from the yogic culture in *Hinduism* and *Buddhism* to the *Jewish Kabbalists*, and from *Chinese medicine* to the *Theosophical* and *Anthroposophical* movements of the West. All these doctrines differ mainly in terminology; they agree that there is an amazing and subtle mechanism that supports the existence of the body and psyche, and in actuality, maintains it. These cultures also agree that only through the power of those hidden systems can one's consciousness evolve.

But why do we need a subtle anatomy? The answer is extremely simple: just as we need the brain and senses for the full perception of the outer world, so do we need these subtle layers of consciousness to perceive the inner worlds of ourselves and of the universe, the invisible layers of existence. The subtle anatomy is a system of complex interactions between the visible and the invisible; it connects the two in the same way that the physical body and the brain connect the subjective perceiver and the perceived object.

The hidden anatomy of man shares many parallels with man's visible anatomy. It, too, contains senses and a nervous system, a brain and a spine, only instead of circulating blood and oxygen, it conducts the vital life force, subtle energies, and mental insights, and instead of breathing, it takes in the universal vital breath, without which all of us would instantaneously die. Through it, man is able to maintain his connection with the greater life in himself and in the universe, and he can also develop new connections with it. It is the vehicle through which man can expand his mind toward the greater universe and acquire an intimate touch with it.

Parts of this subtle anatomy are ever active in us. Yet, for the most part, the subtle layers of our anatomy lie dormant, like a seed of consciousness waiting for its time to take root and blossom. This fact is due to our special capacity as humans: the capacity to expand. Unlike animals, which also have a subtle anatomy albeit much less complex, humans can expand their conscious connections with their own selves and with the universe as a whole more and more.

In many respects, one may refer to this subtle anatomy as *the anatomy of our psyche* or, in an even broader sense, as *the anatomy of our consciousness*. The direct implication of this insight is that by understanding the depths of this anatomy, one may acquire a comprehensive map of one's psyche, through which one can navigate in a much more conscious way.

For this reason, I dedicate this book more to the psychological and transformative aspects of this subtle anatomy and much less to the mystical and esoteric aspects. In dealing with the hidden anatomy, many traditions and respected experts describe in detail the colors, symbols, mythology, and spiritual concepts associated with differing layers of our invisible physiology. Here we use the same information to enlighten the relevance of it to our immediate psychological structure.

Traditionally, the mapping of the hidden territories of our consciousness has been used for the sake of spiritual elevation and transformation, but in this book, this application is only a part of a greater whole. Usually, critically missing from these maps are the psychological, therapeutic and psychosomatic dimensions. Simply put, in our times we need a map of the hidden territories of our consciousness not only for navigation of the physiology of enlightenment but also for the decoding of the unbelievable complexity of our minds.

Our inner world tends to become obscure and mystical, but the moment we can see our inside in an ordered and tangible way, we have easy access to ourselves and a better means for self-liberation.

In order to make the subtle anatomy even more accessible, I also let go of almost all known terminology for the sake of a more direct language. Although the knowledge in this book is tremendously influenced by yogic learning, I have made an effort to lay bare these inner worlds so that you, the reader, can get in touch with it directly, here and now, through the immediate reflection of these insights in your very own psyche.

I even intentionally let go of some aspects of our hidden physiology so things won't become too complex to comprehend. One should remember that just as the visible anatomy is shockingly complex, so also the subtle anatomy holds within it much complexity. However, for the sake of clear understanding, I have made the choice to focus only on the essentials, i.e. those elements which I believe can benefit us the most.

Everything in this book stems from my daily direct experience. I never refer to things that I don't fully embrace in my own consciousness. For the last fifteen years, I have solely and passionately dedicated myself to the direct research of my own and others' dormant potential of consciousness. Through meditative experimentation and intense contemplation, I have managed to awaken the subtle layers of spirit and to realize them fully under the close guidance of the American yogi Gabriel Cousens. Out of this direct realization, I have developed The White Light method, which enables all people to activate and utilize their own inner structures, the chakra system among them. It has become a natural skill for me to reflect the other's present subtle levels of activity in my own subtle anatomy, and this skill has been beneficial not only for guiding others toward their own further development but also for my research in the realm of chakras and other subtle bodies. So, this book is an accumulated understanding slowly extracted from both my inner journey of fifteen years and from learning the inner workings of many other individuals in their journeys toward heightened awareness.

Joyfully, my own experience corresponds strongly with the direct experience of millions of people who, throughout the history of mankind, have dedicated much time and energy to penetrate into the subtle anatomy, to document it, and to use it. What you may not realize is to what a degree this is also *your* direct, daily experience—there are parts of the subtle anatomy experienced by everyone but not acknowledged as such. In our present conditioning, supported by a science that believes only in the existence of one superficial layer of reality, we are well trained to ignore what we "know," but the more we recognize it, the more it grows inside of us and expands to new levels of our own consciousness.

Accordingly, we will begin our journey with the most accessible and the most directly experienced layer of the invisible anatomy: the chakra system. Later on (in the Appendix), we will progress toward even subtler realms of the subtle workings.

Shai Tubali

The Chakra System:
Definition and Functions

Definition

Undoubtedly, the Chakra system is the best known, most widely researched, and most accessible layer of energy. The first documentations of this system go all the way back to the ancient Eastern and Egyptian cultures, about four-thousand years ago.

Simply defined, chakras are mediators of energy-matter interaction. The chakra system is the bridge between the physical body and the subtle bodies and also between the physical body and the vital life force of the universe. The chakras are the key energy centers of the whole subtle anatomy and may be regarded as our basic energetic body. As mediators of energy-matter interaction, they translate material energy into spiritual energy and spiritual energy into material energy.

The main function of the chakra system is to translate spiritual energy into physical energy for the sake of physical and psychological wellbeing. Residing in the central confluences of the energetic nervous system, they connect all the different energies: material, emotional, mental, and spiritual.

One may theorize that every biological system complex enough to conduct a certain amount of consciousness through the brain and nervous system must have a number of chakras. These chakras make the connection between all levels of being for the sake of the living organism possible. Human beings have seven central chakras, the perfect number for human complexity.

The *Nadis*

To better understand the workings of the chakra system, we first have to get to know the *nadis*. The term, *nadi*, means stream, and this is exactly what *nadis* are: channels, or empty tubes, that conduct energy throughout the body. There are physical *nadis*, such as nerves, blood vessels and lymph vessels. The *nadis* we are interested, though, are the subtle ones through which energy flows. These subtle *nadis* are *the energetic nervous system*.

The *nadis* carry energy into the brain, the nerves, the endocrine system, the organs, the skeletal system, and the cells. Yogic tradition identifies about seventy-two thousand *nadis*, of which fourteen are considered central. The well-known meridians from Chinese medicine seem, in fact, to be important fragments of the *nadi* system, and acupuncture points are the meeting points between the meridians and the *nadis*. The *nadis* interact with the physical nervous system and convert subtle energy into material energy for the organs, glands, and tissues. They absorb these subtle forms of energy both from subtler bodies and from the universal life force.

The general definition of the physical nervous system is that it is a complex nerve network through which the body functions as a synchronized whole, with the physical nervous system receiving information of stimulants from the inner and outer environment and supervising all processes related to conscious and unconscious behavior. Similarly, the *nadis* are a complex nerve network through which the energetic and psychic systems function as a unified whole, with the *nadis* receiving information on energetic and psychic stimulants from the inner and outer environment and supervising all processes related to conscious and unconscious subtle activity.

Main Function: The Absorption of *Prana*

The chakras dwell in the seven central conjunction points of the seventy-two thousand *nadis*. In a way, they connect them all. This may be similar to the relationship between the central nervous system, located in the brain and the spinal cord, and the network of nerves around the body (i.e., the peripheral nervous system). The seven chakras are like wheels of swirling energy, rotating clockwise, located in the subtle spine of humans. They constantly absorb the vital life force of the universe and translate it into material energy that can be assimilated into the physical nerves, the glands, and the organs.

Vedic literature calls this vital life force *prana*; Chinese literature calls it *chi*. *Prana* means breath of life, which basically implies that there is a cosmic reservoir of energy that enables all living beings to exist and breathe. Once this energy leaves the body, no life remains, and the body will perish. This *prana* is felt as the warmth of life, and that is why, in its absence, the body becomes a cold corpse. So, *prana* is our basic connection with the cosmos, and as long as it flows into our body, filling the nerves, glands, and organs, we enjoy the experience of life. (There are also physical types of *prana* that flow within our bodies).

So, imagine it this way: the universal life force is captured by the seven chakras; from the chakras, it flows through the *nadis,* and from the *nadis* is assimilated into the nerves, glands, and organs. The chakras function as vortexes, which attract the cosmic energy into the endocrine and nervous systems.

For the sake of simply existing as conscious beings on this planet, the chakras require a small amount of universal *prana*. This is enough to maintain the physical activities and the automatic processes of emotions and thoughts. In this context, one cannot refer to chakras as "blocked" or "open," but rather as conductors of a lot of energy or little energy. The more conscious activity is required for the organism, the more energy the chakras demand from the universe. A tremendous intellectual force for example, creates a greater demand for *prana* to enliven the chakras and, subsequently, the brain and its glands.

When a conscious human being becomes extremely spiritual, the chakras become, accordingly, highly active and conduct much more *prana*. Without much *prana*, there cannot be a spiritualizing process in the body and mind. That's why all spiritual traditions invoke practices that enhance the stream of *prana* into the body and within the body.

On the other hand, we don't need highly active chakras unless there is a specific requirement for it in our bodies and minds. Dr. Gabriel Cousens, a psychiatrist and a spiritual teacher, points out that, in his experience with manic psychosis, patients often describe floods of energy from their vertex. This is not a spiritual advantage but rather another form of imbalance.

Location of Chakras

In the yogic tradition, chakras are believed to reside within the central *nadi*, known as the *sushumna nadi*. Inside these three-layered central *nadi*, at their very heart, exists the *Brahma nadi*, the precise location of the chakras. Since the chakras are really three-dimensional, they are visually similar to a light-funnel whose narrow end starts at the subtle spine. Each one of the chakras radiates in four directions, with the exception of the earth-oriented first chakra, which mainly radiates downward as a lower open end, and the heaven-oriented seventh chakra, which mainly radiates upwards as a higher open end.

The locations of the seven chakras are generally agreed to be as follows:

- The first chakra is located in the perineum, the small area between the sexual organs and the anus. It radiates its influence toward the legs and toward the base of the spine.

- The second chakra is located between the sexual organs and the umbilicus.

- The third chakra is located between the umbilicus and the solar plexus.

- The fourth chakra is located in the center of the chest at the level of the heart.

- The fifth chakra is located in the base of the throat at the level of the thyroid.

- The sixth chakra is located between the eyes at the level of the brow.

- The seventh chakra is located in the vertex of the head, like a skullcap.

Each of the chakras is in charge of its own area, both at the level of subtle anatomy and also at the level of physical anatomy. This means that each chakra absorbs vital life force for the sake of the nerves, glands, and organs located in its own specific area.

Chakras as the Anatomy of the Spirit

The translation of *prana* into physical, emotional, mental and spiritual activities is the most basic function of the chakras, but, as mentioned earlier, the chakras are like bridges between systems with different levels of density or frequency. In this manner, they translate emotional energy into mental energy or physical energy into spiritual energy. They form an amazing bridge between all of our levels of complexity. Just like our digestive system, which translates food into ingredients vital for our thinking brain, the chakras function as the main translator between the physical body and the very complex psyche.

One may regard the chakra system as the perfect bridge between the body and the psyche. As the perfect bridge, this system is in a complete parallel with the physical anatomy. One may say that the chakra system is a metaphor for the body and that the body is a metaphor for the chakra system.

Each chakra is like an organ of our spirit, and each of these organs is a direct copy of a physical organ. Although there is a much more detailed explanation in the sections dedicated to each chakra, a brief overview of this principle is presented below.

The first chakra, located at the base of the spine, is associated with the motor system (which consists of the bones, muscles, tendons, cartilages, and ligaments). Psychologically speaking, it is all about our ability to stand up fully erect and fully rooted on this planet. Being able to stand in full presence and never contract in the face of earthly challenges is the central theme of the first chakra. So, we can see the resemblance between the psychological and the physical; both are reflected and bridged in the first chakra. This is why psychosomatic diseases and disorders associated with the first chakra are mainly connected to disruptions in the skeleton, muscles and joints.

The second chakra, located in the lower abdomen, is associated with the sexual organs, and glands and also with the kidneys. Psychologically speaking, it is about our ability to "flow" in the stream of life's adventure and to enjoy the "juices" of life. The metaphor, again, is quite perfect: the sexual organs provide for our most basic participation in the process of life, which is by definition all about procreation, and the kidneys are responsible for the balance of water in the body, which is parallel to the ability to flow and to thirst, i.e. thirst for life. Accordingly, psychosomatic diseases reflect problems in the sexual organs, and glands and in the kidneys.

The third chakra, located in the upper belly, is strongly associated with the digestive system and liver. Psychologically speaking, it is about our ability to digest information and stimulants and to neutralize outer pressures. Our ability to respond to environmental pressures is not different from our ability to digest food and use the good ingredients while disposing of unnecessary or even poisonous ones. For that we need strength, which in psychological terms should manifest as a strong sense of self. Psychosomatic diseases will be mostly connected to the digestive system and liver, often caused by continuous anger or frustration as a poor response to environmental pressures.

The fourth chakra, located in the chest, is associated with the heart and the lungs, and psychologically speaking, it is about our ability to breathe. Breathing is, in itself, a perfect metaphor: allowing the world to enter deep inside and allowing the self to come out to the world. Isn't it obvious then, that this chakra deals with our *relationship* to the world and to all others around us? Allowing oxygen, as our most basic connection to life, to enter properly and to flow in the body is not different from allowing others to enter our innermost selves and to get in touch with us intimately. Psychosomatic diseases will be from asthma to heart conditions, from angina pectoris to simpler pains in the chest—everything connected with lungs and heart.

The fifth chakra, located in the base of the throat, is associated with the throat and thyroid gland, and psychologically speaking, it is about our ability to connect the outer world and the inner world well. It is similar to the challenge of breathing, but here it is more about expression and communication (vocal cords) and also about the ability to bring vital ingredients from the world inside (the throat being the only entrance of the body through which it can receive oxygen and food). So, the throat is the agent through which the inside can be expressed to the outside and the outside can be assimilated. Naturally, the thyroid gland is involved in this process, being the one responsible for the rate of metabolism—that is, the rate of chemical reactions which allow absorption of materials from the environment and production of energy out of them—basically, responding to the environment while maintaining our own structure. Psychosomatic diseases will be connected to the voice, thyroid gland, tonsils and general throat disruptions.

The sixth chakra, located in the lower forehead, is associated with the brain, mainly the neo-cortex and the pituitary gland, and psychologically speaking, it is about our ability to govern mentally our entire complexity of being (on the physical level, the pituitary gland is responsible for guiding the entire bodily system toward a stable and constant condition, through the regulation of the endocrine system). This chakra is also associated with the eyes, so on the psychological level it is connected with our ability to perceive and to properly interpret what we perceive. Psychosomatic diseases will be connected to headaches and migraines, mental imbalances and disruptions in the eyes and vision.

The seventh chakra, located in the vertex, is associated with the gap between the two hemispheres and the pineal gland, and psychologically speaking, it is about our ability to govern our different states of consciousness (on the physical level, the pineal gland is responsible for the modulation of the two basic states of consciousness, wakefulness and sleep). This chakra controls the entire psyche and, in a way, defines its borders and scope. Psychosomatic diseases will be connected to sleeping disorders, imbalances caused by drugs and psychoactive plants, losses of consciousness, head injuries, dislocation of the spirit from the body and pathology of the psyche (i.e., psychiatric disturbances).

From this brief description we can produce a very important insight: the chakras are, in fact, the central organs of the psyche, and each one of the chakras is meant to regulate a specific need in the human psyche. Together, they create a wholesome map of our spirit: the lowest part of the subtle anatomy deals with the basic challenge of living in the material world; the lower belly of the subtle anatomy deals with our connection with the life force; the upper belly of our hidden anatomy is responsible for the sense of individual power; our subtle heart deals with the regulation of emotions; our subtle throat takes care of all linguistic communication and external expression; the subtle lower brain controls the mechanism of the mental realm, including perception and interpretation, and the hidden upper brain is responsible for abstract interactions with the subtle layers of the universe.

Imprints and Impressions in the Chakras

More than anything else, the chakras function as an energetic system, regulating the connection between the body and the subtle energy of life. They also control, as we could see, the connection between the body and the subtle layers of our own consciousness. This second activity adds a very important dimension to the basic energetic dimension of the chakras: a psychological one.

Because the chakras function as mediators between psyche, or consciousness, and the physical body, they carry within them psychological functions, behavioral attributes and also past impressions. In the yogic tradition, these complexities of functions, attributes and impressions are called 'vrittis.'

Vrittis are the activities of the mind—tendencies, thoughts and desires—in its expression *in the chakras*. They interact with the samskaras of the mind (deep impressions left on the subconscious mind from this life or other lifetimes), which are the root cause of vasanas (habitual, circular mental patterns in the brain). One may say that *vrittis* are just in-between the samskaras and their final expression as vasanas—which makes a lot of sense, because *vrittis* reside in the chakras, which are the mediators between the subtle psyche and the physical body.

We can think of the chakras as channels, or even prisms, through which the unconscious radiates its deepest tendencies, desires and impressions. The unconscious breaks through the chakra system into seven different rays, or layers, while each ray expresses itself as the specific *vrittis* in each and every chakra. In this manner, the chakra system negotiates between our deepest unconscious and the brain.

Vrittis may be imbalanced or balanced, overactive or almost inactive. Since they cause many of the mental disturbances in the brain, it is extremely important to learn how to balance them all—and for that there are many spiritual practices (which will be described later on).

There is another extremely important reason to balance the *vrittis* in the chakras: as we now understand, the chakras are responsible for the absorption of life force, but this function is obscured when the chakra system is heavily burdened with imbalanced *vrittis*. When the optimal flow of *prana* doesn't enter one or more chakras, it causes psychosomatic and psychological disturbances. On the other hand, when the flow of *prana* into the bodily system is optimal, which means completely undisturbed, one achieves a sense of ecstasy and joy, physically, emotionally and mentally.

When one is interested in spiritual transformation, balancing the *vrittis* becomes an extremely important goal, because this transformation requires a tremendous flow of *prana* into the chakras. The chakras then must function at their highest, undisturbed power.

In summary, the balancing of *vrittis* is required in several dimensions of living:

1. Physical health and balance. This balance includes equilibrium between the sympathetic and the parasympathetic systems and also more energy for the glands and organs.

2. Emotional and mental balance. Imbalanced *vrittis* radiate themselves into the brain and create turmoil in it, and correspondingly, when the *vrittis* are quiet, the brain is also quiet.

3. Spiritual transformation. Clearing *vrittis* consciously and unconsciously is an essential part of the spiritual process. Later on in this book (in the appendix) the importance of a complete alignment and synchronization between all seven chakras—as a unified subtle body—will be explained in a more spiritual context.

Human Evolution and the Chakras

It is very possible that at the beginning, when human beings had first evolved on this planet, the chakra system mainly functioned as a technical energetic system, which regulated the interaction between the body and the cosmic energy. The more man has evolved, the more psychological layers have been added to the chakras, resulting in the increasing complexity of past impressions. Later on, even subtler layers have been added to the chakras: the transformative-spiritual impressions, wisdom and capacities. So, perhaps the chakras of man have become more complex in time:

from the energetic functioning to a wholesome map of the psyche, and from the outlines of the psyche to a wholesome connection with consciousness or spirit.

A bolder theory is that the chakra system, as the most basic structure of subtle anatomy, had been created along with the appearance of the complex psyche of humans which finally distinguished them from the rest of the animal kingdom. This theory holds within it the idea that the more spiritual capacities were not inherent or dormant in our race but rather *formed* out of the brain's struggle to learn and understand.

Since the chakras function as storehouses of past impressions, and each one of them carries unique impressions according to its role in the subtle anatomy, we can actually find within this system the whole story of the evolution of the human psyche: the seven layers of the psyche as they have evolved in time. So, the chakras can amazingly reveal both the story of human evolution and the hidden structure of the human unconscious. Accordingly, the chakras reflect the psychological growth of every newborn baby on this planet into mature and integrated human beings.

On a practical level, the first implication of this process is that the multi-layered chakras nowadays are more burdened than ever, and that there is much work to do in order to clear and align them. This is the reason why I wrote this book—to help understand the chakras in the context of a much more complex era than the times in which chakras had been first understood and realized.

***

A profound understanding of the chakras provides us with a clear map of our psyche, and thus, a way to navigate our human complexity. This is probably the reason why this process of learning usually evokes so much ecstasy: we finally get to understand ourselves.

The great advantage of the chakra system is the fact that, in spite of its invisibility, it is the most accessible system of the subtle anatomy. The reason is simple: being the closest to the physical body, the chakras are strongly felt by everyone. All humanity shares sensations such as 'broken' hearts, 'suffocation' in the throat and fear paralyzing our legs. People may advise us not to take things too much to heart, not to keep our emotions locked in the belly, to speak our minds and to free our throat. This accessibility is the reason why in this book I focus almost solely on the chakra system. As the most immediate link to the invisible dimension of the subtle anatomy, they are also the most practical vehicle toward our hidden layers of consciousness.

Perceiving the chakra system as the complete map of human psyche makes it possible to use chakras as keys for perfect balance and conscious transformation. Through this system, we can clearly get a full vision of our journey ahead and also see our evolutionary condition as it really is right now. Most importantly, we can understand our full capacity for growth as wholesome and total human beings.

Part Two:
A Deep Journey into the Chakras

Shai Tubali

***

We are about to enter a very deep journey into each one of the seven chakras. As mentioned earlier, this will not be a journey in the usual mythological and esoteric context but rather a psycho-transformative context.

First, there will be a general introduction to the most important psychological themes of the chakra and also to the major psychological disruptions. Following that, each chakra will be introduced in its four possible levels of development: imbalanced, functional (working but distorted), balanced (working, undistorted but without full spiritual capacity) and spiritually awake (working, undistorted and in full spiritual capacity). For each one of the three later levels I will explain the means to achieve them and to stabilize them (you will find it in the 'solutions' section). This, of course, will present us with a totally different understanding of psychological health beyond the functional level.

Then, other very important psychological factors will be introduced:

- Characteristic emotions and typical reactions.

- The type of trauma accumulated in the chakra, and how this type of trauma may shape the personality.

- The chakra-oriented personality. People can be easily divided into seven personalities according to the chakra system. Through this orientation one can understand his typical perception of life and reaction to life. This chakra-orientation might be extremely limiting in its unawakened state, but in its awakened state, these personalities are being transmuted into unique divine aspects. That's why I will mention names of great beings who were typical expressions of the chakra.

- Masculine aspects and feminine aspects in the chakra. These can reflect back to us our more masculine or feminine bias and further potential.

- The type of happiness. In every chakra we aspire to attain a certain form of self-fulfillment, which seems to us to be the realization of happiness.

- The worldview of the chakra: the understanding of the meaning and purpose of life and other concepts such as death, love and God.

- The evolution of the chakra as it is reflected in the process of growth in a human lifetime.

- Psychosomatic disorders accumulated in the chakra.

- Collective imprints in the chakra: how the collective ideas, accumulated in the chakra system of the human race, influence our own imbalances and tendencies.

- The historical phase in human evolution in which the chakra expressed itself the most at mass level. This is the turning point in which the psychological aspect of the chakra has become a natural collective capacity.

- Important interactions with other chakras. This enables us to map our current journey, not only through one separated chakra, but rather, through its more complex interactions. Each one of us has a specific chakras map for certain periods of life, according to specific life challenges and environmental pressures that awaken different chakras' interaction. The chakras need to respond, then, to the psychological or spiritual pressures by clearing *vrittis* and working in full capacity. That's why being able to read our map is extremely beneficial.

- The chakra in spiritual transformation: the role of the chakra in the context of the awakening process.

- Physical, psychological and spiritual practices most recommended for the chakra's imbalances, challenges and teaching.

Now, fully equipped for this long journey, let us begin.

First Chakra:
The Search for Security

Location and General Orientation

The first chakra is located in the perineum, radiating its influence all along the legs and up to the base of the spine. Since the entire *nadi* system flows out from just beneath the first chakra, it is considered, in the yogic tradition, to be the base of our physiology, both subtle and physical, and also of our psychology. That's why it is traditionally considered the 'supportive base'—its functioning determines the functioning of all of our bodily and psychological systems.

The legs play a great role in this metaphor. Every child struggles to stand on his own feet—this is how all human life begins. Once the child develops the ability to stand on his feet, he takes the leap into a new level of independence, which enables him to more freely get in touch with the world around him. But as a man grows older and gets closer to death, it is very hard to stand; it is as if the life force first leaves the legs and slowly moves upwards toward the brain and then even beyond it.

Being the base, or ground, this chakra is highly connected with the force of gravitation. Just as the force of physical gravitation keeps us attached to the ground, the first chakra keeps us connected with the ground emotionally, mentally and spiritually. This can be quite good, considering the fact that every living organism requires nourishment from mother earth. But, in its imbalanced aspect, the first chakra's tendency for heaviness and density pulls us toward identification with matter and earthly attractions, such as family, food, material possessions, the accumulation of things and a tremendous need for belonging. This implies that as long as the first chakra is not sufficiently balanced, we are doomed to exist only in the earthly and materialistic realms.

The first chakra is unique in its mission to draw out subtle energy from the earth; it serves as an open link to the planet's life force, and that is why it is the only chakra that faces downwards. This strong connection with material nourishment evokes polarities, such as feeling nourished versus feeling disconnected from nourishment. That is why this chakra raises the demand for food, physical health and strength, longevity and the ability to utilize the forces of the earth as a life source. When imbalanced, we will ceaselessly feel an insatiable need for food and grounding, and when balanced, we will use wisely the resources of the earth—foods, herbs, air, water and nature—in order to maintain our health and overall wellbeing.

Basic Psychological Themes

The first chakra is all about survival and secure existence in the world. Its most ancient impressions belong to the prehistoric man, who had to do constant battle against the violent forces of nature, such as predators and radical climate changes, as well as his own kind, through territorial and tribal wars. At those times, man couldn't tell for sure if and when he was going to get his next meal, and he had to make his way through life in a constant existential tension. Life seemed vast, cruel and quite indifferent, and every change could lead to a very upsetting and dangerous turning point.

When we carefully observe a street cat, it is easy to see what living in constant existential tension looks like: the cat moves slowly, examining every moving object around it suspiciously, ready to be struck or shocked by life at any given moment. Most of humanity lives just like this cat psychologically: although the majority of the people reading this book don't need to worry about their next meal and predators surely don't disturb their peace, the psychological fear and anxiety that life is a threatening place is completely there. The predators have changed their form, and violent climate changes have transformed into many forms of change in life, which only means that most of the instinctual and physical anxiety of the first chakra have been transmuted into psychological, emotional and mental forms of anxiety.

The imbalanced first chakra dreads change and resists pain. It aspires for an uninterrupted flow of routine, in which all fixed objects of the mind remain just as they are for eternity. This aspiration is quite problematic in the face of the nature of life itself: since life *is* impermanence, there is actually nothing that can remain solid and stable until the end of times, and since at least half of life *is* pain, pain has to loyally accompany every brief moment of pleasure and convenience.

Resisting change and pain, the one perpetual habit of the imbalanced first chakra, is, in actuality, the experience of human suffering. Gautama the Buddha taught that the end of suffering lies, first and foremost, in the realization of impermanence; thus, seeing the endless cycles of life and death as they are can fill our being with serene equanimity. But the imbalanced chakra by its very nature cannot accept change and pain, and is tremendously hesitant in putting its two legs on the shaky ground of the earth.

Setting my two feet on the ground—on the physical ground of this planet—with a sense of security and trust, might seem like a fearsome challenge for the imbalanced first chakra. If I am constantly, consciously and unconsciously, waiting for the next shock, and if everything that I hold dear is violently taken away from me, my brain will react as a defensive mechanism for the sake of the survival of the organism:

it will minimize the level of presence in the body. For example, it will minimize the process of breathing, because breathing is a part of our willingness to allow a flow of connection with the world. It will also observe the whole of life's happenings through a mental and emotional bunker, interpreting stimulants in an extremely reactive and conceptualized way.

And this is where trauma enters into our discussion. Basically, the brain's defense mechanism is to minimize presence in the body. The brain imagines this defense to be quite efficient, as if this helps to avoid shock. But ironically, this state of no-presence-in-the-body leaves the entire organism quite defenseless in the face of life's shocking moments. Walking on the soil of the earth half-asleep only makes things worse.

Trauma happens whenever there is a disruption in the flow of repetitive stimulants. This disruption is immediately interpreted by the brain as a danger signal. If this disruption seems important enough for the brain, or if it is ongoing, it will accumulate the impression in quite a symbolic way, and the moment it senses something similar approaching the organism, it will send danger signals to the layers of sensations and emotions. Since it accumulates many impressions of this kind, the irritation of endless signals of danger leads inevitably to a constant and very tiresome tension.

The brain's reaction to trauma, caused by an imbalanced first chakra, *minimizes* presence in the body precisely at the moments in which the best reaction would be *maximizing* the presence in the body. Instead of minimizing breathing, withdrawing into shock and denial by freezing the body and mind, and registering irrational conclusions about life, one must breathe fully and gently, embrace the challenge and get into direct touch with the situation, while freeing oneself from unnecessary thinking.

The first chakra has accumulated many such shocks, while its main shock is life itself—the general feeling that life is a dangerous place and that one's relationship to life must be one of minimizing options of danger, doing one's best to avoid the many dangers around and simply managing to live through it all. This chakra has a lot to do with avo*ida*nce of life, and with every moment of trauma or shock, the brain, along with the imbalanced chakra, only confirm and re-confirm conclusions of danger, despair and horror: at any moment everything can turn upside down and there will be no safe ground to stand on.

Psychological Reactions of the Imbalanced Chakra

There are two main reactions of the imbalanced first chakra. The first is the too-grounded personality—the one that develops coarse and stiff earthly qualities, almost like a prehistoric hunter—and the other is the ungrounded personality—the one that develops either anxiety or remoteness from life.

The too-grounded personality is the most common one. Many who carry a first chakra imbalance will seek security and stability in life itself, trying to turn life into a safe place. This effort may very well remind us of the famous and brilliant film *The Truman Show*, in which the perfect routine becomes a parallel to happiness. Happiness, for the imbalanced first chakra, is when everything is the same: every morning you wake up with your family, then go to work, make your way through the day with the same habits and reactions, and then watch TV and go to sleep. This is all just fine, and for those who hope for a reincarnation or a heavenly afterlife, repeating this same routine may seem wonderful—even in the afterlife. The same old life... Of course, there is still the threat of death, and the imbalanced first chakra is either in complete denial of the fact of death (thus becoming traumatized whenever death strikes, even when very old people die) or in complete anxiety.

So, the most basic reaction of the imbalanced chakra is to create an undisturbed stability and to connect it with the sense of happiness. One will find much solace and relief in a safe community, such as home and family, a steady job, even a very boring one, material possessions, eating too much to feel heavily grounded, and tribal identification (i.e., ethnic group, nationality, tradition, religion and so on). In fact, the family and its connections with other tribal circles often become the safest ground for this chakra. Don't forget: in the very memory of the prehistoric man, it was quite dangerous to be alone, while being a part of the herd was always much more protected and secure. That's why this imbalanced chakra is terrified of aloneness in any form.

The more evidence of the horrifying impermanence of everything in life is accumulated in the brain, the more resistance and denial solidify within us in order to protect us from life's cruelty. If nothing lasts for long, we might as well cling to our self-created 'permanent structures.' Over and over again, our brain confirms our basic traumatic relationship with life, but there's always a hope and an expectation that there is still a chance to deceive this tendency of constant changing and ending.

The other reactive personality is the ungrounded one. This personality can either manifest tremendous anxiety or some form of denial.

The many accumulated irrational conclusions about life and people make this personality very suspicious. Since the brain's defense is to compare situations to past memories that were connected with pain, it locates any similar sign of danger and then initiates anxiety or a total shutting down. Although one physical attack by someone surely doesn't mean that everyone might attack us at any given moment, this is exactly what our psychological conditioning signals to our entire body and mind. So, instinctual distrust in everything, even in life's gentler vibrations, is a common reaction.

Becoming so suspicious about life and the environment, and thus cultivating a large degree of distrust, is the major cause of hyper-activity in the brain. This means that a first chakra imbalance is the root reason for the daily turbulence of our thoughts and emotions. We worry too much and do our best to control life's possibilities. Our thoughts move crazily in the effort to avoid future possible dangers. Thought becomes calculative, anxious and burdened with possibilities. Every decision seems crucial, because we are afraid of loosing everything. We hold on to possessions, to our homes and to our families as symbols of security. We feel that if we loose something that we believe we own, we will remain horribly defenseless. This is the core of our repetitive and circular thinking: worry and the effort to control. Although many of us share these characteristics of thought, the anxious personality can suffer terribly from this very common illness of the mind.

The other manifestation of the ungrounded personality is the one which, consciously or unconsciously, rejects the very concept of living on this earth. This personality possesses a subtle or not-so-subtle form of death-wish and a strong sense of alienation from the body; it basically wants to avoid life at all costs.

While a safe place on this earth is a tremendous longing for the first chakra, many times accumulated traumas bring us to the conclusion that we do not have a place on this planet where we can rest our heads and experience a sense of belonging. Some of us experienced a form of rejection while in the womb, thus resisting coming out to this world. In their early years, some felt disconnected from motherly nourishment or even material nourishment. Because of these conditions, we concluded that the world doesn't want us and that there is no place for us in this world. This made us unable to grow out of uterine nourishment and to stand on our own feet. Feeling undernourished, we lose the natural ability to develop our own physical strength and our own erect spine.

Sometimes the imbalance expresses itself in this specific ungrounded way: by proving to myself and to everyone around me that I don't belong; by refusing to earn my own livelihood, to find my own shelter and to support myself through food and other vital ingredients; by feeling uprooted wherever I go, and even by constantly wandering from place to place and restlessly making changes in my surroundings. Our wish to avoid pain can bring us to the other end of the first chakra's emotional scale: the protective mechanism of total detachment.

Many times the imbalanced first chakra develops its own distorted spirituality: a spirituality that stems out of fear and the search for comfort and escape from life's cruelty. At the mass level, this is the function of religious ideas: to provide people with comforting concepts that make sense out of this arbitrary life. Religions go as far as providing people with the promise of another life or another world, in which the evil ones will be punished and the good ones will be rewarded—in this way, life seems more like a passageway, and thus becomes more digestible. We comfort ourselves by thinking that we will meet our dear ones in the afterlife, and that there will be rest and redemption for our souls. Meanwhile, we surround ourselves with soothing concepts, such as "all is God's will," "God has given and God has taken away" and "all is for the best."

True and profound spirituality is simply impossible for the imbalanced first chakra, because, by its very nature, true spirituality must be based upon a positive life experience. When there is great fear how can you relax, let go of the future and be in the here and now of meditation? Spirituality is, then, more like a subtle form of suicide, another form of mental and emotional escape that only helps us avoid full presence in the body. In fact, even new-age concepts, such as being in the here and now and accepting everything as it is, are being misused by this basic fear. It may use detachment and even superiority as ways to turn our backs to life's frightening and demanding nature.

Apart from spirituality, there are other forms of escape. These include different forms of fantasies about another world or life and also addictions (such as alcohol and cigarettes) that support self-forgetfulness and avoidance of life's challenges. Anything that may help the complete avoidance of pain and any form of denial, including apathy and the shutting down of all emotions, can fit into this category.

Solutions for the Imbalanced First Chakra

The most important insight for the imbalanced first chakra is that life isn't meant to be safe at all. Life *is* a dangerous place, and losing everything is imminent. After all, death, as a fact, always lurks just around the corner. Our entire effort to force the outer world into perfect stability is quite futile. We may deceive life and ourselves for some time, even for many long years, but eventually, the nature of life will burst out. Even while the wild nature of life remains dormant, we pay a tremendous price for our constant state of anxiety, worry and tension.

The key solution for the first chakra is to create an inner world of stability. Just like the turtle who carries his home on his back, we must cease seeking an illusory external shelter and realize our very own self is the true shelter. Through practices of presence in the body and meditation (not of an escapist nature!), we allow ourselves to finally enter into the body, fully breathe, and accept the challenge. We agree to embrace life out of this inner stability.

No one can flow with life unless there is a stability within one's self. The first role of the meditative process is to awaken a layer of consciousness that is indestructible and cannot be corrupted by life's ever changing circumstances. This is a level of stillness that can be compared to the stillness and immovability of a high mountain. The more our consciousness expands beyond the limitations of identification with the body-mind complex, the more we can allow ourselves to remain in the body, even in the face of apparent dangers. We no longer need to escape, and we can re-educate our brain so it lets go of the survival function of withdrawal and realizes the importance of presence.

All kinds of meditation techniques, as long as they are practiced in this healing context and are not meant to support a subtle suicide, enable us to learn the secret of presence, to utilize it as a way to embrace life as a whole, to cease avoiding pain and to be willing to experience uncomfortable and even intim*ida*ting moments. Only when this inner stability is achieved can we feel a love of life and fully agree to put both our feet on the ground.

If we have grown into a total hypersensitivity, in which everything seems intim*i-da*ting and overwhelming, it is very important to include practices of connection to the earth. We must re-awaken our sense of having deep roots in the soil of the earth, agree to the harsh experience of physical pain, and accept living in a physical body that is animalistic in nature. This is where some roughness is needed—one could say that we can only face the forces of nature by becoming a force of nature ourselves.

Meditation and other practices of awareness are not enough to heal the imbalanced first chakra. One must remember that we have all experienced many traumatic moments as the result of many years of walking on this planet half-asleep. We have to clear away all of these moments of shock, because they have imprinted us with strong reactions both in the body and in the mind. In fact, we cannot really experience the fullness of this very moment because of all the memory-connections that have turned into powerful imprints, and consequently, into patterns.

The most recommended way to free ourselves from these memory connections is to use techniques that combine therapy, spirituality, enlightenment and psychology because through them we can learn to heighten our awareness even in our moments of lowest awareness, those moments in which we have retreated to an instinctual level of being. The remedy for the negative memory connections of traumatic moments is to implant higher awareness inside of the moments to a degree that one can actually disentangle the memory connections that have been created.

Through the simultaneous inner work of freeing ourselves from past reactions and learning to remain in full presence from now on, we can stop this mechanism of reaction (which, in the east, was considered to be the workings of karma). Slowly but surely we learn how to still our minds, let go of worries about the future, accept the movement of change, get rid of many forms of escape and develop a deeper inner form of spirituality.

The Three Levels of Functioning

The Functional First Chakra

We are able to create, for ourselves and for our dear ones, a shelter and to produce work, money and food. We can maintain family, marital or any other long-term committed relationships, and we develop healthy routine patterns. We possess the natural qualities of patience and endurance, which are highly needed for any genuine building process in the material world. We do not escape life's challenges, even when they are hard and evoke within us many psycho-physical reactions. We don't let our fears stand in our way. Although our brain is clearly over-active, we manage to overcome its high level of worry and stress. We may experience life as an ongoing battle, and we may experience a constant existential tension, yet we support ourselves with empowering concepts and possess a strong will to live. We are able to realize that food is meant, before anything else, to nourish us, though some level of addiction and attachment in relation to food is still clearly present.

The Balanced First Chakra

Our fundamental experience of life is positive. A deep 'yes' bubbles within us in response to the challenges of life. We take full responsibility for our suffering, as we realize that suffering is caused by a lack of presence in which we create irrational conclusions about life, people and ourselves. Our major traumas are resolved, and we learn to develop full presence in the body at all times and in all circumstances. We agree to feel everything without contraction, including physical agony. When a major shake-up comes we welcome it without resistance or anxiety, thanks to our realization that big turning points are gateways to transformation and growth. We are able to become proactive, invite changes into our lives, 'live with death,' and accept and love endings. Our oneness with the constant stream of change enables us to be immersed in the now so we never look back, clinging to past memories, experiences and people. We deeply understand that outer stability is quite unreliable, and we shift our attention toward the cultivation of inner stability, which is much more rewarding. Our ability, then, to meditate and to relax in the here and now, even with our eyes open and while walking in life, is ever growing, and our brains are becoming much calmer. Our practice of spirituality can become a new ground for a true and fearless love of life, in which we don't need to conceptualize in order to embrace both pain and pleasure. Knowing of the indestructible element within us can allow us to fearlessly feel whatever comes our way. God is not a comforting idea, but rather begins to manifest as all of life. We are not afraid of being alone and apart from the herd, and we carry within us a sense of belonging, both to the planet and to the spirit. We connect freely with traditions and all kinds of social and religious structures, including our own family, but we don't have a psychological need to belong. We connect healthily with the forces of the earth—food, herbs, water and nature—and we learn how to consciously use them in a way that actually nourishes us physically and spiritually.

The Awakened First Chakra

When the spiritual capacity of the first chakra awakens, it is the beginning of a tremendous journey of transmutation from matter into spirit, traditionally called 'the awakening of the *kundalini*.' This awakening is the upward movement of the life force stored beneath the first chakra, a life force that is usually only partially used for the mundane functioning of body and mind. Instead of working with the force of gravitation, in service of earthly needs and desires, it begins to awaken its dormant spiritual layers and turn them upwards, toward the seventh chakra, while merging more and more with cosmic *prana* which pierces its way downwards through the crown chakra. We will discuss this whole process in much more detail in the appendix, but for now the important thing to understand is that the awakening of the first chakra—which is the basic realization that 'I am not a body but rather a spirit, a vibrating life force, moving through a body'—begins the entire spiritualization process. The initial inner stability which we discovered in meditation transforms into a tremendously joyful release from earthly bondage. One realizes that the purpose of life is not belonging to the earthly world but rather belonging to the world of spirits, and so, one looses their basic attachment to the sensory world, to material possessions and to the basic psychological instinct of survival. Along with this liberating realization, the life force beneath the first chakra is also being 'shot' again and again through the central *nadi*, the *sushumna*, evoking powerful spiritual experiences, which strengthen one's trust in the spirit even more. This means, in conclusion, that the first chakra, being the base of the subtle spine, controls our entire 'spiritual spine'—that is, our ability to stand on this planet as magnificent spiritual beings. In a way, we realize that matter and earth are just another spiritual dimension, and through this realization, we begin to view our material bodies and the objective physical world in a more airy and less dense light. From this moment of realization on, we are deeply nourished by the most refined 'food' of cosmic *prana*, and we lose any level of attachment to material food.

Polar Emotions

A death wish / clinging to life, anxiety / security, fear / stability.

Type of Trauma

All traumas, at the instinctual level, are stored within the first chakra, but more specifically, traumas that are unique to the first chakra revolve around physical survival and life-threatening situations. This category includes fighting the forces of nature, dangerous diseases, wars, near-death experiences, physical shocks while in the womb and during birth, times in which our dear ones are exposed to a great danger, physical attacks and abuse. There are also financial traumas, in which we find ourselves heading toward the danger of deprivation or hunger, and traumas in which we lose our homes or lands (or move to another country or take on the burden of the survival of a family or a tribe). It is important to understand that since we are heavily influenced by collective consciousness, especially when we have an imbalanced first chakra, we might also be troubled by the physical traumas of our nation, religion or ethnic group.

These kinds of traumas lead us to the conclusion that *life is dangerous.* It may even lead us to feel that being born into this world was a sad mistake. We will sometimes feel so weak in the face of life's challenges that we will actually feel victimized, as if everything in life is meant to do us harm. This might cause anxiety, and gradually, we will begin to wish for an extremely repetitive and predictable life. We might do our best to avoid many of life's experiences and adventures and even become hypochondriacs. Anxiety might express itself through fear of a specific way of dying, such as a fear of heights, animals, cars, elevators, deep water and so on. Our anxiety might grow to such an extent that we perceive *any* kind of life change (i.e., the crumbling of a marriage or a loss of job) as a life-endangering threat.

Type of Personality

Traditionally, the symbol of the first chakra personality type is the ant. This personality is drawn to create stable structures and foundations in the different realms of life. Laying a solid ground and creating perfect structures seems, to this personality type, to be of tremendous importance. This personality is obedient to the law, aspires to settle down, is stable in nature and is very productive. These are the hardworking men and women, mostly salaried employees, who enjoy routine, security, stable income, a house and a family. They are not inclined toward adventures and don't enjoy too many changes. Usually they tend to fit into traditions, such as religion, nationality, heritage and history, and appreciate the sacredness of the land, the cycles of life and the preservation of ancient wisdom.

In general, this type of people is endowed with qualities such as groundedness, patience, endurance, stability in relationships, loyalty, respect and high moral values. However, when they are thrown out of balance, they become anxious or completely dull and apathetic. They might become too grounded, possessive and sometimes even aggressive when they feel they need to defend and protect their 'groups' of identification. They are also prone to inflexibility, stagnation and nostalgia over the past and over minor and peripheral details. They might also demonstrate dogmatism, holding on to rules and laws of any kind. These imbalances can keep them away from any form of profound spirituality, which always deals with a direct communion with the mystery of life. When physically unbalanced, they might suffer from obesity, slow digestion and constipation.

This personality type constitutes a large part of the human population. In the ayurvedic system, they are kapha types, grounded and 'heavy.'

Famous First Chakra Expressions

Moses, Confucius: creators of social order as an expression of divine order.

Male and female energies

The male quality of the first chakra is like the stability and stillness of a high mountain. It is deeply rooted in the ground, both the physical and the spiritual. The female quality is the ability to trust life as if nothing ever occured, to accept everything as it is and to flow wisely in the stream of change. This female quality is river-like.

Type of Happiness

The type of happiness associated with the first chakra is a sense of security and stability, being with family and tribe, and the feeling of having a place on this planet to which they truly belong.

Life's Meaning and Purpose

Life is all about order, health and balance. Family ties are most important, followed by being loyal to outer circles of identification, such as religion and nationality. Love is family and, sometimes, faith in God; Death is a sad event; God may be a comforting father figure.

Ages of Development of the First Chakra

From the womb to the age of seven, the most characteristic period in development is the struggle of birth and the baby's first year, during which he fights to settle in and relax inside his body. This is the time when we adapt ourselves to the world around us through a growing sense of belonging to our body, family, community, tribe, and nation. Inevitably, we experience total identification with primordial instincts and the physical body.

Psychosomatic Disturbances

The human spine is a great symbol of our ability to stand fully erect on this planet and on our own two feet. Correspondingly, since the first chakra controls the entirety of the skeletal and muscular systems, all disruptions connected with the spine, joints, tendons, ligaments and muscles have a psychosomatic link to a first chakra imbalance.

Also included in this category are chronic exhaustion, chronic back pains, injuries, paralysis and the inability to become rehabilitated (after injuries, surgeries or long diseases). In short, everything that is connected to an inability to overcome physical struggles and to stand back on our feet is included in this category.

Obesity, in the context of psychosomatic imbalances in the first chakra, is the expression of the too-grounded personality, while anorexia nervosa is the expression of the ungrounded personality. Anxiety attacks are also the expression of the later personality.

Collective Imprints

The first collective imprint is the accumulated traumatic experiences of the race: natural disasters, world wars, massacres, hard violence of any kind (natural or human-inflicted), plagues, long periods of starvation, and great financial crises. All of these memories make us conclude, collectively, that life is indeed a dangerous place—which is a good enough reason for constant existential tension.

The second major collective imprint is the societal inclination of gravity toward and attachment to the earthly elements of our being. This imprint is based on the assumption that only matter exists (this is also the basis of our scientific materialism). We are encouraged to become heavily attached to 'permanent' and 'fixed' social structures, such as families and nations. Biological connections are regarded as supreme forces within us, and death is our collective enemy.

One last major collective imprint is the common religious spirituality. Totally opposing the materialistic view, here we are encouraged to look beyond this world and to prepare ourselves for the other, better world, be it paradise or some other redemptive dimension. The material realm seems like a passageway, and material existence is considered low and degraded. This imprint creates within us an unconscious 'no' to life on this planet.

Evolution of the World

The chakra first developed with the evolution of all biological creatures and on into the prehistoric man and woman. It is rooted in the genesis of human culture, and is all about man's primordial relationship with nature—his struggle and effort to adapt to the violent forces of nature.

In those times of evolving human culture, consciousness was a very basic existential feeling without any individual mind, only tribal mind. Time was a perpetual existence, in which every day seemed like the first day. Consciousness was in harmony with the world around it, just like an animal that is deeply rooted in its surrounding nature. Naturally, every newborn baby experiences this passing stage of primordial consciousness.

Common Interactions with Other Chakras

Along with the second and the third chakra, the first chakra is the seat of primordial sensations and the instinctual relationship to the sensory world. Correspondingly, these three, when awakened, create a mature relationship with the world, in which we experience a high level of independence and inner strength. We become less easily influenced and rather self-sufficient.

The first chakra connects all the other six at the level of traumatic registration. When the basic layer of the traumatic relationship with life is removed from the first chakra, it gives way to the healing process in all other chakras.

In the Process of *Kundalini*

The first chakra is considered to be the first granthi, or knot. *Granthis* function as locks that prevent the flow of energy until the nervous systems, both physical and energetic, are truly ready. When we untie this first knot, we liberate ourselves from the imprisonment that was caused by the illusion of belonging to the sensory world. This is the initial step for the force of *kundalini* in the process of self-spiritualization.

Recommended Practices

As the first chakra imbalance is all about resistance to change and pain, most of the recommended practices aim at changing this fundamental resistance.

Before anything else, it is most advisable to, from time to time, take a sober look at your life up to this very moment and to ask yourself: was there really any good reason for all the energy wasted on worry and tension? Can't you see that life has its own peculiar way to always, somehow, sort itself out? There is nothing practical or sensible about worrying; try to gain this wisdom by simply observing each and every past trying experience: didn't it sort itself out? Life is like an endless stream, and as such, it always moves swiftly, and never stops.

One has to try his best not to resist pain, because resistance turns pain into suffering. When pain occurs, allow it to be and to flow within your body and mind, reminding yourself that this is a natural and inevitable part of life. Try not to protect yourself by bringing up all kinds of comforting and reassuring mental concepts. Techniques, such as vipassana meditation, can help you create a healthy disassociation from emotional and physical pain. You can even invite pain intentionally into your life, welcoming it with a ready heart—this is a great gesture of fearlessness. Always be willing to experience pain to its fullest, and then, after exhausting its teaching potential, let it go.

Any practice that involves facing death and integrating it into our lives is important for the first chakra. You can feel the presence of death in the midst of life whenever you experience endings of any kind. When something you hold dear—a relationship or a job, for example—subsides and fades away, you can feel the sweetness of death in the last few precious moments with them.

Meditation is extraordinarily essential for the balancing of the first chakra. Deeply meditate in order to realize, again and again, that which is not subjugated by time and change, that which never dies. As long as we feel that we totally depend on changing circumstances, we are inevitably doomed to be fearful and miserable.

Aside from a daily practice of meditation for fearless living, we have to go through other various practices to enable full presence in the body and spirit: practices for clearing major traumas (possibly also from past lives) through psycho-transformative techniques; practices of connection to the earth and to the animal kingdom; practices of presence in the body and deep grounding, and practices for creating stability in life while still initiating conscious changes and adventures from time to time.

For the ungrounded, escapist personality, who often encourages unnecessary changes in order to avoid pain: practice committing to one thing or one place for a long time (a job, a land or a long-term, responsible relationship), and also, intentionally look for coarse and demanding situations, so you don't become too gentle and vulnerable.

For those who choose stability, even if life's structures are completely distressing: practice taking your chances and creating a big change for yourself.

Understanding the vital nourishment from the forces of the earth is essential. Look for better ways to utilize the amazing vibratory and healing forces of nature through natural foods, pure water, herbs, physical activities and direct connection with the soil through gardening or communion with nature.

Second Chakra:
The Search For Joy

Location and General Orientation

The second chakra is located between the sexual organs and the umbilicus. It governs the sexual glands and organs, including the uterus, and also governs the kidneys. It is interesting to note that, within that area, there exists what Chinese medicine recognizes as '*jing*', the kidney essence that is the material basis for the entire physical body and considered to be the fuel on which the body lives and from which the body draws power for all activities. Correspondingly, in Ayurvedic medicine the term '*ojas*' describes the vital life force and reserve of vital energy. Just like '*jing*', this life force is equated, at least partially, with 'the fluid of life', and is also connected to the function of the kidneys. Semen, for example, which is the seed of creation, is connected both with *jing* and *ojas*. These two terms can give us a sense of what the second chakra is all about: it is the seat of the life force in the subtle body.

Also, it is not a coincidence that Japanese martial artists concentrate on what they call the 'Hara': the vital spirit and force that resides just below the navel.

Another connection is the fact that adrenalin, which among other attributes is the hormone of an over-excited sympathetic nervous system, is secreted by the adrenal glands that sit atop the kidneys. This is related to the body's responses to peak life experiences that are very often over-stimulating, and sometimes verging on dangerous. The adrenal gland also balances stress in the body in general, as it secretes cortisol—another 'stress hormone.' This level of kidney functioning correlates with the very experimental and experiential character of the second chakra.

The navel is a powerful symbol of the connection or disconnection to the greater life force. When we were fetuses, we were nourished through the umbilical cord; then it was cut off, and we had to develop an independent connection with the nourishment and energy of the external universe. We could no longer rely on this inner, safe environment; we were forced to rise to our feet and to learn how to suckle from the great 'mother' of life. Naturally, this ability to develop an independent connection to the life force depends on our experience with maternal love and support, both in the womb and in our very early childhood.

This chakra's direct relation to the sexual organs, the centers of primordial pleasure, makes it, before anything else, the 'pleasure chakra'—the one that regulates psychological issues revolving around pleasure and loss of pleasure, as well as attachment to orgasmic peaks and fear and avo*ida*nce of such peaks.

Basic Psychological Themes

Close your eyes for a brief moment, and try to imagine what it was like in the 'time' of the big bang: condensed, singular energy bubbling and fizzing, and then... in a great explosion, which was probably like a cosmic orgasm, this unitary energy began to rapidly expand and unfold, diverging into many different and even contradictory forces, and at the same time, passionately forming alliances between identical/different particles—short lived alliances that slowly but surely created planets and creatures. This is, so to speak, the second chakra of the universe: the creative fire of the cosmos, which pushes everything first toward erotic merging and then toward breaking apart in order to create even more complex unions; it is the power of creation, passion and eruption.

The second chakra focuses on our participation in this process of creation and procreation and on our involvement in life's play of energies. It is the fire of life force within us, wishing to burst out and connect with the greater life force of the universe. This life force creates within us the urge to become an active partner in the great celebration of life, and would have us explore every little bit of every variety of experiences offered to us by nature and the senses, be it joys and pleasures, peak experiences and wild experiments, or the expression of creativity (such as biological creativity, giving birth to a child, and also subtler forms, like the various arts).

The first image that comes to mind when describing the second chakra is spring time: imagine the soil fertile, opening itself like a womb toward the open sky and tender sun; imagine the fields of flowers, with all their sensual gorgeous colors bursting out from this soil; imagine the bees buzzing with excitement, while pollinating flowers... All creatures, including sensitive humans, become more sensual at springtime. The whole atmosphere is a celebration of sex and procreation.

Another great visual of the second chakra is the image of a woman giving birth, while her husband escorts her in this journey with eyes wide open in wonderment. No one understands this miracle of life: how is it that from a sperm cell fusing with an ovum a whole human personality comes into being, and we, as mother and father, get to become the vehicles of this great mystery of life? The most basic bliss that is being experienced at the moment of birth is found in the feeling of oneness with the forces of creation; it is a peak of creativity, and our second chakra rejoices.

Life is full of possible experiences. In fact, from the second chakra it is viewed almost as a Dionysian feast. There is a vast spectrum of possible joys and pleasures, which one may regard as 'the juices of life.' We are equipped with senses that allow us extreme experiences, and naturally, when the second chakra is healthy, it wants to take them all in.

Indeed, when we were small children, and maybe even in our later youth, it all seemed quite fun. Life seemed like a great playground and life's possible experiences like magical gateways. Our joy of living was based on this sense of having many open possibilities and the feeling that we were allowed to experiment. This is what we often refer to as innocence—and, correspondingly, as the loss of innocence.

Slowly but surely three different blockages have restrained and narrowed our joy of experimentation. The first one was morality; our parents and other authorities disproved of our different experiences—representing the imbalanced 'higher', 'social' chakras, which suppress the natural energies of the lower second chakra. While we played innocently with the different energies of life, they showed up with sour and angry faces, calling us a 'bad boy' or a 'bad girl', and telling us, often quite violently, that what we did was actually wrong and forbidden. There wasn't much logic in it for us, it seemed more like the whim of adults rather than rationalized thinking. Perhaps it was us playing with everybody's shoes in the house, or touching our genitals while becoming overwhelmed by the simple flow of pleasure; whatever it was, we had to succumb to these whims of strange morality and stop doing what we were doing, or learn how to do forbidden things secretly and in the dark.

Morality follows us like a shadow during puberty and onwards. There are numerous should's and shouldn't's that escort us wherever we go, limiting our possibilities and freedom of experimentation. Basically, to be a 'good person' means to fit to social custom, so we do our best to be considered 'good'—the problem is that, too often, being good equals minimizing our life force, and therefore, limiting our joy of life. We teach ourselves to repress our passions, since too much joy, being overflowing with energy and total experience of the senses, is simply 'inappropriate'. Eventually, we become our worst persecutors; we are divided into two persons: the sinner and the oppressor, and we begin to hide facts even from ourselves.

Morality in religions and social structures is all about conforming oneself to a given order. Ever since the biblical story of *Genesis*, in which the eating the forbidden fruit expelled human beings from the garden of Eden, and in which self-awareness implied that one would become ashamed and guilty of one's naked body, we have been given an almost endless set of moral rules that makes us afraid of our own body, the life force and the different energies that are swirling inside of us.

One may very well regard the second chakra as the seat of the suppressed libido. Religions and the designers of social structures have never been fond of the idea of sexual freedom. We have been taught that there are many low impulses that we should deny and transcend for the sake of holy marital security and stability. Religions have regarded sexuality as low, ungodly and evil—in short, immoral. To be more accurate, the problem was never procreative sexual intercourse in itself, but rather, sexual *pleasure*. The thing that most troubles us, consciously or unconscious-ly, is that our sexual urges are inherently pure and innocent. The sexual drive is ex-tremely blind to 'good' and 'bad'; it simply moves toward the object of attraction in order to merge. As young boys and girls, we were intimidated by adults who warned us to avoid graphic sexual scenes in the cinema, to avoid exposing our bodies, to direct our passion only toward heterosexual attraction, to shy away from 'strange' combinations of partners, to fear the 'beastly' elements of sexual desire, to avoid too much ecstasy and overflowing orgasmic sensation, to be ashamed of masturbation and to aspire to a 'Catholic' holy marriage. Indeed, sexual fears and suppressed de-sires play a major role in the second chakra's psychological spectrum.

The second blockage that hinders the balanced functioning of this chakra is traumatic experiences and irrational conclusions that resulted from our joyful ex-perimentation. Every child is taught to avoid touching flames, and that makes per-fect sense, but what about the many burns caused by playing with the metaphorical fire of life? Fire, as the metaphor for passion and desire, is exciting and powerful, but it can also scorch and leave marks of great distrust and disappointment. A young girl can joyfully play with a partner and try out different sexual sensations, but then her uncontrolled partner might become harsh and even rape her; a young boy can try to penetrate a partner but prematurely ejaculate or, embarrassingly, have no erection at all; a teen boy might experience pure pleasure with another boy, resulting in a total failure to fit his sexual pleasure into his family's set of moral values; someone can have a terrible experience with psychedelic drugs or jump happily from a cliff only to break his head and almost die. Many such experiences may lead us to the sad conclu-sion that whenever we venture into bold and daring, or even playful territories of life, it might end in a great danger or even death (or in an earth-shaking discovery about our true nature). So, our brain and the imbalanced second chakra will warn us from then on not to take too many risks and to 'settle down.'

Even the simple experience of falling in love may end up as a traumatizing ex-perience—we give in to a complete ecstasy (to the 'butterflies' in our belly), but then we are 'shocked' when we are rejected. We then promise ourselves that we will *never* fall in love again and that we will avoid the pain of risking and losing so much. We reject the fact that, as far as pleasure is concerned, pain is on the other side of the coin and always will be.

There is yet another important sub-category for this blockage: in very unfortu-nate events, such as sexual abuse, our blockage is not the result of our own hunt for pleasure, but rather the result of a forceful invasion. These events—including rape, pedophilia, incest, sexual humiliation and so on—will leave traumatic imprints on the second chakra, forever connecting our most powerful organs of pleasure to pain or even punishment.

The third kind of blockage is not inflicted on us by others, but is rather a result of our brain's poor functioning. Since the central function of the brain is to maintain the organism's safety and survival, both physically and psychologically, it accumulates two major types of memory connections: the first type links certain situations with possible danger—leading to the resistance and avo*ida*nce of pain, which is the cause of suffering in the first chakra—and the second type connects certain situations with possible pleasure—leading to attachment to convenience and pleasure, which is the cause of *desire* in the second chakra. This is the reason why every moment of joy and pleasure is carefully registered in the brain, and turned into an object of desire. Desire simply means: wanting to repeat an enjoyable experience over and over again, or wanting to further enhance the same experience. When the brain gets used to an experience, it is no longer satisfied by repetition itself, so it strives to increase the sensory stimulants. (On the physical level, while the intensity of the stimulus increases, the brain regulates and diminishes the number of receptors, and thus we need more of the stimulus in order to achieve the same level of joy.)

Naturally, this effort to perpetuate every moment of joy and pleasure gives birth to many kinds of addictions and obsessions. For the imbalanced second chakra, there is a great confusion between pleasure and happiness, so it is always on the hunt for every possible way to increase pleasure—but the disaster of self-destruction awaits it on the other end.

Because of these three major blockages—morality, traumatic experiences and the workings of desire—we might become disconnected from our natural life force, which also means that we become disconnected from the celebration of life and nature. Yet, there are other factors that may cause a state of imbalance, such as being born with a low *jing* or feeling disconnected from the creative power. This later factor might include various blockages, from infertility to the famous 'writer's block.' Whenever we feel that we cannot be a part of the creative flow and whenever our creative urges feel 'stuck' within our belly, we are at risk of becoming depressed.

There are several ways to participate in creation in life. The most common way is, of course, sex and procreation—this is the physical level of creation. The second common form of participation is through the various arts and any kind of creative ideas—this is the emotional and mental level of creation. Ingrained in this creative impulse, there is a much subtler impulse, which one may regard as 'the merging impulse.' This is a spiritual urge to merge with life and to lose all barriers in an ecstatic and cosmic 'orgasm.' The tantric teachings, for example, are about transmuting the sexual drive into a spiritual merging. We are being urged by this impulse to move from physical, emotional and mental unison with nature and life, to the final, subtlest form of lovemaking. This is, in platonic terminology, the workings of the 'lower Eros' and the 'higher Eros.'

When we cannot 'give birth' to anything—be it a baby, an idea or a spiritual longing—our second chakra doesn't fulfill its most basic drive.

Psychological Reactions of The Imbalanced Chakra

Morals and religious ideas, the first type of major blockage, inevitably lead to feelings of sin, guilt, shame and fear of punishment. Morals make us fear our own natural energies and feel that they are unpredictable in nature and might lead us into dangerous, humiliating situations or to shocking discoveries. As a result, we begin to limit the flow of life's juices both within us and outside of us. On the psychosomatic level, this limits the flow of energy in the second chakra, and might result in both depression and problems with the flow of water and liquids in the body in general. On the mental level, it leads to rigidity and dogmatism as an escape from the sensual dimension.

One may think of the image of the suppressed monk, who tries his best to transcend his 'evil' and ungodly impulses. Instead of transmuting the life force, he shies away from it, and this results in a freezing of the life force—life cannot flow from the lower to the higher level within him. He escapes into rigid thinking and false purity, and he idealizes this state of freeze.

The moment we turn off the inner fire, we become lifeless and depressed. The more we conform to being small, 'nice' and invisible, the more we narrow our range of freedom in all directions and block our ability to feel that everything is possible. Slowly but surely, we become 'outsiders,' those children who stand outside of the game, watching all the other children playing with joy. In fact, we are not truly alive, because from time to time, life demands experiments outside of the realm of accepted morality. All life begins with senses and pleasure, and only through senses and pleasure can one build a joyful and life-loving spirit.

For example, even the choice to become a monk must be followed with a very conscious and welcoming effort to work with our basic drive toward pleasure—otherwise, one may ironically move even further away from the path of spiritual merging.

In cases of traumatic experiences and blockages of all kinds of creative expressions, our usual reaction is to shut down our participation in life's flow—in other words, we become depressed. When we conclude that it was indeed a grave mistake to even try to participate wholeheartedly and totally in the creative process, we simply turn off our life force and withdraw from the constant movement of life. Depression is the reaction of the complete outsider; it's a silent protest against the life force that only wishes to flow in joy. It might lead to boredom and emptiness, dullness and chronic fatigue, loss of sexual desire and an inability to fully enjoy the orgasmic experience. A 'loss of appetite' is a great metaphor for this state of 'revenge' on life.

There is, of course, the other side of possible reactions as well: the development of a compensating addiction, such as obesity or marijuana.

The third blockage, the mechanism of desire, is a big problem for many people. Although desire is a universal problem, caused by the lower functioning of our present brain, there are those who 'catch it' more badly than others. For example, when someone represses his natural energies due to moral or religious ideas, it will, ironically, increase desire. This is because the life force is always desperately seeking ways to channel itself, and if it doesn't find natural ways, it will divert its course and become a twisted mental obsession or addiction that will force its expression 'in the dark.' In the case of traumatic experiences, the avoidance of life will create an addiction to 'safe' pleasures like food.

Another type of desire-ridden people are those who are extreme cases of the second chakra personality type. Artists, poets, musicians and actors are very often prone to self destruction. Their inner fire is overflowing, and they become addicted to ecstatic sensations. Eventually, through various tragic circumstances, this inner fire consumes them.

Basically, we all suffer from some level of addiction to pleasure and develop the habit of perpetuating moments of joy. Our brain has not adapted to make a clear distinction between pleasure and happiness. So, there is a great lesson for us all in the second chakra, though it may not be easy to learn; we must allow our life force to move freely and naturally upwards until it is alchemized in a spiritual transmutation.

Solutions for the Imbalanced Second Chakra

The most profound teaching for the imbalanced second chakra is that our joy of living does not depend on powerful experiences or peaks of pleasure. The joy of living must spread into every moment, express itself as a totality and creative involvement at any given moment, and, in actuality, be a non-causal feeling that awaits us from within. Totality does not lie in any experience, but is actually *an attitude* that fully embraces whatever comes its way.

This teaching includes both moments of pleasure and moments of pain, even moments of pain inflicted on us as a result of our search for great pleasures. The imbalanced second chakra is completely dependent on the experiential dimension of life and a total connection between experience and joy. If we are hurt by certain experiences, we believe that this should teach us to avoid further contact with life's flame. If we enjoy certain experiences, we believe that our joy depends completely on them, so we start to enhance them more and more. The lesson is that *joy is not pleasure* and also that joy cannot be taken away from us just because we get hurt from time to time or because our pleasures for some reason fade away.

This insight brings to mind the image of a child who bursts with the joy of living until his pleasure is taken away from him or he experiences pain. All of a sudden, the face is filled with disappointment and anger. This is because of the fact that, as a child who is bound to sensory stimulation, there is no separation between joy and pleasure; the two totally depend on each other. The problem is that most humans have never really grown out of this phase.

Our main solution is to locate within us the ever-existing flame of life, which keeps burning in both moments of pleasure and moments of pain. It may not be natural for us to look for this independent flame in moments of pleasure, since we are so used to being consumed with pleasure. Yet, this practice has to be done precisely in these very challenging moments in order for us to realize, again and again, that we are never cut off from the life force, and neither are we connected to it only through fleeting moments of pleasure. We are the life force; we are life, thus we can never be cut off from life. Furthermore, we have to realize that what we're looking for in intense moments of pleasure and peaks of excitement is the internal emotions and sensations that follow these moments. This means that our longing is not for these experiences, but rather for these feelings, feelings that can be easily evoked through an inner, uninterrupted connection to the life force. We are the vibrating, joyful dance of life, right here, right now.

We should do our best to untie memory connections created by unconscious moments of traumatic experiences. We must untie, through spiritual therapy, all rigid moral ideas that we have absorbed from society and authority figures. Working with the life force should be a very attentive and sensitive process of listening that doesn't allow any kind of prejudice. We also must untie all traumas that revolve around disconnection from the creative process. If we discover we are infertile, that doesn't mean there are no other ways for us to participate in the great flow of creation. Of course, we should also untie all memory connections that have resulted in the terrible conclusion that we mustn't live an adventurous life because we could get hurt. Even if we have been victims of rape, this does not mean that all sexual encounters are inherently dangerous.

Finally, we must untie our addictions and obsessions through the understanding that they are mere substitutes for true joy. For this healing, we will have to realize that we have created an addiction not only in the mental or emotional spheres but also in the physical sphere. Our bodies must also recover by reconnecting with the natural joy of being alive and breathing.

Life is a celebration of creation from moment to moment, and a play of energies. It must not be *too* serious. There are many ways to recover the sense of playfulness of the *true* inner child. Innocence can be regained. The 20th century spiritual teacher Osho, who was a natural-born second chakra awakener, helped many thousands reclaim their rights for joy and celebration. Through his dynamic meditations, which include wild dancing and cathartic experiences, people can liberate themselves from the burden of morality and unbind their bodies from all restrictions. The whole of humanity will look much better when all sense of guilt, shame and sin—the remains of rigid religions—is removed from its collective second chakra. Sexuality is innocent. Pleasure is as godly as anything else, and even the most heavenly joy must sprout from somewhere—in our case, from our earthly soil.

We should always take care that our daily life doesn't become disconnected from pleasure. A certain level of bodily pleasure, in which we get in touch with the sweetness of life, is extremely important. In Sanskrit, the term, *Rasa*, means *juice* or *essence* and is connected with the mental state of joy, evoked through the various arts. As long as *Rasa* is consumed moderately in order to avoid overstimulation of the nervous system, it is an essential form of nourishment. Sexual pleasure, fun, laughter, nature, tasty food and creative habits are also good examples of nourishment for the second chakra. Life is abundant with pleasing experiences, and whenever we connect with such experiences, we can also connect with life's generosity and with the sensual echoes of the non-causal joy of living.

At the same time, we must develop the sensitivity needed to make a clear distinction between moments of joy, and the wish to repeat or enhance those moments—which is desire. We should learn how to enjoy moments in totality, with no guilt and with no reserve, but also without clinging to them. When the pleasure is gone, it must be completely gone, without a trace in our minds.

The capacity to enjoy in totality and then to totally let go can be achieved through various aspects of a balanced second chakra, such as the moderate consumption of pleasure and the wise distinction between pleasure and joy (realizing that joy is our true aim), but more than that, it is possible through the understanding that, because of our ability to enjoy totally, fully, and without reserve, no imprint is left on the body-mind complex. This is, after all, the basic law for both traumas and pleasures: be there fully and wholeheartedly. Being one-hundred percent present is the remedy for irrational memory connections and also for desire.

An interesting example of a person following this rule is the great philosopher Socrates, who knew very well how to enjoy the company of Athens' most beautiful boys, and at the same time, to avoid clinging to their beauty, using it consciously for further transcendence. The joy of the senses becomes, then, a good friend of the spirit. So there is really no need to suppress it, but rather we should 'surf' on its wonderful waves as long as they last. Perhaps this is what Osho envisioned in 'Zorba the Buddha,' a new man who can enjoy the richness of the senses without loosing his total independence of spirit.

Since pleasure is connected with excitement, on a deeper level, what we really cling to is the *feeling* of excitement. Our life is, too often, boring and dull, so we develop a subtle addiction to over stimulation and peak experiences (even negative ones). Again, this addiction is to be solved through the excitement of life itself, and through our ability to enjoy the subtle wonders and magic of every moment in this universe. In Terry Pratchett's *Hogfather*, Death, who is thrilled about humans, tells his granddaughter in amazement: "Human beings make life so interesting. Do you know that in a universe so full of wonders, they have managed to invent boredom?"

The non-causal joy is, in a way, a feeling that we are never separated from life's creative process. We don't need to constantly get in touch with it through pleasures; we don't depend on pleasure to feel that life is indeed a celebration. We don't even need to constantly be creative, in the lower sense of the word. Bursts of creativity often make for wonderful moments: it may be a moment in which you realize that you are pregnant and that your body has become a vehicle of the creative universe; it may be the feeling that music is being born through your hands, or it may be a moment when you think of a thrilling story that holds in it the creation of a parallel reality. In moments of creativity we are one with the creator, and we get in touch with the 'why' of creation—who needs to know the intellectual answer to the mystery of God's creation when one can actually *feel* the reason whenever the creative impulse pounds in our bellies?

In the process of balancing the second chakra, one great requirement is realizing one's own potential of creative manifestation. We cannot go through life without contributing creatively to this process; contributing, not because we have to out of financial need or because we wish to be famous and important, but for the simple reason that, through the creative action, we experience oneness with life, with the bees and the flowers of spring time, with the stars, and with the wonders of our own bodies. Life, after all, is a creative burst, and one can never know life intimately without conscious participation.

But even here one must not depend on these bursts of creativity for the sense of tremendous oneness with life. True oneness with life stems from non-causal joy, while creative bursts can evoke only temporary joy and short-lived experiences of oneness. Creativity, as an extension of life's joy, must spread all over as a moment-to-moment quality. To be creative does not mean to write two books a year or to become a mother of thirteen children. In the gaps between one writing session and another there may be great spaces of dullness and emptiness, and when children grow they take really good care to clarify that they are no longer the parent's creation but rather their own creation. True creativity does not lie in our creations; creations go through us, and after they have used us as vehicles, they can leave us empty and bored.

Here lies the reality of creative living and the creative mind: every moment can become creative through our total engagement with it. Creativity is a quality, not an action. In fact, our most important creative project ever will always be the process of turning our life and being, as a whole, into a shining masterpiece. Discovering how to perfect ourselves at all levels, and how to excel in the human experience in all possible dimensions, is surely our greatest creative challenge.

In addition to dispersing joy and creativity throughout each and every moment of life, the second chakra contains another important energy—sexual energy—which is also destined for diffusion. Since our most powerful organs of pleasure are the sexual organs, and since sexual moments are very often our connection to perfect ecstasy, many people develop a fixation with sexuality. This fixation is not to be healed through suppression, but rather through the understanding that our entire experience of life must be sexual and orgasmic—a continuum of lovemaking so to speak. All addictions, and specifically sexual addictions, are, in truth, a longing for oneness and self-forgetfulness. So, we need to learn how to stop limiting the joy of living to narrow channels of pleasure, creativity and sexuality, and to begin seeing those channels as mere echoes of the real, wholesome thing.

The Three Levels of Functioning

The Functional Second Chakra

We are generally quite happy and allow life's juices to flow within and without. Mostly, we are capable of avoiding the bottomless pits of depression. We are willing to experiment from time to time and to be curious and adventurous, even when there is some fear of danger. We are not too rigid, and are able to have a good laugh and get a little wild. Of course, sometimes we get hurt, but we are able to rise up again, willing to continue living without dramatic conclusions about life. We may have some addictions and obsessions for pleasure, but they don't prevent us from functioning in daily life, and most of the time we maintain balance. We can enjoy sexuality and feel quite sexual. Generally, we feel at home in our bodies, even though negative body image might overshadow our physical ease. We are able to appreciate beauty, aesthetics, fine arts and good style, and we can cherish moments in nature. There is at least some amount of creativity in our lives: children, arts or initiative in projects.

The Balanced Second Chakra

We have an impressive level of non-causal joy. We enjoy moments of pleasure without obsession and struggles to preserve it. We are quite free from the workings of restless desire, so our minds are clear from images of pleasure that pretend to be images of happiness. We are willing to experiment at any time, are not afraid of consequences, and light-heartedly enjoy the new sensations that new experiences bring about. We don't take unnecessary risks; we only take risks when we feel that the experience is important for our evolution. We feel no limitations in regards to life's countless experiences, and yet we choose from them consciously and freely. We are joyful even when nothing is happening, even when we sit in a corner and do nothing. We have no addictions whatsoever. Sexuality is wonderful, and yet we can live without it when it's impossible to have a healthy and natural expression of it. We are deeply receptive to encounters with true beauty and aesthetics, such as sacred unions with nature. There is a high level of creativity in our lives, not only creative action but also creative thoughts and attitudes toward situations that demand our attention.

The Awakened Second Chakra

In the awakened second chakra, all life force is transmuted into an uninterrupted state of non-causal joy. We overflow with the true happiness of oneness with life as a whole. Both biological urges and creative urges are transmuted into the urge to merge with the wholeness of life. Sexuality and creativity are mere expressions of this higher merging impulse. Life itself is a great play of energies, and since we are one with this play, we lose interest in pleasures and pleasing sensations, and we also lose interest in creativity that is meant only for the sake of self-fulfillment. We experience urges to create only in connection with the greater whole and in the service of humanity. In fact, our urge is one with the creative fire that has given birth to the universe.

In the awakened chakra system, the second chakra is in charge of the merging impulse. This impulse is the basic drive toward union with the greater reality. In the awakening process, it flows upwards, moving along the chakras and injecting them with this impulse to merge, making it their one and only drive. The longing for ecstasy, expressed in sexuality, pleasure and creativity, is then fulfilled in the ecstatic dissolution of all separation into perfect oneness.

Polar Emotions

Passion / depression, desire / loss of appetite, creative excitement / boredom.

Type of Trauma

Traumas can be caused by daring to experience and experiment, and daring to live up to one's desires and urges, resulting in deep hurt, disappointment, and even physical injury. Traumas can occur when an adventure or a peak experience turns into a life-threatening situation, when falling in love proves to be a humiliating experience, and when sexual encounters result in pain. Also included in this category are innocent experiments, for which we are horribly punished without understanding why.

In cases of sexual abuse unconnected with our own attempts to experiment, our sexual organs can become traumatized, and our irrational conclusion will be to connect sexuality with pain and punishment. There are also traumas created when we are forced into an endangering adventure.

Some of us may have gotten carried away and aggressively abused others sexually. Realizing our misdeeds, we have concluded that sexual urges are inevitably dangerous and necessarily lead to aggression and exploitation.

The general irrational conclusion of this entire range of traumas is that 'experience is dangerous,' and the inevitable psychosomatic reaction will be fear in the face of risky adventures, peak experiences, powerful feelings and wild sexuality. This effort to avoid life's most powerful experiences might cause depression, loss of creativity, inability to feel sexual pleasure (frigidity), sexual dysfunction, addiction, obsessive thoughts of desire, and a reluctance to feel ecstasy and over-flowing joy.

Type of Personality

Traditionally, the symbol of the second chakra personality type is the butterfly. The best representative of this personality type is the artist: extremely romantic in spirit, over-passionate, over-heated, addicted both to arts and to pleasures, subjected to mood swings (and loves it!), always on the hunt for new adventures and new sensations, and admiring of beauty, aesthetics and good style. Second chakra personality types often suffer from some level of bipolar disorder: in the morning they wake up totally depressed, and in the evening they become exhilarated. They are hasty and impulsive, easily bored, easily excited, attracted to the decadence of sensuality and may be addicted to sex and drugs (sometimes even to adrenalin-provoking extreme sports), highly orgasmic, and drawn toward experiencing everything powerfully and dramatically. This type loves comfort, soaks in self-indulgence, spends lavishly, and enjoys showing off. An individual of this type is said to be 'all over the place,' very unstable in relationships, and attracted mainly to short-lived relationships, falling in love easily. In general, this personality distastes all types of stifling structures, really enjoys parties and celebrations, is attracted to law-breaking and to the shattering of taboos, and is quite fond of scandals. They are always looking for states of self-forgetfulness, but are quite unhappy with spirituality and meditation, because they cannot, and will not, transcend their passion for experience (trance-like shamanic rites may be more appealing in their eyes). Many poets, writers, painters, musicians and performers 'live' in this chakra. In ayurveda, they would be considered a pitta type, which is connected with the fire element—when unrestrained, the fire consumes its vehicle, and the vehicle falls into a self-destructive mode.

The second chakra personality type can be a very inspiring model of totality and 'joie de vivre.' They are open to the many possibilities of life and to the intensity of each moment, feeling life to its fullest and not being too moral, connecting healthily to their natural energies, having a poetic view of life and acknowledging beauty and nature. However, in extreme cases (although it is in the very nature of this personality type to be extreme), this personality will express complete narcissism, have a complete inability to truly engage in long-term relationships, develop destructive addictions and obsessions, and will lead a very unstable and unhealthy lifestyle.

Famous Second Chakra Expressions

Arthur Rimbaud, Jim Morrison: capricious, poetic, and ecstatic.

Male and Female Energies

The male quality of the second chakra, which is connected to semen, is found in the impulse to create, to literally spread new seeds of creation in the form of ideas and initiatives. It is this urge that compels us to participate in the process of creation.

The female quality, which is connected to the womb, is found in the pure joy of living and the ability to fully enjoy the different pleasures of life, to literally take them in. Ecstatic communion and merges with the forces of nature are also a part of this female quality.

Type of Happiness

Pleasures, total use of the senses, peak experiences, adventures and creativity; feeling like an integral part of the total celebration of life through creative contribution and joyful delights.

Life's Meaning and Purpose

Life is a play of energies, which can be fully comprehended only through bold experimentation and passionate engagement. Life is to be found in its extremes of joy and pain, and must be, at least to some extent, lived dangerously. Love is the ecstasy of falling in love, and death is another extremity to be played with. God is nature and is to be found in the eternity hidden in every flower and every force of nature.

Ages of Development of the Second Chakra

The second chakra is developed from the age of seven to the age of fourteen. This is the time when we first feel our conscious urges of experimentation, and also when we first encounter the half-moral, half-whimsical 'should's and shouldn't's' of our elders and other authorities. We realize that there are limitations to the realm of possible experiences and discoveries, and we develop our desire mechanism, which strives to eat the forbidden fruit in the dark and develop ways to escape punishment.

For many of us, this is still the time of magic, and we are attracted to fantasy stories and mythologies, and we imagine life to be filled with magical occurrences. At the same time, realizing that life is filled with prohibitions, we begin to loose our joy of living and the innocence of direct contact, and we sometimes even become depressed. Our initial contact with sexual feelings and the process of puberty quite embarrasses us because of the strange combination of pleasure and morality, excitement and disappointment.

Psychosomatic Disturbances

The first physical aspect of the second chakra is the entire reproductive system—from the prostate gland to the semen, from the ovaries to the womb. This system is our most basic way to participate in creation. When there are psychosomatic disturbances on this level of participation, all kinds of sexual dysfunctions, physical or psychological, might appear: premature ejaculation and erectile dysfunction, abnormal menstrual cycles and the inability to enjoy orgasm or even to ejaculate, infertility and various dysfunctions of the womb.

Another form of physical aspect is connected with the kidneys' main function, to control the water balance in the entire physical body. The flow of water in our bodies is a perfect metaphor for our life's natural flow of energies, and our ability to allow life's juices to move freely and innocently. Many times, when we are too subjected to moral codes, and when we feel guilty and sinful about our temptations and desires, we might damage the functioning of the kidneys. The psychosomatic expression of this might be chronic pain or infection in the urethra, kidney stones or prostatitis. Water is the conductor of life, and it is also connected with physical thirst, which is also, metaphorically, the thirst or desire for life.

The third physical aspect of the second chakra is the adrenal glands, which, among other functions, secrete adrenaline to stimulate the sympathetic nervous system. Adrenaline is the body's source of the 'fight or flight' response to threatening or stressful situations, and it's also a coping mechanism for handling the emotional and physical pressure caused by such situations. Naturally, living on the edge of life, and experimenting too much with trying situations, can end up exhausting the adrenal glands, which are connected with *jing* and *ojas*. Also, traumatic experiences can lead the body to think that whatever it encounters is inevitably dangerous and that it must be avoided at any cost, making the body respond with an over-secretion of adrenaline (and other stress hormones).

It is essential to free ourselves from the fear of experience and, at the same time, to take care not to exhaust ourselves with overstimulation of the senses. Finding the middle ground and being willing to enjoy life's juices while leading a basically peaceful life is the solution to over stimulated adrenal glands and also for the maintenance and enhancement of the vital essences of *jing* and *ojas*.

Collective Imprints

Our cultural heritage, a strange mix of monotheistic religions and secular rebellion, leaves us with very contradictory imprints on the second chakra. In our Western society, we are ceaselessly exposed to overstimulation of the senses, and at the same time we carry many taboos and restrictions on certain experiences (such as drugs and sexual experimentation). We are heavily encouraged to hunt for pleasures and enhanced feelings, resulting in our cultivating various collective addictions, such as pornography, while upholding many sanctified institutions, such as holy marriage. This consciousness of sin and morality, implanted by monotheistic religions, along with our consumerism and desire for material pleasures, creates within us a constant tension between 'good' and 'evil.'

Added to this strange mixture is the long history of sexual abuse, especially by men (the penis is connected with abuse). This engenders an unconscious fear of unleashing the 'monster of sexuality' again. On the other hand, for the over-cultured people we are, there is always the inherent attraction to regress into the free, unrestrained, primordial and Dionysian forces. Our culture, especially through the various arts, deals quite a lot with the somewhat dangerous attraction of decadence.

Evolution of the World

The second chakra developed in the time of the first tribes in ancient history. It had mainly developed through tribal consciousness: the gathering of people for the worship of the forces of nature as Gods; the celebration of the various forces, the power of fertility, the seasons and nature's great cycles in tribal ceremonies and artistic expression; shamanism as man's collaboration with the forces of nature; the discovery of healing and magical herbs; the power of tribal dancing; sex as a primordial force moving through humans; the body remaining naked or almost naked as a natural expression of life; oneness with the material universe, and no separation from the great whole, mother earth and genesis.

Common Interactions with Other Chakras

The second chakra is strongly connected to the first chakra since both deal with the primordial fear of life. The only difference is that the fear of the first chakra is of physical danger, and in the second chakra, it is the fear of the possible results of experiences. These two fears intersect in experiences that result in physical pain.

The second chakra also connects to the third chakra at the level of the libido and id versus ego. The ego is the mediator between our urges and desires and society's morality, and it too often suppresses the natural energies, instead of gently regulating them. The teaching here, especially in cases of too much guilt over sin, is that sometimes it is better to loosen up and allow the energies to flow freely. It's important to maintain a balance between self-discipline and joy. Another connection with the third chakra is the development of authority over oneself, stemming out of the inner freedom to sometimes disregard moral limitations and allow ourselves to freely choose out of life's possibilities.

A strong connection is also to be found between the second chakra and the fourth chakra. This is where feelings, such as 'I am bad,' 'I am impure,' 'I am not worthy' and 'I don't deserve certain things,' come into the picture because of experiences connected with sin and punishment.

The second chakra is the origin and base of the creative urge and the ability to enjoy and appreciate the various arts. However, in every complex artistic expression the urge alone starts in the second chakra; the creative act itself is a collaboration between the fourth and the sixth chakra, and the final outcome is processed and released through the fifth chakra.

The second chakra is the origin of the merging impulse, which aspires to dissolve all boundaries and to disappear into oneness. In the second chakra this will manifest through artistic expression, sexual attraction, communion with nature and peak pleasures and experiences. However, the more the second chakra transmutes, the more this merging impulse releases its gross energy toward the seventh chakra, in which the loss of boundaries occurs in its most refined expression, and in a purely spiritual and transformative context.

In the Process of *Kundalini*

The second chakra is an integral part of the spiritual foundation of the three first chakras. When these three synchronize and align, a solid spiritual foundation is created, enabling us to move safely from our foundation toward the heavens. The second chakra contains one of the three most basic qualities of the inner self. These qualities are stability (first chakra), joy (second chakra) and power (third chakra).

Recommended Practices

The holistic balancing of the second chakra consists of three fundamentals: a liberating spiritual practice (through which we awaken the non-causal joy); a purification (of traumas and morality), and a balanced lifestyle that embraces both intensified pleasure and a general, restrained way of living.

Spiritual practices can be directed toward the realization of non-causal joy. Spiritual practices can transmute our longing for limitlessness, ecstasy and freedom into the world of the spirit. When this is done, along with an intense purification of traumatic experiences and conditioning of moral codes and obsessions with pleasure, one's joy of living can be released. The best spiritual practices for the healing, balancing and awakening of the second chakra are those that aim at the development of non-causal joy, such as tantric transmutation (refining pleasure into spiritual energies), spiritual inquiry on the nature of desire, spiritualized lovemaking, and ec-static, trance-like experiences.

In creating a balanced lifestyle for the second chakra, it is first of all essential to maintain a moderate level of pleasure and joy, through laughter, dancing and singing, Osho's dynamic meditation techniques and other dynamic meditation techniques, sexual pleasure, good foods, body care, beauty and arts. It is also important to leave everything behind from time to time, to break the routine and to consciously go out for an adventure—anything that will 'surprise' the mundane brain. Communion with nature is tremendously important for the second chakra's health, as well as having enough time for leisure in general. From time to time you can re-enter the world of the inner child through imagination or even through wholeheartedly playing with kids and enjoying their magical perception.

Being creative—writing, composing music, painting and so on—is an essential way to share beauty with life. Try not to express egoic and negative emotions and ideas through creativity, but rather aim for beauty and oneness. Aspire to reach a time in your life when your livelihood and creativity become one and the same. Always remember that our greatest creative project is to turn our life and ourselves into a moment-to-moment masterpiece.

On the other hand, it is also important to maintain a high level of the vital essences (*jing* and *ojas*) through practices of moderate living: moderate stimulation of the senses, moderate work and creative activity, and a balanced lifestyle, having tantric-like sexual activity, minimizing ejaculation (ejaculating only every once in a while), sleeping well, eating natural foods, enjoying herbal support (especially adaptogens, such as ginseng, reishi and ashwagandha), using breathing exercises and practicing gentle sports, such as dynamic forms of yoga.

If your main issue in this chakra is struggling with obsessions and addictions, try to practice enjoyment without attachment; experience the pleasure totally, with a guilt-free spirit, and then completely *let it go*. If these obsessions include obsessive sexual hunger, instead of fighting it, try to channel this powerful energy toward creativity, service for others and spirituality (essentially, this is the same energy in different forms).

For those who are used to suppressing all passions and excitements, it is advised not to rush, but to overpower the urges of pleasure through refining spiritual practice. If your main issue in this chakra is a fear of experience, then from time to time consciously choose to experience states of limitlessness and ecstasy (through wild dancing, unrestrained sexuality, nude swimming, powerful sports, trance-like meditation, shamanic rites, and so on). If you suffer from a very guilty conscience, then play intentionally with the forbidden fruit while telling yourself, 'as long as this does not harm anyone, I am allowed to do it'; question the limitations of the existing morality, and try, through trial and error, to re-define its frontiers. If you tend to drown in depression, you can try stimulating and warming herbs, spicy foods and aerobic physical activity.

If you are a spiritual or religious aspirant, do your best to develop your connections with the spiritual dimensions of life while, at the same time, letting the earthly energies flow naturally from within. Spiritual evolution is actually blocked when one suppresses the natural energies. Trust that when the time is right, you will effortlessly drop some of your earthly desires—avoid tyrannizing your present needs and urges through a rigid spiritual self-image.

Shai Tubali

Third Chakra:
The Search For Power

Location and General Orientation

The third chakra is located between the umbilicus and the solar plexus. It governs the entire digestive system (mainly the stomach, liver, pancreas and bowels). Correspondingly, the third chakra functions as the digestive system of our psyche, absorbing the many different energies of life and directing them appropriately, while trying to push away pressures and hostile stimulants. This makes it the psyche's main protector, a shield of strength which prevents all kinds of over stimulation (like 'immunity' versus 'toxins' if using the physical equivalents). Of course, the chakra's ability to fulfill this function completely depends on the level of power in the chakra.

Basic Psychological Themes

The third chakra focuses on the issue of power. How much individual power do we own or feel we own? Do we suffer from a sense of weakness, or do we perhaps misuse our power and turn it into force? How do we express our power over others, over the energies of life and over our own inner energies? These are the three key questions that determine our third chakra's balance.

Power can be measured on a vast scale of feeling and expression. At its first end is the feeling of total weakness, to the point where there is an absence of self-existence. In the middle is the use of power for very specific and right aims, where power is just a tool of expression. At its other end, you can find megalomaniac, self-aggrandizing and arrogant feelings expressing themselves through aggressiveness, exploitation and control. At this end, *power* transforms into *force*.

There are three different levels of power issues in the third chakra. The first is concerned with our feelings of power within ourselves; the second is all about our feelings of power in our relationship with life, and the third is about our feelings of power in relationships with others.

The first level, the innermost one, is, before anything else, connected with the basic sense of 'I AM.' The degree of this most basic sense of self-existence, or self-presence (which is the grounds of any true individuality within us), actually determines the degree of power we have. When we feel almost non-existent, we will also, inevitably, feel very powerless; when we feel all-encompassing, it might lead to an over-active sense of power.

In psychological terms, this sense of 'I AM' is called the ego. The ego's function is to mediate between the id, the natural forces of man, and the super-ego, society's needs and moral values. When the ego is weak, it cannot control the natural forces from within. In the chakra system's terminology, this means that the third chakra cannot handle the flow of energies, desires and urges of the second chakra, and the instinctual forces of the first chakra. One needs an ego powerful enough to regulate one's desires, creative impulses and most basic feelings.

A weak sense of power implies that one has a very small capacity for self discipline and self authority. One is overwhelmed by the different and contradictory energies swirling within, which also means that this person cannot direct their energy toward one goal and one fulfillment. The ability to concentrate and direct our energy toward a specific goal's fulfillment is what one may regard as our 'will.' So, when we lack this ability, we inevitably lack willpower. In order to have willpower, we must develop the ability to overcome some forces from within, especially laziness, sudden urges, fear of failure, disbelief and fear of pain. These are our 'enemies' from within, and we have to conquer them before anything else can ever happen.

The second chakra is all about desire, while the third chakra is about ambition. Desire is an urge that stems out of a feeling; it can be very short-lived. Ambition is a quality that has to have a solid base built on the capacity to endure; it demands patience and long-range focus. For this, we need a strong sense of 'I AM'—you can never truly *want* until you really *exist*.

A strong sense of 'I AM' will bear the fruit of free will and free choice. As long as you are non-existent, you are being devoured by your natural impulses, so you cannot really choose—you are your natural impulses. On the other hand, once your sense of self solidifies, you are free to select out of these natural forces, and more than that, to direct the body-mind complex toward a higher goal that doesn't belong to the instinctual and impulsive realms at all.

The Armenian genius mystic, George Gurdjieff, claimed that, while it is commonly assumed that everyone owns a self and a will, most people on this planet do not exist yet, and, therefore, cannot own a true will. Every person, he asserted, consists of many 'I's,' fragmented and contradictory selves, and is actually a sort of battlefield in which every small 'I' takes over for short periods of time. The thought that this total fragmentation could ever bring about an expression of true and free will is one of man's worst misconceptions. For us to *develop* a true willpower, we need to practice self-remembrance and make a continuous effort to overcome our first and second chakras' instinctual habits. Only a total conscious effort can produce a real selfhood that can master and direct the various psychological and physiological energies.

The feeling that we don't have enough power to gather our energies and control them with willpower is very common. Sometimes this feeling goes as far as to prevent us from being able to even develop our own views and opinions. We can easily be pressured and carried away by others' points of view, and we may simply adapt to follow those in power. Since we feel we don't own our sense of existence, we will experience transparency and feel as if we have no unique identity. We will become what others say we should become; we will simply adjust and 'flow,' in the negative sense of the word.

On the other hand, when there is an overuse of power on this inner level, we might become our own greatest suppressor. In this case, the ego will control the id's energies in the most rigid and dogmatic way. It will dominate the natural energies instead of carrying out its true function, which is to regulate them all. It will suffocate pleasure, creative urges and simple feelings of life, and it will command the body-mind complex to work toward different missions and goals, as if in an army unit. Our personal identity will then control the natural life force, and thus prevent any possible 'surprises.' It will limit our freedom to move in all directions of life, and will focus only on the ambition to become someone. Its interest will not be in finding *uniqueness*, but rather in defining its own *special* and separate identity and qualities. This is when willpower is everything, and self-discipline becomes harsh.

The second type of power issue in the third chakra concerns our communication with life's great stream of change. An imbalance in the third chakra will almost always result in a feeling of powerlessness and helplessness in the face of the immense forces of 'destiny.' We feel that we do not control life's events and cannot really influence them at any level; we feel victimized by life, as if life is an arbitrary and whimsical being that would never negotiate with the poor helpless creatures it controls. Since we are totally in the hands of this terrible being, hoping for its mercy, even imagining ourselves fulfilling any kind of dharma (our most potent service to the world) is quite impossible. No, we are forever being swept away by the stream of karmic events, and we simply cannot rise up from this stream and claim our basic right to make an impact. We lack a sense of control over our fate, and so we believe that there's no point in thinking of free will and choice. Naturally, this leaves us with a lot of frustration.

On the other hand, we might imagine ourselves to be in total control over destiny and the flow of events. This is another form of illusion because all of us do have some level of influence; yet, life functions as an intertwined whole, filled with interconnections that we cannot fully fathom. Sometimes our only choice will be to have the most enlightened attitude possible toward a specific event. When we imagine that our willpower determines everything, we will awaken an inner aggression and a domineering attitude.

This leads us to the third type of power issue, which is concerned with our relationships with others. If we feel weak in front of others, we will not be able to stand up and claim our individuality. Being an individual demands enough power to face tremendous pressures from society—even friends and family—and still refuse to give up. Sometimes others will put pressure on us in order to change our mind, making us conform to society's moral values and behaviors. When we feel that submitting ourselves to this pressure would betray our authenticity and our innermost, individual moral values, it is usually best to say 'no.' However, even though we may *feel* uncomfortable with society's values, we will often be too scared to face the consequences of detaching ourselves from the crowd.

Too often we carry within ourselves both unconscious and conscious memories of struggles for independence that ended in catastrophe. This implies that true individuality is quite dangerous, not only because it might alienate us from all others, but, worse than that, because it might lead to physical dangers, such as exile, prison and death.

We might also grow fearful of all kinds of authoritative figures, feeling totally helpless in their hands, and trying to adjust ourselves to fulfill their 'requirements.' Being dominated by another is a big sign of an imbalance in the third chakra, because it shows that we are being identified as weak— be it by a romantic partner, a teacher or a business associate—and that others will soon find out how to control our minds and bodies for the sake of their own fulfillment of power.

On the other hand, we might be the abusers ourselves, enjoying dominance and control over others. This might be through the misuse of power as an authoritative figure in any relationship with helpless others—for example, when we are parents or bosses. It might also occur when we trace weak-mindedness in seemingly equal partners, whether romantic partners or just friends. In any case, enjoying an increased sense of power by taking others' power is a sign of an imbalance, calling for deep healing from within.

Another effect of an increased sense of power in our relationships with others is that we become addicted to the feeling of individuality. Not only are we not afraid of expressing our unique positions, but also, we totally miss the fact that, in a balanced state, our highly evolved individuality is supposed to serve others. Being totally ignorant of this purpose, we tend to focus on our special expressions, special opinions and special points of view, and we hurt others out of the belief that we must always be true to ourselves.

In summary, imbalances of the third chakra revolve around the polar feelings and expressions of power. The imbalances will always be connected to opposites: feeling non-existent or having too much self esteem; feeling inferior or superior; feeling a total lack of control and influence or always trying to be on top of things; having no ambitions or being too ambitious; having no opinion or being too opinionated and too critical; submitting to forceful individuals or forcing yourself on others; being pressured easily or putting pressure on others; choosing to remain small and invisible or aspiring to always expand and become more visible and powerful; having no identification or being extremely self-defined.

Psychological Reactions of the Imbalanced Chakra

Persons who suffer from a decreased sense of power in the third chakra tend to be extremely scattered in life, having no real aim and always feeling that self-fulfillment is a far away, imaginary destination. Sometimes these people suffer from sudden outbursts of anger, since anger is the last outlet for power. Ingrained in this anger is a terrible degree of frustration.

These people will be troubled with issues of self-image and self-definition: "Who is the true 'me'? And what do *I* really want?" Mostly, they will seek answers for these questions from the outside, hoping to be relieved through the confidence of an accepted authority, such as a priest, channeler, expert or guru.

The most common action of a weak third chakra is just hanging on, forever waiting to develop enough power to act. Meanwhile, these persons will do what they are told to do, and will define their 'individual' preferences through stronger minds. This type believes that trying to choose and decide on one's own, and then following through on decisions with the endurance of true willpower, will almost always lead to failure and disappointment. This, of course, doesn't leave much space for taking initiative and working on independent projects. It is best to follow others' power and charisma. This state of following can lead either to total laziness, where one needs to be pushed further by others, or to an excessive diligence, where one is motivated by the drive to please others. Dissatisfaction in the workplace is quite often present, either at the back of this type's mind or clearly and consciously.

Many will find some type of authoritative figure to submit to, and some might even develop an inclination toward all sorts of masochism. Masochism can be purely sexual, but it can also become a tendency to engage in abusive relationships. These people might be fearful of taking on a powerful position and being in charge. After all, they mostly wish to be invisible and to take on others' expressions of power.

Some, even in their adult life, will still be in conflict with their parents and other authoritative figures from their early childhood, living or dead; they will continue to rebel against these figures and struggle for independence, whether the struggle is real or merely in their head.

The weak third chakra personalities are easily pressured and are quite afraid of what society thinks of their acts and deeds. How people will react is a tremendously important factor in their decision-making. They will also be extremely vulnerable to pressures and stimulants, like others' anger or dissatisfaction, and they will feel powerless to defend themselves against feelings and demands that surround them.

Excessive power in the third chakra creates personalities that identify themselves as 'doers'. They are quite addicted to work, career, status and recognition, but, unlike with an imbalanced first chakra, they don't do it for the sake of security and a stable routine, but rather for self-expansion. This imbalance is more of an addiction to conquering and enhancing the sense of power through possessions and money, or through persuading the masses to consume their products. These people enjoy the increased sense of power achieved through the fulfillment of aims and goals, while forever making more aims and goals. The main way that this type identifies itself is through what they do, what they have already achieved and what they wish to achieve.

Naturally, these people are most prone to outbursts of anger and even rage. If their agendas do not go as planned, or if others do not submit to their will, they can literally loose their minds by trying to forcefully manipulate and divert life's flow.

Excessive power leads to excessive tension, which can cause both psychosomatic diseases and an unhealthy lifestyle. If this type wants to achieve something, it can't sleep too well, it overworks and overstrains itself, it eats badly and it never finds time for other things. Shortages in time are always a problem for this type of imbalanced chakra. This tension can make one want to relax through different kinds of addictions: food, sex, television, drugs and alcohol are only a few examples. This is not the same addiction tendency that is expressed in the second chakra; this addiction is not created out of the wish to experience things strongly, but rather out of the wish to distract oneself from the tremendous pressures of achievement. It's very easy to locate this imbalance in the general quickening pace of the western culture.

Achievement can also make someone quite uncaring. Money and position become of greater value. Love and emotional expression are not as important—who has the time for it? These people become like dispatched arrows, seeing only the targets of life; this leads to obsessive thoughts, which bind targets to happiness. The obsessive thoughts can also culminate in frustration (when things don't move in the 'right' direction), anger and manipulation.

For this type, life is seen from the angle of natural selection and the survival of the fittest; there's no room for equality. This type believes that there are those who are superior and those who are inferior, and this is how it should be; in fact, this is 'nature'. This kind of imbalance will express itself through a subtle, or a not-so-subtle, sense of superiority: 'I am a *somebody*, you are not.' Arrogance is inherent in this type, as well as criticism (and even abhorrence, up to the point of sadistic expression). They are only envious of those people who are in better positions and, when needed, they will flatter those in power and express a pretentious admiration, but only so they can get what they want.

If we are this type, our position of power is our identification. If power is taken away from us, it will literally leave us with nothing. We exist because of our expression of power, whether we are a great Indian shaman, a powerful yogi who has achieved siddhis (supernatural abilities) or a stock market manager. We cannot see our work and power in only a functional role and as a service in the play of life.

When the excessive tendency of the third chakra connects with the spiritual dimension of life, it is expressed as what one may call 'a spiritual ego.' This ego is an over-ambitious drive to gain spiritual power, rather than a drive to dissolve all separation and to merge. Spiritual experiences are viewed as power intoxication, enlightenment is interpreted as the absolute expansion of the narcissistic self, and the various powers that can be gained through self-control (from telepathy to walking on fire) seem very appealing. Spirituality, then, will be perceived as the ability to manifest whatever one wills; in other words, it will be perceived as mind power. This is how the idea of the power of positive thinking has gained unbelievable popularity; people actually imagine that they can attract anything they want through thinking.

In general, men tend to express the excessive aspect of the imbalanced third chakra (over ambition, power abuse and anger), while women tend to express the weak aspect of the imbalanced chakra (sense of non-existence and low ambition). Both energetically and physiologically, this trend makes sense; the masculine testosterone is the hormone of conquering and power, and the motherly oxytocin is the hormone of relationships and dependency.

Solutions for the Imbalanced Third Chakra

The key solution for imbalances in the third chakra is to understand that power is not about outer force and control, but rather about self-presence and self-control—a genuine self-existence, which is to be achieved through a conscious effort, purification and meditation. Power must be transmuted into the ability to organize and to perfect ourselves; the self-definition, which depends on doing, must be transformed into a self-definition of being, and the control we exert over others should be redirected toward self-mastery. By attaining complete self-control and realizing a truly integrated self, we will no longer seek an outer expression of power and will use power only when truly needed.

When we have a low sense of power in the third chakra, we must understand that we should not *try* to become someone in the outer plane, but rather turn our energy into the creation of a wholesome and integrated self. Clearing traumas connected with the suppression of our own power and submission to others' power is essential. We also have to complete our rebellion against our parents and other powerful figures, since this is not about them at all, but about us. Aside from healing our sense of non-existence, the third chakra also calls for action.

Practices for the development of self-control are of high importance. There are a great variety of practices in this field. Practices that aid in self-discipline, such as waking up early or responsibly organizing one's day, are one example. Demanding meditation techniques, powerful gymnastics and conscious eating are also good examples—along with anything that requires our ability to transcend urges and impulses, such as laziness, boredom, distractions and so on. Effort, followed by some level of discomfort, is the great trainer of the imbalanced third chakra; ejaculatory control for men, or even abstinence from time to time can be a good exercise for this.

However, using practices to develop self-control is only one important action. Other important actions are developing stamina in the face of great challenges and pressures (sometimes even creating such challenges intentionally) and focusing on one goal alone until it is achieved. We don't have to go all the way at once and move to the other pole of excessive ambition. We can decide only on one goal or one challenge at a time, and practice through this one challenge an inner strength that can withstand all efforts, discomforts and encounters with outside pressure. From practice to practice, we will be able to maintain a higher degree of willpower, until it becomes a habit of our personality.

Practices for developing stamina include taking on voluntarily responsibilities and accepting power-positions. Another interesting way to develop stamina is to stick to something that we believe is true and to remain loyal to it, even in the face of terrible societal pressure, and even if it means loosing empathy. When others' opinions put too much pressure on us, we can simply use them to reflect our own doubts and the weakness of our own 'psychological spine'.

Staying loyal to our inner truth does not mean becoming forceful in order to 'defend' it. Actually, it is the other way around: as long as we suffer from weakness in the third chakra, we are at risk of attacking in order to defend ourselves from stimulants, which we interpret as dangerous 'invasions'. So, we must keep in mind that inner strength never needs to defend itself.

We also have to gather enough energy to be active in the world, not only to persevere, but also to manifest our own powerful expression. We must cultivate the aspiration to dare, and become a contributing and influencing presence in the world of time and space. For that, we should start listening to ourselves, without escaping to experts and friends, and without any dependency on the strength of others, until we realize our own potential for dharma. We can start by simply asking ourselves: if there were no limitations whatsoever, and no societal pressures and opinions, and if I owned a tremendous reservoir of energy, how would I have acted in this world? How would I have expressed myself in the world if there was no sense of restrictive destiny and there was only my free choice?' However, when we listen to these questions, we must not be safely sitting in a quiet corner and contemplating them, but rather acting and making mistakes, and out of these actions and mistakes will rise up our true individual inclinations.

Basically, we can regard this kind of balancing process as the development of the more masculine inner feelings: a foundation of confidence on which one can build a complete individual self.

When we have a sense of excessive power in the third chakra, expressed through too much frustration and anger, it is a call for us to stop and to realize that the meaning of life will never be completely fulfilled through achievements and possession of power alone. Power can be intoxicating, but not fulfilling, and it will always leave a deeper sense of hunger and dissatisfaction. In spite of Nietzsche's claim—a classical third chakra doctrine—life is *not* motivated by the will of power alone.

This means, first of all, that our sense of self-existence cannot be gained through doership. When our existence can only be confirmed by what we did, do or plan to do, it is actually not a real existence at all. Our identity in life is only a vehicle of expression, while our sense of self must be deeply rooted in being. So, we must shift our sense of existence from our obsession to become somebody to the eternal presence. This means that whatever we do in the world, from within we will always be the same. Meditation teaches us how to become all-pervasive, not at the level of doing, but rather, at the level of the true, all-embracing self.

This means that we need a more feminine type of meditation. Absorption into eternal reality will dissolve all our self-definitions and our feeling that we have to 'do' in order to exist. Along with this clinging, arrogance, self-aggrandizement and 'specialness' will also fade away.

We also have to consciously clear space and time for important things in life, which have nothing to do with our steadfast movement toward achievement. We have to experience life, as much as we can, as an open and spacious being, in which self-fulfillment is only one tiny expression. For that, we could spend some time alone in nature, without any interference. Experiences like that can greatly rejuvenate us.

Secondly, we must learn to accept that life's flow is mostly out of our control. There are many cases in which our only choice is to respond with a wholesome attitude. There is a limit to our influence, and sometimes the only thing left to do is move along in harmony with the forces of life.

Always trying to manipulate life according to our agendas and targets is not only exhausting, but also completely out of tune. While ambition is a good thing, we must learn to distinguish between harmonious ambitions and inharmonious ambitions. Whenever we push forcefully against life, we will experience a terrible frustration. Frustration is completely gone from our lives the moment we develop enough wisdom to want only as long as it is in harmony with life's flow, and to stop wanting the moment it becomes a violent struggle against the simple facts of life. It is nice when our ambitions find fulfillment in life, and yet, it is unnecessary—life is a vast phenomenon, and when we cling to only one aspect, we miss numerous others.

Indeed, it is wonderful to have grand visions in our mind's eye, but grand visions always demand careful and slow unfolding. Frustration will emerge, in this context, in our desire to hurriedly reach the point of completion—but, again, this is not what life is all about.

The last level of power abuse we need to balance is our control over the weaker beings in our life. Here, we must divert our effort to control others toward a greater self-mastery. Whenever we feel anger—which is basically a result of our wanting others to act and behave exactly the way we want them to—it means we loose control over ourselves; we cannot master our own lower energies. So, our great challenge is to conquer anger and to transmute it back into pure presence. Even when someone attacks us psychologically and emotionally, our main concern is the level of self-control with which we respond. This is actually a deeper practice of non-violence.

Of course, there's no need to become obsessive about controlling your own energies and to make a new third chakra career out of it. This will, again, be more about the 'joy' of achievement. We must learn how to regulate and channel our lower energies just as a wise king would run his kingdom: peacefully, gently and lovingly. We don't want to strangle our life force with another rigid identification.

In summary, this kind of third chakra imbalance can be resolved through the understanding that there is really no need to use our power to control life, others and even ourselves—power is an energy to use for good aims, and it is definitely not the center of our identification. In this case, we can regard the balancing process as a movement toward more feminine inner feelings: our individual power aligns with all other forces—life, other people and energies within ourselves—in a way that only allows it to be used when necessary -when our active involvement is actually needed.

The Three Levels of Functioning

The Functional Third Chakra

When our third chakra is functional, we have a proper level of self-identity. This measure of self-identity is enough to enable us to have our own views, inclinations, choices and ambitions. Thanks to this average feeling of power from within, we are able to face pressures and outer demands, and we can stand up for our individual beliefs, and sometimes even separate from the crowd to represent a very unpopular position. We also feel that we have some degree of influence on life's events, and are able to monitor our basic urges and drives enough to lead ourselves to wake up early, go to work, fulfill our duties and responsibilities, and complete long-range missions. We can surpass our laziness. Generally, we are quite reliable, thanks to the medium level of integrity in our minds. Yes, we do have our moments of complete rage and loss of control when things don't happen as we expected, and yes, we do have issues with power, such as fear of authorities and dependency on stronger minds. We can also be very critical and aggressive toward others' choices and actions, and have either inferior or superior tendencies, but generally, we know how to suppress these issues when we are called to action.

The Balanced Third Chakra

Our feeling of self-existence is rooted, not in doing and outer identities, but rather in being. Even in the face of physical or emotional contraction, we can still maintain this solid presence. We are also able to easily surpass lower impulses of desire for food and sex. We have begun to develop the true spiritual self, which transcends all known identities and is independent of the time and circumstances of life. This self is powerful, but not in the familiar sense of power; it is not forceful or defensive, it doesn't need to protect its own individuality, and it knows how to flow with life *while* fulfilling harmonious ambitions. This powerful spiritual self cannot experience rage, because it doesn't have frustrated ambitions. It is always just in the middle between being and becoming, ambition and flow, individuality and service, resistance to pressure and total openness, self-discipline and spontaneity, and confidence and humbleness. It can quite effortlessly have tremendous and world-wide visions, and yet it only moves through the harmonious channels. It uses its power only when it is needed for creativity, for constructive manifestation or to stay loyal to one's authenticity. There is almost no drive for self-enhancement, but rather for ambitions that can actually serve humanity as a whole. Whenever this type finds itself in an authoritative position, it will demonstrate authority in a way that does not lean on force.

The Awakened Third Chakra

The great mission of creating an integrated and unified self, with one will and one drive, is completed in this person. The self is transcendent, free of time and space. The sense of power is transmuted into pure life force. This self is uncontaminated and uncorrupted by the pressures of time and 'becoming,' and therefore, has a tremendous spiritual strength and solidity. The body, the basic drives, and the life force are all under the guidance of the inner master, who can actually direct the various forces and is not bound to the power of fears, desires, thoughts and emotions. This is like being re-born in a simultaneously simple and complex new stage of consciousness, in which all the contradictory forces in the body-mind complex become a harmonious, fully functioning system. When this chakra fully awakens, it binds with the two lower chakras, becoming one spiritually awakened, indestructible self. Furthermore, after the full awakening of the four higher chakras, the power of this chakra will no longer be used by an individuated self, but rather by greater cosmic drives.

Polar Emotions

Powerfulness / powerlessness, ambition / frustration, control / helplessness.

Type of Trauma

The traumas accumulated in the third chakra are societal traumas from whenever we encountered societal forces that pressured us to a degree of breakdown. In this are included, encounters with abusive and humiliating authorities, being in an environment which suppressed our individuality or was hostile toward it, being in a harsh environment, in which we couldn't stand and digest outer pressure or negative energy, and any other suffocating encounter with tyranny, power positions or a controlling society.

Of course, we probably have plenty of examples from the time in which our individuality most aspired to evolve: adolescence. At that time, we struggled to individuate ourselves, while feeling pushed back by parents, teachers and other authorities. Very often we were surrounded by abusive classmates or other teenagers, who, just like us, struggled to define their own individuality through belittling others. If we were too 'different' and exceptional, we probably met with a lot of pressure to become 'like everybody else,' or, in other cases, we became outcasts. Sometimes we were punished for being stubborn individuals and standing up for our beliefs.

Inevitably, meeting abusive people led us to conclude that people are dangerous, especially those who are high in power and position. This might imprint our chakra with a great sense of non-existence and powerlessness, a fear to take on responsibility and a fear to use power ourselves, even for the sake of self control. We might even develop a strange form of rebellion, in which we shirk any kind of responsibility and continue to act like little children, only to show that we still do not listen.

This type of trauma can lead us to act in two main polar ways, depending on our constitution. The first reaction is to further conform and to long to be embraced by a dominating father figure; we might become addicted to the sense of security bestowed upon us by confident authority figures. This can even lead us to a masochistic desire! The second possible reaction is greater individuation, outcasting ourselves from any group and any society, and insisting on always being 'independent,' even if that means sacrificing the possibility of being healthily influenced and touched by others. This can make us very suspicious toward any kind of social embrace, especially idealistic closed groups.

In rare cases, this type of trauma will lead us to look for weaker people that we can dominate and abuse as a twisted way to compensate for our own loss of power.

In a totally different kind of traumatic experience, we ourselves were the aggressors, using force in order to abuse others. Realizing, in retrospect, the ramifications of our misdeeds, we conclude that to be powerful is to be dangerous, thus we limit our presence and suppress the fire element of our self-expression.

Type of Personality

Traditionally, the symbol of the second chakra personality type is the deer. Nowadays, the best representative of this personality type is the businessman: forever busy, extremely ambitious, always in a hurry, competitive, always trying to better his status, looking hungrily for the 'top' and enjoying the accumulation of money for the sake of an increased sense of power and control. The businessman can also be quite manipulative, devious and even violent. What he does is his complete identification: 'I do—therefore I am.'

Originally, the third chakra personality type was best represented by the warrior, the hero and the conqueror. In some places in our world it still is a more authentic symbol, but it seems that, in our Western society, war has changed its form: it became more sophisticated, and is not about direct physical fighting, but is rather a matter of mind control. The businessman fights for money and status, not for land and honor, and his weapon is his cunning mind. 'Strategy,' now means developing ways to move eloquently and smoothly in order to get what you want. Instead of empires, we have an ever-growing tendency toward world-wide corporations.

For both cases—the warrior and the businessman—it is all about reaching targets and conquering them. So, naturally, included in this definition are also mountain climbers, Olympic candidates who aspire for the highest achievement, and also great rebels, such as Che Guevara. Heavy rock music, like heavy metal, which expresses rebellion and outbursts of existential anger, is a good example too. Also included in this category are the Shaman, the Yogi and the magician, who are all attracted to developing esoteric skills for the sake of power. Even in 'Star Wars,' the attraction toward the dark side of the force is synonymous with the attraction toward power for the sake of power.

Today, our entire Western society is colored with the fire element of achievement and competition, and has the tendency to obsessively improve and become. When a society revolves around moneymaking, it reflects excessive power in the third chakra.

In the Ayurvedic tradition, this personality type is the pitta type, the fire element. It is the same element as in the second chakra, only here it is not aiming at powerful experiences and sensations, but rather at targets and impressive attainments.

At its best, the third chakra (especially when combined with the fifth chakra) gives shape to great individuals who are powerful enough to change the world, and who are not swayed by any popular convention. However, when this personality type is imbalanced, it is arrogant, aggressive, raging and destructive. It will use all the powers it has accumulated in order to destroy an apparent enemy, but it might, simultaneously, burn itself.

Famous Third Chakra Expressions

Alexander the Great, Che Guevara: ambitious conquerors and warriors.

Male and Female Energy

The male energy of the third chakra can be symbolized by the sword: a powerful force that can break through any kind of obstacle and move persistently toward a goal. It never wavers, for it has a tremendous aspiration and the energy to follow it. We need this male energy when we have a vision that we wish to manifest in the world of time and space.

The female energy of the third chakra can be symbolized by the shield. Just as we need a sword, we need a shield: the sword is needed for offense, while the shield is needed for defense. So, the female energy equips us with a protective shield, which can actually push away any kind of pressure and over stimulation. It can equip us with stillness when someone offends us, and it can equip us with persistence when we are being pressured to let go of our authenticity.

Type of Happiness

For this chakra, the experience of happiness is evoked by attaining world wide recognition or some highly valued award, gaining a great position or an impressive amount of money, managing to conquer a long-expected goal, or acquiring some desired powers. It is about getting something that symbolizes success or reaching the top.

Life's Meaning and Purpose

Life is a process of natural selection, a subtle and not-so-subtle battlefield in which those who express the strongest capacities and aspirations win. Life is about overcoming obstacles, facing challenges and fighting our way to success. The feeling of increased power is the most amazing affirmation of self-completion. To be ambitious is to join life's true movement. Life's purpose is to succeed in conquering whatever we believe is worth conquering. Love is also an attainment, a possession; Death is something we hope to one day conquer and overcome through the power of medicine and technology; God is the greatest experience of power. God is the almighty, all-powerful being that we may believe in or aspire to become.

Ages of Development of the Third Chakra

The third chakra develops from the age of fourteen to the age of twenty-one. After the quite suppressed, vulnerable and amenable time of the second chakra's development, this is the time of rebellion: we insist on individuating ourselves and clearly defining our borders as separated egos. This is when we encounter our strongest drive for self-definition and, at the same time, society's most powerful pressures: parents who give their last fight to influence and shape our personality; teachers who burden us with studies, which we are very scarcely interested in, and, of course, friends and class-mates, who create many great dilemmas of conformity versus individuation. In some countries, at the age of eighteen the army also creeps in, shaking our world through encounters with harsh authorities, the worship of power and the struggle for self-control.

In this battlefield, we begin to develop our willpower, trying out one goal or another to see whether we can actually get the things we want or not. Life is not nice at these times: it keeps pushing us away from our desired goals, and too often leaving us with shattered dreams and frustration. Sometimes we feel so weak that we dream of committing suicide as a last cathartic expression of self-power. Mostly, these are just thoughts of revenge, and we settle for milder bursts of rage, especially when facing our bewildered parents.

Defining ourselves can be quite confusing. Who are we really? Our personality is quite loose, so we don't have the protective shield of certainty that grown-ups seems to own. We try to trace, out of our second chakra's adventures and experiments, a more continuous feeling of ourselves, but still we're not so sure: 'What kind of man or woman should I be?' 'What does it mean to be like my parents or to clearly distinguish myself from them?' 'And when I have a fleeting attraction toward my closest male friend, does this *feeling* mean I'm gay?'

So, this period is characterized by the effort to harness our inner wild energies and to divert them toward a steadier self-expression.

Psychosomatic Disturbances

Psychosomatic disturbances in the third chakra are almost always connected with parts of the digestive system: stomach, liver, pancreas or bowels. They might be caused by either a great psychological debility—when we find it hard to 'digest' impressions, and when everything seems like pressure to us—or by the misuse of power—when we become too ambitious, and therefore, too stressed and angry.

When weakness is the cause of our issues, our digestive system will not demonstrate the integrity needed to push away the burden of stressful impressions. This means we won't be able to get rid of toxins (a function of the liver) and keep pace with the level of outer stimulation—which can lead to stomach and bowel imbalances. If our environment is psychologically hostile, or at least perceived to be hostile, we will be unable to neutralize negative impressions. This might cause chronic problems, from IBS to bowel infections, and from heartburn to peptic ulcers.

When the misuse of power is the psychosomatic cause of our disorders, they will be connected with anger and over ambition. Of course, anger and over ambition can extend themselves and develop into further problems, such as high blood pressure and heart disorders, or even heart diseases. Another complication is our need for a compensating lifestyle, which leads to imbalances, such as food deficiencies and sleep disorders. An over use of stimulants, such as coffee and drugs, in order to 'keep going' is also common and may lead the body to dependency and toxicity.

Collective Imprints

Our deepest collective imprints are those connected to tyrants, from emperors to dictators, who charismatically and forcefully managed to control nations and kingdoms. Since they brought along terrible disasters, a profound fear of powerful people has been ingrained in the hearts of all of us. Fascism of all sorts, even that which is subtly expressed in our own nations and armies, has also become synonymous with the love of power. Empires and giant corporations evoke suspicion; anything that aspires to grow for the sake of self-expansion seems dangerous. Any kind of collective force is considered quite hazardous, as it might lead to the suffocation of the individual. This is why we are also very afraid of any effort to build an 'utopian' society—sometimes we will even call these attempts 'cultish,' as a synonym for 'evil.'

We are all quite bruised from the shocking abuses of power, especially by men, throughout human history. This fear of the destructive potential of power leads us, too often, to avoid it ourselves. Men have weakened themselves intentionally, suppressing their energy, and choosing to become 'sensitive,' and sometimes even hyper-sensitive, just to avoid this danger. This might not be very beneficial for the world's development: by confusing power and force, we limit the energy that is highly needed for any further healthy revolutions in our culture. Sensitivity is a wonderful quality—combined with constructive power, it can actually help change the world for the better.

On the other hand, slowly but surely the suppressed groups—women, homosexuals, blacks and so on—begin to claim their own sense of power and identification, overcoming the eons of the weakened third chakra.

Apart from the issue of power, another huge collective imprint is our ever-spreading materialism, which conditions us all to chase after money, status, achievements, publicity and an enhanced sense of external power. We are taught that 'time is money,' and following that, we become neurotic beings, running around on this planet and imagining that we are going to accomplish something important very soon if we keep going. Our society also sanctifies individualism, so we all focus on gaining our 'own' power, thus creating a very isolated and limited sense of self.

Evolution of the World

The third chakra developed at a mass level starting in the time of ancient Greece and, even more, the Roman Empire. Thus, it developed from the will to conquer 'the entire world,' that is, through the birth of imperialist desire. This desire was born in the minds of ambitious individuals who felt the urge to stand out while most of society was of a second chakra mentality (focusing on the worship of Gods and nature, tribalism and ritual). These individuals felt the burning urge to become Gods themselves, and quite often they disgraced the Gods only to aggrandize themselves. Alexander the Great is a perfect example for that: his drive to conquer the world became an uninhibited force—this is the third chakra 'at its best' (at least its shadowy best).

This means that, along with the desire to stand up and to conquer, the sense of individuality became stronger too. Daring to separate oneself from the second chakra mentality was an act of self-definition.

Always striving to overcome competitors was, according to Nietzsche, the driving force behind the great cultural quickening that occurred in ancient Greece. Evolving through struggle, which extends itself to Darwinism and even the capitalist era, is this chakra's approach to the world.

In regards to nature, the transition at the mass level from the second chakra to the third chakra was expressed through the final detachment from nature. Worship and surrender to the forces of nature were replaced with the effort to control nature, overcoming its energies within and without, and the use and abuse of it for the sake of human needs and desires. Thus, nature became a tool.

The separation from nature began with the monotheistic emphasis on the inferior flesh versus the superior spirit, and also with its emphasis on conquering the earth, which is viewed as 'our destiny as the center of creation.' Technology, of course, is another layer of this separation.

Common Interactions with Other Chakras

In traumatic events, the first chakra often connects with the third chakra, since encounters with power abuse usually weaken both, on the instinctual level as well as on the level of our sense of self-existence.

Interactions between the balanced second chakra and the balanced third chakra support a capacity for livelihood: the much more conscious impulse to create combines with wise discipline, and the individual will synchronizes with the cosmic will.

One interesting connection between these two chakras is the twisted blend of sex and power. This calls for a deep healing, which can liberate the sexual impulses from all images of power.

The most important interaction is between the third and the fourth chakras. Actually, this combination or alignment leads to the third chakra's resolution; it's when the crucial question, 'how can I use my power in the most proper way?' is being directly and deeply answered. This fusion of power and love, and energy and emotion, brings us to the understanding that developing our individual power is important—but only so it can finally take the form of service. We are not meant to acquire power only for the sake of increasing our own sense of individuality, but mainly to become strong enough to help others. Our confidence is a quality that can support many others who are weaker than us. A great king is one who constantly asks himself: 'how can I serve my people?'

When this fusion begins to take place, several things happen: the information that the third chakra receives from outer stimulants is interpreted by the fourth chakra through the worldview of love; the emotional balance and the transmuted energy of lower emotions created by the self-control of the third chakra will merge into universal love; additionally, one will actually be able to serve with great sensitivity, selflessness, a clear conscience and morality. We cannot give if we don't have energy, and the third chakra is essential for that. Only then, supported by the more refined creative impulse of the second chakra, can we actually insist on finding or inventing work that is profitable, loving, successful and beneficial for all mankind.

We can see the infusion of these chakras through the symbolic union between the lion and the lamb, or, in Nietzsche's terminology, between the lion and the child. In the opposite direction, the split between the two chakras has been expressed over and over again in the various arts, mainly literature and cinema. This is the classic struggle between the temptation of pure power and love or service, as presented, for example, in *Star Wars*, *The Lord of the Rings* and *Harry Potter*.

A great outcome of this fusion is the sense of synchronization between our individual will and the divine will. Although we have grown to be powerful individuals, we let go of our attachment to personal desires and open ourselves up to receive higher guidance. Giving one's energy away for the sake of the whole is a sacrifice that sweetens our third chakra.

An alignment of the third and the fifth chakras is necessary if we ever want to actually manifest our ambitions. The third chakra gives the energy and the power of ambition, while the fifth is the gateway to actual manifestation—where the inner dream becomes fulfilled.

An alignment of the third and the sixth chakras is required for the integration of the different parts of the self. The third chakra can integrate inner energies through discipline and willpower, thus radiating a sense of a united self up to the sixth chakra. Since the sixth chakra monitors all thoughts and emotions, it can only direct its power of attention with the help of an integrated third chakra. Correspondingly, when the third chakra is imbalanced, the sixth will express, as a result, the total disintegration of thoughts and emotions, and therefore, a disordered and disorganized life.

Lastly, there is the interesting connection between the third and the seventh chakras. While the third chakra is master over the primordial forces of the two lower chakras, and the sixth chakra is master over all thoughts and emotions, the seventh is master over the entire psyche. This means that the third chakra is crucial for the awakening of the inner master. In other words, the first essential layer of the inner master is to be realized through the third chakra.

In many traditions the common teaching is to give oneself to God, but, if there's no one there—which means that power is lacking in the third chakra—how can one give that which does not yet exist? In order to actually be able to give away one's power to the higher scheme, the third chakra must, first of all, generate tremendous self-power.

In the Process of *Kundalini*

When this chakra awakens in the process of *kundalini*, it marks the final opening of the first granthi (a knot which prevents or allows free pranic flow in the central column). Untying the first granthi means initial, yet irreversible liberation of the self, that is, freedom from earthly bondage. The moment this granthi opens up, the first three chakras unite into one. This link is the birth of the spiritual self, a self that cannot be destroyed by time and circumstances. Once this self is created, it is an unbreakable spiritual foundation, upon which we can safely build all further development. We cannot fall back, because the first three chakras, which previously were the great hindrance of all spiritual evolution, now function as the psychological 'ground' and 'floor' of our spiritual building. This new solid self is stable (first chakra), joyful (second chakra) and powerful (third chakra).

Recommended Practices

All practices of self-discipline and self-control suit the third chakra: from controlling our food intake and diet and our sexual habits, to controlling overflowing emotions and automatic reactions (such as pain, fear or anger), and to controlling any types of urges and impulses, such as laziness and the tendency to shirk from commitments, projects and great challenges.

Since our habit is to quit most practices after a short while, all kinds of spiritual practices, when followed regularly and seriously, build the third chakra. Anything that demands effort, *especially* when we don't feel like doing it, is suitable—a conscious effort, which gathers energy precisely when the urge is to disperse it, can build intention and willpower.

However, we must also keep in mind the importance of balance between the flow of life's juices (in the second chakra) and the transcendence of impulses and urges (in the third chakra). Being able to control the powers of desire and laziness does not mean that we drop our experiences of pleasure and stop taking healthy breaks throughout the day. A certain degree of enjoyment must be preserved, even in the times when we struggle to defeat lower tendencies.

For those who tend to have excess power in the third chakra, the most important practice is to start being, rather than becoming and doing, in order to replace the addiction to outside force. This includes meditating, spending time alone without any kind of doing, going on retreats in nature, clearing time to enjoy life and loving relationships and doing all sorts of service. Usually this addiction includes violent outbursts, so practicing non-violence, meditative therapy and other techniques that can transform force into power, is also highly recommended.

Those who tend to have a weakness in the third chakra, aside from the already discussed practices of discipline, should learn how to intentionally increase their level of inner power. This can be done, for example, through the various martial arts, which support the creation of the protective shield of the third chakra.

The Fourth Chakra:
The Search For Love

Location and General Orientation

The fourth chakra is located in the middle of the chest at the heart level. It governs the heart, the lungs and the thymus gland. The lungs transport oxygen from the atmosphere into the blood stream and release carbon dioxide from the blood stream into the atmosphere. At the same time, the heart provides a continuous blood flow through the circulatory system, thus allowing oxygen into the body, while eliminating carbon dioxide from the body. This constant exchange of vital in-breath and out-breath hints at a psychological parallel: oxygen and carbon dioxide are a metaphor for allowing the world to enter into oneself and allowing oneself to go out into the world. It's the borderline of our *relationship* with the world: the constant stream of connections between 'I' and the 'other,' 'me' and the 'world.'

The thymus gland is also interesting in this context. Being in charge of the adaptive immune system, especially at young age, it is the physiological parallel to our defense mechanism, which is supposed to help us whenever we get 'shocks' at the emotional level in any kind of relationship. Naturally, the energetic equivalent of the thymus gland is the storehouse of all traumas in relationships.

Finally, the fourth chakra extends to the hands. Through our hands we participate in the endless exchange between 'me' and the 'world,' giving and receiving. This hints at the psychological challenge of the fourth chakra, learning to balance giving with receiving, and finally, transcending them both.

In the chakra system, the fourth chakra is exactly in the middle, dividing the lower three chakras and the higher three chakras. This has great significance: it makes the fourth chakra the connecting point between the more earthly energies and the more spiritual energies, between the more instinctual or primordial human parts and the intellectual or cognitive parts. Naturally, this makes the fourth chakra a bridge between the lower and the higher chakras, and in a way, uniting heaven and earth. Perhaps this is why some have regarded it as the 'seat of the self.' In the *kundalini* rising, the fourth chakra's awakening is also the middle point of the entire process. This seems to correspond quite well with the central functioning of the heart as the preserver of life.

Basic Psychological Themes

The fourth chakra's focus is relationships of all kinds. In every 'me' and 'other' there is a relationship, a subtle tension of attraction or repulsion, and in this basic tension vibrates a whole stream of feelings. This makes the fourth chakra not only the seat of relationships, but also of all feelings that revolve around relationships. While the three lower chakras contain more instinctual and primordial feelings—such as anxiety and longing for security, pleasure and desire, and weakness and power—here we find the great emotional entanglement that arises out of complex communions.

Relationships are everywhere you look: they can be between me and my body, me and my dog, me and my lover or me and God (at least, me and the way I perceive God). Relationships are a very dual notion, which allows a whole world of contradictory feelings into the picture. There is a border which separates the self from any other, and which forces the self into an emotional inquiry about others: 'do I care about this other, or do I ignore it?' 'Should I be sorry for it, be compassionate toward it, embrace and love it, attach myself to it and be depended on it, or just leave it behind?' 'Do I let it in, or should I shut my heart's doors and turn off all emotions?'

This, inevitably, puts the fourth chakra in charge of the entire spectrum of love. There is a vast potential evolution in the understanding of the nature and scope of love: from biological love to the love shared by equal partners (lovers, friends and creative associates alike), and then from spiritual love, which is the expression of unity, to love as the meaning and the motivation of life itself—and finally, love as the fragrance of our very own beings. Slowly but surely we merge with love itself.

Throughout this evolution of love, our basic psychological tension revolves around the feeling that something is lacking or absent; that somehow we are not whole and complete within ourselves, and therefore, love is something that we need and even demand from others. Relationships then become a matter of dependency: we always look for outer completion, for something that might fill up the void. Moreover, given that we cannot give abundantly, we end up feeling miserly since our deep experience is that we don't have enough for ourselves. This feeling that we have nothing to give and always need others to give to us stems from the empty, or 'broken' heart.

This emptiness and poorness of the heart could be the result of a few different things. First of all, it could be the result of traumas in which we felt abandoned or neglected. Whenever we feel deeply unwanted and betrayed it creates some kind of a bottomless pit of hungry neediness, and we need to be reassured by outer elements (be it parents, God or a lover) that we are, in spite of everything, loved and accepted. Until we receive our long-expected reassurance, we will be quite suspicious and distrusting toward almost everyone. Even those who wish to embrace us will, quite often, be furiously rejected.

Sometimes our heart is empty not because we have been neglected, but because we ourselves have deeply hurt dear ones through ignorance, aggression or irresponsibility. This might haunt us so that we simply cannot forgive ourselves, and do not feel worthy to even ask for forgiveness. This is another form of trauma, which is caused by the shock of being an aggressor, and realizing what we are able to do when trapped in deep ignorance and self-forgetfulness.

A second important reason for an empty heart is having a totally unstable structure in the lower chakras—especially an undeveloped individuality in the third chakra. As I explained earlier, the first lower chakras create, in a state of balance, a stable, joyful and powerful self. As long as we do not have this kind of integrated and wholesome self, we simply won't be able to love in a rich and fearless way. We will be too busy trying to solve our most basic issues, and we will only use (or better, abuse) our relationships as mirrors reflecting these issues.

Simply put, we are totally unavailable. As long as we do not possess a wholesome sense of self, we will not have a 'me' who can actually love and express sensitivity toward another. Having an incomplete basic structure causes one big problem: the foundational imbalance extends into our hearts and twists our emotional center. This is why we have fifty and sixty year old men and women who express a level of emotional communion that is more suitable to three and four year old children. This is *not* the result of a unique trauma—after all, almost everyone has it—but rather, a general and complex lack of true inner selfhood.

The fourth chakra cannot develop and organically mature as long as the first three chakras are keeping us busy with the more basic issues, such as fears, worries, desires and control. To actually be able to love, to actually make ourselves available and be filled with another's presence, we need a complete and wholesome heart. Since our heart is damaged and broken, we will forever depend on others to make us wholesome and complete. This dependency is the cause of all conflict in relationships. Only by meeting the other halfway, as an independent and complete heart, can we own the freedom to love. If we demand love, because we only feel complete when we receive love from another, we create a tragic connection between these momentary enjoyable interactions and our inner sense of completion.

One last important reason for having an empty heart is a lack of true spiritual development: most of us do not express interest in broadening the meaning of love, which means that, in a way, we refuse to hear the teaching of the fourth chakra. Remaining only in a biological and sexual context of love actually disconnects us from a tremendous force, and lets us enjoy only tiny drops out of a vast ocean. Even our biological connections can benefit from this expanded notion and experience of love. As long as we deny this teaching, we will be able to love our dear ones only in short-lived bursts of generosity.

Psychological Reactions of the Imbalanced Chakra

A sense of lacking and emptiness in the heart chakra can bring on two main psychological reactions: focusing mainly, if not only, on oneself, or tending to focus only on another person. In both cases, this is the result of an emotional dependency on outer completion through another.

Focusing on the self, which is basically the narcissistic way of living, is the most common level of expression in human relationships. When this narcissistic self encounters the 'other', it cannot truly recognize or appreciate its 'otherness'. The main focus, if not the only focus, of this self is the way this other can serve them or give them what they need. The other is merely a vehicle, which they use in order to extract some benefits into their life.

It is important to understand that the narcissistic self is not necessarily in love with himself, but can also hate himself. The essence of emotional narcissism is the self-focus, being deeply involved in how *I feel* and in the way you make *me feel* at every given moment.

For the narcissistic self, the other does not really exist as a separated entity. This type of recognition inevitably would require the recognition of a totally different set of needs and wants. The other is but an extension of one's own self, and that is why possessiveness, jealousy and revenge are always intertwined with narcissistic 'love'. The other belongs to 'me', and since he is 'mine', he must keep delivering the emotional reassurance he is meant to deliver. If he doesn't—if he rebels against his 'natural' job in my life, or even abandons me—it brings about the very opposite of love: hatred and grudge.

Of course, when we were young children this was our natural position, but most grown ups remain in the narcissistic position for the rest of their lives. The more they concentrate on their wants and needs, the more they feel their emotions are a bottomless pit of neediness. The narcissistic self always feels dissatisfied and always feels the need for more approval, greater embraces, more support, and more reassuring love and compliments. 'I need you to give me the feeling that I am wanted, needed and loved'—this is the basic demand, and since this type of self also grows to be hyper-sensitive, it thoroughly examines the level of love and caring in every word and every gesture. Since this neediness is fault-finding by nature, it will always find enough evidence for a lack of love on the other side of the relationship. Of course, people of this type are perfect and know how to love and respect; therefore they happily appoint themselves to be others educators on the path of love-realization.

The arrow of attention always points at the self: "even when I love and give, the other only mirrors back my own great generosity." The general scope of feelings ranges from emptiness and stiffness of the heart to dissatisfaction and discontentment. We are momentarily satisfied when we receive enough emotional nourishment, but soon we'll need more and the other might not be as available. Since in our experience we have totally depended on the other for emotional nourishment, as if our heart is missing something on its own, we will put the entire weight of our emotional imbalance on the other's shoulders, blaming them for leaving us 'alone' and 'broken hearted.'

The narcissistic self might also reach a state in which it simply cannot engage in any kind of deep and demanding relationship, so it will choose to live in solitude, to engage only in short-term relationships or even to stay in a very neglectful partnership. This self will simply shut the doors of its heart, create its own world of false 'independence' and feel nothing. There will be a terrible hardening of the heart, making it totally uncaring. It will intentionally avoid the possibility of dependency and emotional attachment, and it will turn the individuality and power of the third chakra into an object of worship. Inevitably, it will find strange new kinds of 'relationships' as sources of compensation: money, status, sex, food or self-fulfillment.

Our damaged self might also express itself in the opposite way: through an obsessive inclination toward self-sacrifice and devotion in all kinds of relationships, or in one particular kind of relationship. The tendency to forget oneself in a relationship, to devote all one's energy to another (sometimes to the extent of endangering our health) and to be unable to be alone, is also a sign of a lack of self. Since we do not possess a sense of completion, we look for affirmation through the presence and gratification of others; we exist only as long as the other exists. Sometimes we may support this behavioral pattern through religious and spiritual morality—'losing oneself in love'—but in reality, deep inside we will feel dissatisfied and unfulfilled. 'What about me? Who will look after me?'—will be our silent distress, since something will definitely be missing. Everyone enjoys the company of self-sacrificing personalities, because it's always nice to have someone at your service. That is why society quite often supports this behavior, but if we ever want to feel wholesome and content, this is certainly not the way to live.

In general, men tend to develop the psychological reaction of the narcissistic self, and women are more inclined toward self-forgetting and sacrifice. Biologically speaking, this is due to the psychological expression of testosterone (the ability to act impersonally and in a target-oriented spirit) and oxytocin (the urge to define oneself only through relationships).

The phrase 'unconditional love' is very well known, and yet, beyond the cliché, we must face a very direct and bitter reality: the love of the damaged self can very easily change into horrifying violence and hatred. When the heart is incomplete, it will develop a dependency that always has two opposing emotional sides. Somehow everyone agrees to live and bear this strange mixture of love and hatred, affection and violent jealousy, and passion and revenge—and, in between, the more introverted and milder twisted forms of 'love': sorrow, immediate insult, disappointment, self pity and the shutting down of all emotions.

The general idea of love for the damaged self is the experience of total dependence on another. Sometimes we fight it and try to escape this dependency by creating more independent communions—for example, an 'equal' relationship based on give and take—and yet, even then, we cannot escape this vast range of violent emotions; violent either toward the other or toward oneself. Only by owning an inner sense of wholeness can we actually escape this emotional vicious circle.

On the religious level, for example, we have developed a very complicated relationship with 'God.' We expect him to love us just as we are and to receive our prayers and requests. We give him our moral behavior and obedience to the law, and in return we expect some benefits: mercy, material possessions, or even the mere feeling that we are not alone in this universe. Since God seems to be silent most of the time, and we remain in this Godless and merciless human realm, we might end up feeling betrayed and unprotected. Where is God when we need him? Why doesn't he respond to our prayers? We might develop several ways to cope with this 'silent betrayal,' such as feeling abandoned and becoming frustrated atheists, developing a contradictory and ambivalent relationship with God, praying even harder or imagining that our prayers are received in spite of all apparent evidence, and so on.

A totally different example is the biological love of a parent toward his or her baby. This biological love is totally arbitrary: if someone in the hospital would have mistakenly brought us a different child, we would not have been able to notice, and we would have immediately begun to develop a 'unique' love toward him or her. Shortly after that, we would feel that this was indeed the nicest child ever. When we raise a child while our sense of self is damaged and incomplete, we will also depend on the poor boy or girl to help us achieve our own sense fulfillment and happiness. When this child grows up and begins to confront us and to express his or her own separated personality, we will feel disappointment and anger: the temporary oneness will be broken, and once again there will be an interruption in the flow of love.

Solutions for the Imbalanced Fourth Chakra

The key solution for imbalances of the fourth chakra is understanding that true love stems only from an unbroken *wholeness* and never from *neediness*, and that it is fulfilled not through what we *receive* but rather through what we *give*.

This solution requires an evolution in our understanding of the nature of love. As long as we link love with specific people and with experiences that are bound in time and changeable—a tendency of the damaged self—the flow of love will be interrupted and broken. People can die or leave; the intensity of falling in love can fade; a relationship can suddenly become very demanding and be filled with obstacles, which can lead to hardships on our side; our child can rebel against us and tell us that he 'hates' us, and God can be indifferent when we are in a terrible agony. For the damaged self, which believes that love is about receiving, this is the cause of great sorrow.

Love can never be broken. Love is an uninterrupted flow, which may or may not express itself through our hearts, and yet, it is always there, as a cosmic sun that never dies. When we are too busy hindering it with neediness and emotional materialism, the rays of this sun cannot be felt by us and aren't able to express their light through us. Indeed, it is well known that we can easily block the sun's all-encompassing light with a single palm covering our eyes!

When we realize that love is a cosmic sun that always shines, we will perceive that its reflections in our lives, through people and experiences, are merely momentary expressions of love's light. Then we will begin to communicate with this uninterrupted flow, and this communication will be the only true source of healing for the imbalanced fourth chakra: someone will 'die on us,' and we will still experience love; our partner will abandon us, and we will still experience this light. Love's light is in fact an inner flow that we can communicate with directly, without the mediation of objects and people. Love comes from within, as an inner revelation, and it is really not an experience but rather a constant state. In this context, we can even say that we do not experience love, but *love experiences us*. We are merely vehicles for that flow.

By the power of this magnificent insight, our heart chakra is finally free from all bondage; it is now free to become a complete true self, which never waits for love to come and never fears that love might leave. Of course, when a dear one dies, some level of longing will remain, but even this longing will be sweet and tender. When the heart is whole and complete, all emotional entanglement will be over. The complex emotions, which usually cloud the brightness and lightness of love, will be gone. Your love can never turn into hatred, your affection can never transform into revenge, and your warmth cannot suddenly become pure rage. The three lower chakras will not be able to abuse love's light and to rob its purity.

The moment these hard emotions are banished from the heart's realm, we will not need to be narcissistic. In fact, we will become extremely available to the other's presence, since our hungry emotions will be absent. We will also be free from the psychological tendency to completely forget ourselves in relationships, since all relationships will come into their right proportion in this new context of the vastness of love. The need for self-defense that follows miserable dependency upon outer completion will be gone.

There is another part to this key solution. The wholeness of the heart chakra leads to freedom from neediness and dependency, and this freedom leads to a new state of availability. This availability is in a natural relaxed state, a state in which caring, sensitivity and warmth are only by-products. This implies that love is, indeed, unintentional; love is not an agenda to be imposed upon people and situations, but rather a state of openness, which is always ready to share and always willing to give.

Reaching this state of openness is the beginning of our communication with the meaning of life, and the fourth chakra is the gateway to this meaning. Everyone somehow knows that without love, life has no meaning, but when this is interpreted through the filters of the damaged and incomplete self, it leads back to the same old dependency on others. The meaning of life is to be found in the very opposite state of dependency: its message, as I pointed out earlier, is that love is fulfilled, not through what we *receive*, but rather, through what we *give*.

The fundamental questions that underlie the entire spectrum of emotional materialism are: 'What's in it for me?' 'What can it give to me?' and 'How can this serve my need for happiness and wholeness?' Whatever experience of love we may extract from this materialistic approach, it will never fulfill love's 'desire.' Love never asks, 'what's in it for me?' but rather, 'how can I serve the other, or even all others?' The arrow of true love always faces *outwardly*.

This maturation of the heart chakra leads to an uninterrupted contact with the meaning of life. We never ask for anything from God; if we pray, our prayers ask, 'How can I serve you better? How can I give myself away even more?' We don't need love, we give it; we let it shine through our complete heart chakra. Then and only then do we realize that our deepest yearning was never to receive, but only to always be able to give.

This is a synchronization of the heart chakra with the cosmic sun of love. In a way, our heart chakra becomes a small sun, radiating abundantly everywhere it focuses its attention. This small sun, if it wasn't constricted by the limitations of the body, could give and give tirelessly, twenty-four hours a day. In fact, it has no choice: once awakened to its own fullness and capacity, it shines just like the sun—always, and with no intention to do so.

The heart's realization of its own wholeness transforms the nature of our relationships: we understand that when we are not there, love is, and when we are there, love is not. We understand the true meaning of self-forgetfulness—leaving behind the illusory state of the damaged self and moving into the state of self-wholeness, in which we are empty enough to be completely filled by the other's presence. This availability makes way for a whole new set of awesome emotions.

This might seem like a huge task, but that's only because our damaged self seems *completely* real. It tells us that only when we heal completely, can we ever make ourselves available. Yet, even if we don't negate the need for healing—surely every one of us had his or her share of heartaches and disappointments—the amazing fact of love's wholeness is that it is already there!

Every young mother knows this type of wholeness. Before the act of giving birth, the young woman is perhaps quite narcissistic and even spoiled, but the moment her baby comes into the world, instincts tell her that she—her entire world of wants and needs—must momentarily 'vanish' to make room for the baby's world of wants and needs. She disappears completely, making herself empty in order to be filled by the other's presence. Amazingly, at least in most cases, in spite of all her fatigue and weariness, the woman is overwhelmingly blissful after becoming a mother. When contemplating the meaning of life, one would realize that this is not that surprising—in fact, it's pretty simple: true happiness is to be found not in our own happiness, but rather in our ability to make others happy.

This is not only valid for peak experiences, such as fresh motherhood. This fulfillment is realized whenever we don't have time to think of ourselves, because we have to dedicate our entire energy to others. Usually this happens in times of emergency, when we don't have any other choice but to be self-sacrificing. Whenever we do that, our heart chakra reaches a momentary state of balance, softly awakening its own dormant wholeness. This is probably the best mark of our inherent divinity: there is something in us that makes us complete only when we function as a radiating selfless love, just like our sun and just like God. Concentrating on ourselves immediately makes us feel miserable and empty-hearted—isn't that the clearest sign of our destiny?

The greatest practice of the fourth chakra is moving out of oneself and becoming totally available to another. Even though conditioned thoughts will tell us this is impossible unless we first get everything that we need from the other—all love and reassurance, a sense of safety and unconditional acceptance—we will soon realize that we can actually take this leap at any given moment. There is a level of being in which life is all about the self, and there is a more progressed level, in which life is all about equal and conditional giving and receiving. Yet, for all of us, there is an open possibility to devote our being to another, and to immediately experience great bliss—a by-product of getting in touch with the meaning of life. Just think of moments in which you made someone happy. Isn't it more thrilling to give someone a gift than to receive one? If your answer is 'no,' search more within the depths of your heart; you will probably find that you harbor a strong belief that you have to be given everything before you join the celebration of love.

In the Kabala teachings, the most fundamental practice —or even the most fundamental way of living—is to 'receive in order to give.' This means that we must open ourselves and be filled by the great wholesome divine light, and then, overflowing, we will be able to give. Love is simply a cup, which is too overflowing with nectar to keep within as our own treasure; we give because we have too much, and the more we give, the more we realize that the source of love is endless, and the cup keeps overflowing.

That is why balancing the fourth chakra requires spiritual evolution. Spiritual practices can expand our experience of love and free us from the fixated belief that love is merely biology, sex and romance. Practices in which we get to know the awesome wholeness of love, put all our exalted notions about love affairs and even parenthood into proportion—they are still only pale echoes of the divine light!

In the inner process of balancing the heart chakra, we have to heal traumas that revolve around all kinds of wounds and scars from relationships. Forgiveness that flows from self-wholeness beautifully awakens the heart. This is why it is advised to forgive through spiritual therapy. Following that, it is very important to thoroughly investigate and understand (through mind techniques, for example) any expectation or need to be loved and any projection on your dear ones. One more essential practice is clearing the three lower chakras, which, as we mentioned earlier, is an absolute necessity for the heart's balance.

There is also the inner work of clearing self-hatred—our inability to accept ourselves. Self-condemnation might be our favorite habit (and religions do support it quite passionately—after all, the very birth of humanity was apparently followed by sin, and we *did* fall from grace). This can be the result of an injustice or a harm we did to others, a trauma in which we absorbed other's hatred and negativity, or a general outer judgment that we have assimilated. Again, being too critical and judgmental—with the self divided into two halves, the judge and the condemned—reflects nothing but a lack of wholeness in the heart. In this case, we should not strive to move in the opposite direction. This might just be a new trap, since in so many respects loving oneself is not different from hating oneself. Both are forms of narcissism, which stem from the same unstable structure of the three first chakras. So, when self-hatred is cleared, there will be a transcendence of both emotional sides, and an immediate leap toward the wholeness of love.

Apart from the inner work of spiritual practices and psychological healing, one can balance the fourth chakra through two great outer practices. First and foremost is service. We have to practice love which is not biological and romantic, that is, love that isn't connected with our lower three chakras. Service, which forces us to extend ourselves beyond the familiar limitations of 'love' as we know it, is a wonderful practice, and it is in its highest expression when we serve something that is clearly greater than our own lives.

The second practice is for the narcissistic self, who forever escapes commitment in love, and to whom 'love' connotes 'falling in love.' Although the entire entertainment world—cinema in particular—supports this idea, in reality, love is demanding and requires a careful and daily cultivation of sensitivity. To balance the fourth chakra, we have to take on the burden of love—committing to give ourselves away, even and *especially* when we don't feel like it.

The Three Levels of Functioning

The Functional Fourth Chakra

We are able to commit to long-term relationships, and we do not try to escape from the hardships and the burdens of relationships. We are able to express gratitude and regret, to forgive and to ask for forgiveness. We are also able to experience true intimacy and deep emotional exchanges. It is possible for us to suppress our narcissistic self when an act of selflessness and sacrifice is required. Of course, we might drown, from time to time, in emotional needs, but we can overcome these floods through the realistic understanding that life is not about us, and we are not the center of creation (although that would be nice, at least from time to time). We do our share of service in the world, since we understand that, as a part of the whole, our meaningful existence is about what we can contribute to the general web of life. Our understanding of love is still mostly limited to biology, sex, romance, family and friends, but we can also show acts of compassion toward people who do not belong to our inner and immediate circle of caring. We are tolerant and pluralistic, and we aspire to create peace in our surroundings and in the world in general.

The Balanced Fourth Chakra

We experience wholeness in our hearts, so we are quite free from emotional materialism and attachment. Our arrow of attention effortlessly turns outward. We feel ourselves overflowing with non-causal emotions (which can be regarded as soul-qualities), and this leads us to ecstatic sharing and gives us a great capacity for true intimacy with many people. When we meet someone, our attention and energy naturally turn toward listening to their needs and understanding their perspectives. Selfless service is our natural attraction, and we actually feel it is inseparable from our definition of the meaning of life. We feel both passion—an emotional engagement with life as a whole—and compassion—a feeling that our hearts can never be closed and sealed in the face of other's misery. This compassion might even result in some pain, because of our ability to empathize deeply with the pain of others. Activism in the world is very natural for us. There is a deep heart-based knowledge, that results from a spiritual connection with the divine, which links us with the meaning of life; this heart-based knowledge remains lucid, even when our mind forgets and becomes confused. We experience a constant flow of spiritual longing, and an attraction toward merging with the wholeness of life; this longing and the experience of love are our direct connection to divine realms. Our relationship with God moves from belief and obedience to the longing to merge and unite with him. Love, for us, is a universal phenomenon, and we experience a unifying urge—an urge to bring heaven into earth and to create a world peace in which we all transcend our self-preserving tendencies.

The Awakened Fourth Chakra

The awakened fourth chakra is all about the growing revelation of inherent unity. Constant awakenings to the fact of oneness take place here, and through these awakenings, we cease holding on to the notion of 'me' and the 'other.' This means that, essentially, this is the beginning of the end of 'relationships.' Indeed, the other is myself, my extended self, just as my arms and legs are parts of my whole body. Humanity, including all sentient beings and the whole universe in general, is an interconnected web of oneness—and the more we know it, the greater our responsibility grows, since we are part of that one and only being, and there's no one else to rely on. The awakened fourth chakra releases a tremendous reservoir of energy, which enables us to become giving suns that never tire of giving. We always 'know' the truth in our hearts, and our hearts, minds and actions are totally in tune with the insight that the only good reason to breathe and live is to give. The Bodhisattva vow, which binds our own happiness and liberation with everybody else's happiness and liberation, is an example of this awakened heart. The heart, as the meeting point between all polarities ('this' and 'other'), connects our earthly elements with our heavenly elements, and, in this connection, enables a constant flow of grace from the heavens to the earth—manifesting a divine reality in this world of time and space.

Polar Emotions

Emotional emptyness / emotional wholeness,
need to receive / wish to give, narcissism / love.

Type of Trauma

The emotional trauma occurs whenever a painful disappointment follows a powerful relationship. In this are included parental abandonment or any kind of abandonment by dear ones, the physical loss of dear ones, and sudden betrayal, or even apparent betrayal, by someone we trusted or even devoted our life to—this may even be a spiritual authority or God himself. This also includes times when we needed approval and love but got rejected by significant others. In traumas of the fourth chakra, we are unable to let go of the heartache caused by memories of love and the loss of love.

The fundamental conclusion reached through heart traumas is: 'It is dangerous to become attached to someone or to something.' This conclusion is accompanied by the feeling that we are alone in this world and that there is no real love in the entire, indifferent universe. From then onwards, whenever we open ourselves to another in intimacy and vulnerability, it will make the brain send signals of warning to the entire body and psyche—after all, if we attach ourselves too much and become vulnerable, we might pay a terrible price.

Many emotions are connected with these traumas. We might become vengeful, and be filled with grudges and hatred, and this, in turn, can lead to aggression in relationships. We might also become very suspicious, jealous, possessive and domineering, fearing that at any given moment 'our' love might be taken away from us (unaware of the fact that love is a mysterious force, and we cannot control its rising and subsiding). We won't be able to believe that someone can actually love us, and at the same time, we will violently demand love from others. Of course, we might completely shut down our emotional system, stop feeling and start connecting only on an intellectual level.

Type of Personality

Traditionally, the symbol of the fourth chakra personality type is the antelope. Basically, this personality type perceives life as an exchange of feelings, as a space of sharing—receiving and giving. These are the people who put relationships as the top priority. This type is very sensitive and highly emotional; they connect to life through powerful emotions, and that is, in fact, what's most real for them.

There are a variety of expressions of this personality type. In its simplest form, we find the people who constantly dwell on family and romance. Raising children and loving a man or a woman are the most powerful and meaningful experiences in life. The more complex form of this personality type is found in activists and social idealists, those who engage in powerful forms of giving and consider this the center of life. An even more complex form of this type is found in people who tirelessly devote themselves to selfless service and actions of universal compassion, and who very often create international movements for the sake of healing the planet and cultivating world peace. This later type of person is usually driven by great visions, which revolve around the idea of 'bringing heaven to earth.' There is yet another expression of this type, which is based on loving God through devotional and spiritual practices (in the yogic tradition this is called 'Bhakti Yoga').

In the Ayurvedic tradition, these people are considered to be mostly a Vatta type, which means they are connected with the air element. In an imbalanced expression, this personality type will demonstrate hyper-sensitivity, hysterical emotionalism, tremendous jealousy and possessiveness, which might become violent at times (in the effort to defend this hyper-vulnerability), and this personality type will experience an inability to think logically and separate itself from blinding emotions and an obsessive and narcissistic dwelling in the world of emotions.

Famous Fourth Chakra Expressions

Jesus, Mother Theresa: unconditional love as the direct expression
of divinity in human beings.

Male and Female Energies

The male aspect of the fourth chakra is the activist approach of world rectification: being totally engaged in changing the world for the better, constantly giving, and constantly bestowing the grace of love and care. It is seeding the world with the inspiration of love, sometimes even screaming its gospel from the rooftops. It is important to understand that when the curtain of indifference is removed from the heart, and the heart remains exposed to all the misery in the world, the only possible expression of a true heart's empathy will be action.

The female aspect of this chakra is an unconditional, absolute acceptance of everything: embracing all sentient beings at their own level of development no matter what, even if they have been harmful to themselves or to others. It is a tremendous level of acceptance—seeing the inherent good in everything just as it is. One can even say that this is 'seeing the world through God's eyes.' This female aspect is amazingly healing for the wounded hearts that encounter it, and can be symbolized by the image of the divine or universal mother.

Type of Happiness

The experience of happiness in the fourth chakra is found in sharing highly positive feelings with others. In this conjunction between 'me' and 'the other,' there is a tremendous flow, which overwhelms us with beauty, grace and selflessness—and whenever we are able to experience it, we get in touch with what seems to be the only meaning of life. Love, intimacy, service and devotion are the energies that fill us with happiness. We feel happiest whenever we forget all about ourselves and all barriers between 'me' and the 'other' are removed; as well as when taking part in great peace movements, changing the world for the better, or experiencing total oneness with all that exists, through a spiritual revelation.

Life's Meaning and Purpose

Love is the one and only true motivation for life. It is the first cause, the fuel, the meaning and the purpose of life. There is no meaning to life when our hearts are empty and when we don't do our best to deeply engage in emotional exchanges with others. By serving a higher cause, we are fulfilled. We have all come here to become love in human form. Love is eternal, and by connecting to it, we overcome death. Of course, God is love, and He can be directly communicated with through our hearts and our own noble expressions of selfless love.

Ages of Development of the Fourth Chakra

The fourth chakra develops from the age of twenty-one to the age of twenty-eight. During the development of our third chakra (ages 14-21), we are completely focused on the integration of our individuality, and our separateness from all others. If we followed this process diligently and had our share of rebellion and freedom, the natural and inevitable next stage is to return to the society from which we separated, and to begin developing real relationships *based* on our newfound individuality and independence.

In the fourth chakra's development, the young man or woman is called to complete the growth process by acknowledging the presence of others, and handling demanding relationships with care and respect. We cannot continue with our narcissistic habits; love and momentary infatuation must be followed by commitment and true respect for the other's needs and worldviews. It is no longer about our immediate impulses and desires, and the others do not exist as mere servants or supporters of our journey. We cannot make ourselves comfortable in our former position of financial dependence and childish living—we are now called to contribute to society and to slowly locate our own unique way to serve the world.

In this period, there is usually a struggle between our narcissistic habits and the new outer demands. At first, we might become extremely insulted, frustrated, angry, and disappointed when others refuse to focus on us and abandon their own strange needs and demands. Of course, we might keep our childish behaviors for much longer than we should, even for the rest of our lives, but this means we won't ever face the challenge of the fourth chakra, and that it will remain poorly developed within us (quite often people will revile us for this uncaring behavior). It is highly important to understand that, while a child's narcissism—the inability to recognize others' autonomy—can sometimes be quite amusing, when adults behave in the same manner it is one of the clearest indications of improper psychological development.

Psychosomatic Disturbances

Psychosomatic disturbances in the fourth chakra are mostly connected with disorders in the heart and lungs. Since the heart and lungs represent the exchange of vital breath and air—which is man's most fundamental relationship with the world—their psychosomatic disorders will, first and foremost, revolve around the inability to breathe properly; asthma is only one good example. All kinds of pressures in the chest might also imply psychosomatic issues. Heart disorders can be connected to difficulties with intimacy, forgiveness, compassion and the letting go of past heartaches (and also an over-achieving third chakra, which strains the entire organism and overshadows the deep challenges of the fourth chakra). Shutting down all emotions or suppressing deep emotions, whether positive or negative, can be very destructive to the flow of energy in both the lungs and the heart.

The thymus gland, being the one responsible—especially in early childhood, when it is physically active—for the immune system, is, psychologically, the heart's defender. If it cannot stand the pressure of accumulated emotional traumas it might express itself psychosomatically, through diseases connected to a weak immune system.

Collective Imprints

The development of religious morality is the most powerful collective imprint in the fourth chakra. On the one hand, there is always the feeling of not being good enough and not being accepted in the eyes of God—after all, our first step toward humanity was God turning his back on us and making us fall into earthly existence. This is one good reason for collective self-hatred, and religions quite often maintain this image, thus supporting collective second and fourth chakra imbalances. On the other hand, there are plenty of moral codes regarding our attitudes and actions toward others. These moral codes demand respect, love, compassion, service for the community and so on, and yet we, as humanity, have not assimilated these values too well, and nowadays, secular society rejects many of them. This leaves our heart chakra empty, as it is not filled by new inner codes. We are a strange mixture of the remains of religious morality (the sanctity of marriage, for example) and the secular third chakra's rebellion against our ancestors.

In our present, materialistic and extremely competitive society, it is very hard to avoid emotional materialism and narcissism. Everything becomes a commodity that we can easily consume and throw away, so our level of communication is deeply challenged. Combining this atmosphere of mutual exploitation with the absence of moral values creates a great hole that must be filled.

The second major collective imprint is man not accepting many kinds of 'minorities' (black people, women, homosexuals—these are just a few examples), denying their inherent divinity and dishonoring them in many respects. Fortunately, this imprint is being slowly corrected and healed in our Western society.

Evolution of the World

The fourth chakra developed mainly through the evolution of morality. Morality, being the regularization of human relationships in the context of higher values, created a foundation for moving away from the narcissistic self and recognizing the 'other.' Without morality, the still childish brain would create an even more chaotic sphere of human relationships.

Morality is, basically, cultural support for higher qualities, such as honor, sacrifice, devotion, non-violence and commitment. In principle, moral codes have existed for many thousands of years. Confucius and Gautama the Buddha are impressive examples from the east, while in the west, it seems that the development of morality has reached its highest influence in the last two thousand years through the increasing power of monotheistic religions. Monotheistic religions have set two levels of moral codes: one between God and man, and one between man and society. These two sets quite often intertwine.

It seems that the evolution of morality reached a certain peak in the rise of Christianity. The Roman Empire was basically a third chakra regime, power and glory being its center of attention. Christianity elaborated on the monotheistic notions of the Bible, yet it also got rid of the vengeful and extremely critical father-like Jewish God. Jesus was a prominent advocate of the notion that God is expressed, through human relationships, as unconditional love; obedience to the law became less important than the direct and pure power of compassion. Although in the Middle Ages, and many other centuries, man excelled in not listening to this profound teaching, it was still probably the root cause of the New Age, in which God is now considered to be more of an inner consciousness, which expresses itself, in human form, as love.

Through the monotheistic belief structure, the notion of the individual soul has been increasingly strengthened: the soul is a spark of divine light, which embarks on a long journey, in order to return to its creator in a purified and elevated form. The individual soul maintains an independent relationship with the 'Father,' a relationship that requires a profound commitment to moral conduct. In its personal process of development, it must cultivate right intentions and actions, obeying the everlasting law of reward or punishment. Meanwhile, it longs to attain a worthy position in the afterlife. This notion of the soul has greatly developed in the heart of human beings, encouraging a sense of responsibility and individuality in our relationship with the divine.

Common Interactions with Other Chakras

The first and the fourth chakras intersect in traumas of betrayal, abandonment and the physical loss of dear ones.

The second and the fourth chakras intersect in sinful feelings, which too-rigid moral codes may arouse. We feel that we are not allowed to have experiences, and when we do dare to have an experience—or even simply *want* an experience—we are 'bad' and even evil. These sinful feelings accumulate in the second chakra as a suppression of life force, and in the fourth chakra as self-hatred.

An extremely important interaction between the third and the fourth chakras was discussed at length in the third chakra section. Generally, the fourth chakra is the deepest solution for the third chakra: being the center from which we choose our focuses for devotion and dedication. It teaches the third chakra how to dedicate its accumulated power to the whole. This means that the fourth chakra gives purpose and context to our developing individuality—we become more and more individual *only* so we can contribute more to others and to life as a whole. Love is then realized as the highest form of power.

There is a common interaction between the fourth chakra and the fifth chakra when feelings in the heart overflow and reach a point when they need to be expressed outwardly. These can be either negative or positive feelings, but they have to find their expression through the gateway of the throat. However, when the fourth chakra opens up, it gives way to the balance of the fifth chakra, since we begin to use our voice only for the expression of harmonious and unifying inner urges.

Another major interaction is the one between the fourth and the sixth chakras. Together, these two create what one may regard as the 'wisdom of the heart,' a state in which there is no longer any difference between love and intelligence, intellect and heart-knowing, or feelings and knowledge.

In the Process of *Kundalini*

The heart chakra has a tremendous role in the process of the *kundalini* unfolding. Before anything else, it is the center of longing for and devotion to the spiritual journey itself—it is the center of the love of truth, or the love of God, from which we express our aspiration to attain a perfect union that transcends all relationships.

The heart chakra is just in the middle, between the three lower chakras and the three higher chakras. As such, it is the meeting point between heaven and earth, and it has the power to unite them into a God-like human being. It does this through the power of soul qualities, which are divine and human. That is the beauty of love and all its expressions: it is just in between divinity and simple humanity; love is the power that connects heaven and earth.

The fourth chakra is the second Granthi (lock or gateway of energy)—again, just in between the first, most-earthly Granthi (first chakra) and the third, most- heavenly Granthi (sixth chakra). This puts it in the middle of the *kundalini* process. When the *kundalini* reaches the heart, we are in the midst of our awakening: just between separation and oneness. There is a thin relationship barrier separating us from divinity. Here we experience oneness with all that is, and it expresses itself through an abundant, uncontrolled love that has no one object of attention.

Recommended Practices

As described earlier, mainly in the 'solutions' section, the most important practices of the heart chakra are actions of compassion. This may include the variety of religious and spiritual practices of compassionate service, and all other kinds of activities for the sake of world peace and collective healing. The fourth chakra can never evolve unless it experiences actual involvement and engagement in things that are higher and bigger than our own little lives.

Too often, spiritual practices tend to lead the practitioner toward self-immersion. This might increase unwanted narcissism, and put the heart chakra into deep and eternal sleep. So, one must take care not to fall into the spiritual narcissism trap. Practices, such as the Bodhisattva Vow, in which we remind ourselves that the only logic for spiritual evolution is, indeed, evolution for the sake of all sentient beings, can be not only heroic, but also very helpful for this purpose.

At the deeper internal level, deep emotional healing must take place in order to open the heart and to keep it from closing again. The purpose of the healing is not to feel strong or immune, but rather to agree to be totally vulnerable and exposed. This is actually a new type of strength. Clearing all kinds of traumas from the first four chakras can gradually open us up to this new state of being.

Practicing Bhakti Yoga and other kinds of spiritual devotion—be it toward a teacher or toward a God—can be extremely powerful. Devotion can express itself through non-materialistic prayers, sacred singing and meditation on beloved objects of union. Another spiritual practice is veganism, which is a gesture of love and an expression of oneness with all animals on this planet.

Deep meditative states, reached through contemplative meditation or any other mind technique, should be entered in the context of the realization that we can be completely self-satisfied, and free of all emotional needs, without the support of any other. This is a paradoxical realization since only by immersing ourselves in these states of total aloneness can we experience the wholeness of heart out of which we can awesomly love.

One beautiful practice is imagining that we literally lost our heads and that we physically perceive all reality through the eyes of the heart. When reality is seen through the eyes of the heart, we cannot help being selfless and compassionate.

At the level of romantic and family relationships, we can practice what can be regarded as the 'Tantra of the heart,' which is basically turning our arrow of attention toward the other and emptying ourselves in order to be filled by them. This does not mean ceasing to express our own needs, but rather connecting more and more with a state in which the inherent wholeness of our heart reveals itself. Remember: we don't have to wait to love selflessly until we are fulfilled ourselves—this is only a misconception, for love, by its very nature, is an immediate possibility, here and now.

Fifth Chakra:
The Search For Communication

Location and General Orientation

The fifth chakra is located in the base of the throat. It governs the throat, the thyroid gland and the mouth. In many respects, this chakra is the bridge between our inner world and the outer world. Physiologically speaking, the throat is the only passageway through which the body can receive vital ingredients, such as oxygen and food—which also makes it responsible for allowing materials from the world into the body. That is why the throat, being exposed to harmful micro-organisms, has 'guards' in the pharynx (the tonsils) and in the mouth (saliva) to prevent them from entering. Another physiological aspect of this chakra is the vocal cords, which enable us to express thoughts and emotions through speaking and singing. Lastly, there is the mouth, which enables us to eat, to speak, to sing and even to be intimate through kissing.

The psychological parallel of these three elements is our ability to connect well between the outer world and our inner world. It is similar to the challenge of the fourth chakra, but there is one major difference: the heart is still a part of our inner self, while the throat is all about expression and communication—first and foremost, linguistic and verbal communication. So, more directly put, the fifth chakra translates inner feelings and ideas into outer manifestations; it is the agent through which the inside can be expressed to the outside, and at the same time, through which the outside can be 'let in.'

Naturally, the thyroid gland is involved in this process. It is responsible for the rate of metabolism, the rate of chemical reactions that allow absorption of materials from the environment and production of energy out of them—basically, it responds to the environment while maintaining our own structure.

In the chakra map, the fifth chakra is located just in between the fourth and the sixth. This makes it the 'bottleneck,' which can either block or enable a free flow between these two very important chakras. The fourth chakra, the governor of emotions, and the sixth chakra, the governor of thoughts, meet in the middle in the throat chakra. The throat gives way to both emotions and thoughts through its final vehicle, the mouth.

Basic Psychological Themes

The fifth chakra focuses on the ability to communicate and to express our innermost being properly, accurately and directly. It is the translator of the other six chakras. Whatever is accumulated within the other six chakras—experiences, creative urges, will, individuality, caring, emotional involvement, knowledge, wisdom and spiritual realization of all kinds—will seek a way to be expressed from the innermost to the outermost. It won't want to stay secretly locked in the inner world, since the act of sharing is also the act of materialization. Nothing wants to slowly suffocate as an inner abstract feeling; life is all about creation and *participation*. For this, the six chakras depend entirely on the fifth chakra, and naturally, if it is imbalanced, this process of realization will be disturbed and even blocked.

I may have a tremendous creative power in my second chakra, and yet it will be unable to move upwards and to be expressed outwardly. Or I may have a great feeling of love in my fourth chakra, which will remain there, stuck, because of my blocked fifth chakra. I can carry within my sixth chakra an overwhelming amount of wisdom, but my wisdom will remain locked within me. If my fifth chakra is balanced, it can release a song, a beautiful and vulnerable gesture of love, a book or an amazing teaching for the masses. So, the final release of everything within me—from my deepest needs to my greatest gifts—completely depends on the balancing of the fifth chakra.

At this stage, we understand that the fifth chakra has far reaching implications, and a much broader meaning beyond the mere ability to speak our mind and inner truth. It is the chakra of realization, manifestation and materialization. It transforms abstract feelings, thoughts and even visions, into tangible, visible and communicative forms and structures. This makes it a highly important chakra in the process of self-fulfillment.

The fifth chakra, supported by the sixth chakra, is both the editor and the translator of our inner story. It is responsible for choosing the most suitable structures of communication—the structures that will most enable others to hear us and to understand us. It is an editor: at every given moment, it chooses what should remain inside and what should come out. For the fifth chakra, the great challenge is to find and realize the perfect middle point between talking too much and talking too little, tracing the exact time to speak out and the exact time to clear space for the other to be heard, and identifying what must come out—preventing suppression—and what doesn't *really* have to come out. Without us noticing it, the fifth chakra is in a constant state of questioning. After all, there is a vast spectrum of thoughts and feelings within us; a tremendous question is: what should we pick up from this endless stream and reveal to others by voicing it?

When the fifth chakra is in a state of imbalance, it will, inevitably, be unable to properly select from the inner world, and to *edit* us in a good way. This can create either too introverted a personality or too extroverted a personality. The chakra will be unable to identify what is merely a passing and unimportant emotion versus an emotion that is essential for constructive sharing and growing intimacy. It will not recognize the right moments to stand up and stick loyally to our opinions and the right moments to 'suppress' our opinionated mind. Of course, it will also have a hard time choosing, out of the many options, the right path for self-fulfillment. Basically, this level of imbalance results in the inability to bring out the authentic parts of our inner self and to let go of the inauthentic parts of our inner world. Sometimes, suppression isn't such a bad idea!

This imbalance does not stop there. It also makes it very hard for us to *translate* ourselves in a good way. Translation means putting our inner feelings, thoughts and even visions into accessible structures, which most (or at least many) people can understand and appreciate. When this process of translation is damaged, we will be unable to reveal the more abstract and elusive world of ours to others in a clear and lucid way. This will leave both sides frustrated: we will feel that we can't transfer our ideas the way we experience them within—sometimes we will even feel that we want to express one thing, but what comes out is a totally different thing. Others will feel that our messages are confused, incoherent and unsystematic.

The ability to edit and translate ourselves very much depends on the state of our sixth chakra—which is the editor and translator of our thoughts—and the third chakra, which determines our level of inner integration. If you're interested in learning more about this concept, you can either go back and read the third chakra's basic themes section or move forward and read the sixth chakra's basic themes section.

Suffocating or feeling stuck is very typical for the imbalanced fifth chakra. We feel as if our innermost self is locked up and suppressed, and that we cannot let it out in a simple and direct way. There is a strong sense of a border between our inner world and the outer world, almost like a very tense border between two hostile countries. We think one thing, but we cannot articulate it correctly, so we either remain silent or express it through very clumsy wording; whether we feel love or emotional pain, on the way out, it somehow all becomes twisted and wrong. There is no feeling of flow, or of spontaneity; we accumulate so much emotion and frustration, and it all just builds up toward an explosion, typically a self-destructive one.

Everyone has a basic need to be heard by others. This can range from expressing emotional needs to artistic expression, and from voicing our opinion to leading crowds toward just causes. By being heard, our unique inner world is recognized by others; we are no longer caged and in isolation within ourselves—we are liberated by the power of sharing. The moment this need cannot be met, a tremendous barrier rises between us and the world, leaving us with frustration and sadness—and, above all, suffocation. We are literally unable to become fulfilled, since our experience of self remains stuck in the more abstract realms of inner feelings and visions.

This state of stuckness can stem from various causes. One major cause is to be found in the field of traumas. Perhaps we found ourselves in a society that could not accept or appreciate our unique voice, so we were harshly silenced or even mocked by the 'crowd.' Even if no one harassed us, we might have 'read' our surroundings and realized that it would be best to silence ourselves. Gradually, we have learned that we shouldn't expose our opinions and beliefs, but rather conform ourselves to the general worldview. If this trauma included some psychological or even physical threat, we might, throughout our entire life, carry a fear of being exceptional—a fear of sticking out too much. We might diminish our presence to the minimum level of functioning necessary for surviving and living in the world.

In this category of traumas that might have silenced us, are also included times of injustice, when we were condemned by society and felt we didn't get the chance to really defend ourselves and voice our own side of the truth. This can happen in court, in encounters with blaming and mocking journalists, or even through neighborhood gossip that condemns us without listening to our own version of events. When we were children, we were often judged wrongly, or at least so we felt, by our parents and teachers, and we didn't have the chance to be heard.

Another major cause is damage in one or more of the four lower chakras. We should keep in mind that the higher the chakra is, the more its balance depends on the lower chakras. So, to understand why we carry this sense of suffocation (which is usually followed by a real, physical sensation of suffocation, as many of us know), we should closely examine the origin of the sixth chakra's imbalance. Perhaps it originates in the first chakra, where we worry that, in the act of expressing ourselves, we might loose our basic security—our job, our family, our community or our land. It might originate in the second chakra, fearing the surge of life force that could arise from within, along with the outer appearance of our true self. It could also stem from the heart, where we fear intimacy and true reliance on others.

However, the greatest obstacle stems from the third chakra. In fact, the third chakra affects the fifth chakra in the most crucial way, since the level of our strength and the integration of our individuality determines our ability to voice our unique inner world and to stand behind it fearlessly and vehemently. As long as we lack a sense of individual power, there will be no one there to claim our right for expression and communication.

Psychological Reactions of the Imbalanced Fifth Chakra

As discussed earlier, two polar personalities grow out of the imbalanced fifth chakra: the introvert and the extrovert.

The introverted personality, which chooses to suppress its voice, will 'express' itself in taciturnity and withdrawal. It will be unable to communicate emotions, either positive or negative, and this creates a problem for intimate relationships. Each and every kind of overly expressive gesture seems dangerous to introverts since they fear being exposed to others' reactions and are reluctant to take center stage, even for a short while. Introverts find solace in their ability to understand themselves. They will be extremely cautious when asked to take a clear stand on just about anything—after all, this might engender great turmoil. They have tremendous stage fright, and their heartbeat will reach an unbelievable pace whenever a crowd's eyes are on them, waiting to hear what they have to say or to demonstrate. Leading others is an impossible task, considering the required level of visibility.

This brings 'shyness' into the picture. Shyness is nothing but the hesitancy to show oneself, out of the fear of others' reactions. It is a quality that has to be carefully examined, since it encompasses a sense of impending danger whenever an outer demand to be seen is presented. It is the irrational, unconscious belief that exposure leads to danger.

When the introverted personality must speak up, too often their messages sound confused and incoherent. For the speaker, it is quite clear what they are trying to convey, but others usually remain bewildered. They are not sure what they are expected to say or to demonstrate, so they either say what they believe will conform to others' expectations or say something that makes sense only in their own inner language. Naturally, these messages will carry weak and low energy, so they won't harm or shock anyone; the inner truth can be dangerous in so many ways.

Many times the introverted personality will find itself caged (out of its own free choice!) in suffocating social structures. Suffocation is felt in the fifth chakra whenever we find ourselves stuck in places or with people that don't allow us to be who we really are. For example, we might get stuck in a romantic partnership in which we cannot express our true selves. We will gradually suppress all our urges, whether they are creative, sensual or experiential ones. We might hold back very important things for years or even for a whole lifetime, a suppression that gradually sucks all the life force from this relationship.

Mostly, the introverted personality will find it hard to fulfill itself in extroverted forms of communication, such as appearing on stage or leading groups. This can limit its possibilities of self-fulfillment and creativity, and leave the person with great frustration at being unable to trace its own unique voice.

This personality knows no true spontaneity. It can only know sudden outbursts of rage and other frustrated emotions, which stem from long-held suppression. This, of course, leads to the wrong conclusion that a direct and truthful expression of inner feelings and beliefs will always result in hurting others, so, we might as well remain silent. This personality's last resort is to cry. A child expresses himself in tears because he lacks linguistic skills, but even grown-ups, when feeling unable to express themselves in the face of life's challenges, can escape into sorrowful tears.

In contrast, the extroverted personality seems to connect its very existence with constant communication. It over-uses communication, because in every gap of silence and aloneness there lurks the dread of death and nothingness.

This kind of personality cannot regulate the flow of expression from the inner world to the outer world. Thoughts and emotions come out quite uncontrollably. It simply cannot edit itself, so while the introverted personality buries both authentic and inauthentic selves deep inside, the extroverted personality will externalize almost every passing and unimportant emotion or thought, as if it was an essential self-expression. It will be unable to distinguish between the authentic and the inauthentic, and it will all seem the same—after all, the important thing is that they didn't keep it locked inside, which means that they were truthful, intimate and open, doesn't it...?

The extrovert can be extremely interactive always having something to say about everything. It has comments and opinions and, of course, it must always say the last sentence in every conversation. What's important for this type is to stick out, since sticking out equals existing, being recognized and being seen. That is why this type is inclined toward gossiping, being opinionated even on unimportant issues, and proving to everyone that 'I am the right, all-knowing one.' It loves quarrels, even when they will clearly lead to a dead end. It will demand to be heard, and usually it will be boisterous; its voice will exceed in tone and strength in every conversation. It will also demand 'justice,' because it very often feels deprived of attention—'you are not listening to me, and this is not fair!'

Since extroverts tend to suffer from lack of self-control, they often appear tactless, using humor inappropriately, unintentionally causing insult, and exhibiting an inability to be quiet at moments that clearly demand listening, withdrawal, or respect for others. Extroverts are frequently addicted to leadership positions, even at the family table. They tend not to listen to others and continue to lead, even in romantic relationships, where an equal exchange is necessary. Since extroverts can magnetize their listeners, they can be prone to manipulative behavior, trying to direct others' attention and support.

Naturally, most of us are a mixture of these two personalities. Although nowadays the extroverted personality is much more dominant—in this age of endless communication, when no one remains alone for a single moment, we collectively express a severe lack of control in the process of externalization.

Solutions for the Imbalanced Fifth Chakra

The key solution for the imbalanced fifth chakra is to use our voice only when it clearly serves the purpose of mutual growth and development, that is, only when it supports the greater good of the whole. This is the basic definition of the balanced fifth chakra: using the voice only for service, and only when it will lead to constructive ends. This is also the deepest meaning of the known Buddhist 'right speech.'

The question, of course, is how to determine what is the greater good and what is not. Another question is: how can we express egoic needs, which seem essential to us, and still follow the principle of the greater good?

For this, there are a few important guidelines. First and foremost, whatever we express, there has to be total self-responsibility. This means that we express ourselves in a real, non-violent way; we do not force anyone to accept or to obey our opinions or feelings. We clearly know that these are only *our* feelings, opinions and worldviews, and therefore, no one is expected to follow our demands—not even a partner in a romantic relationship. Whatever comes out of our inner world is ours, not theirs.

If we keep this in mind and understand it deeply, we can freely express our wants and needs. (Of course, even here some common sense editing will be necessary.) It is important not to suppress the flow, but rather to let it out and naturally let it take shape out of real interactions. So, we must be willing to make mistakes and also to pay for them.

When we keep the balance between natural flow and complete responsibility, we can progress by asking: 'Will these words truly encourage development?' and 'Will these words drive all of us toward more constructive lives?' These questions are, actually, the best editors ever: they teach us that our inner world should be externalized only when it promotes elevation and progress in our environment.

Of course, introverts and extroverts use different approaches to reach this goal.

The introverted personality cannot even express its own wants and needs. Therefore, it shouldn't be too quick to put the key solution into action. This type of personality needs, first, to overcome the tendency to suppress and suffocate itself. So, its initial lesson will be to artificially express its wants and needs, in spite of the predicted reaction. It should express itself even at the risk of making mistakes: say very unpopular things, agree to unintentionally insult others from time to time, and demand justice when its voice is left unheard. The most important thing is for this personality to connect with the feeling of suffocation in the throat and to 'ask' it what it wants to convey and what it feels it cannot convey. This personality must trust that 'right speech' takes shape only through making mistakes, and only through true and direct experimentation. Sitting in a corner and brooding will never bring about the long-awaited true spontaneity. So, only after some time of experimenting and feeling comfortable in this process of externalization, can this personality move on to a more progressed level of balancing for the fifth chakra.

The extroverted personality should use the power of purifying silence. It must learn to disconnect itself from all levels of communication, to remain alone and to keep silent. Instead of gossiping and expressing opinions, it can withdraw its 'case' from time to time and simply listen to others. It can ask itself: 'Is what I'm going to say really necessary? Will it help anybody and support them in their *own progress*?' Before any externalization during major conflicts, it is best for this personality to go through a spiritual therapy session to examine the level of responsibility it can take in this situation. Rushing to complain is one of this type's greatest tendencies. In general, relaxing the fifth chakra and allowing it to let in some vital knowledge and 'otherness' can be extremely beneficial.

We must keep in mind that true spontaneity is not the same as the common so-called 'spontaneity,' in which we express ourselves mechanically and automatically. True spontaneity is the result of deep cleansing, self-responsibility and genuine listening. We have to deeply cleanse ourselves, since the quality of our inner world determines what will be externalized through us. If our inner world is balanced, we feel much freer to express ourselves without self-monitoring.

Because of this correlation between the quality of our inner world and our ability to freely express ourselves, we will have to go through a clumsy stage of awareness, in which we carefully observe the process of self-editing. This might feel, at times, like a state of over-awareness, yet it is essential to have this transitory stage between automatic expression and true, responsible spontaneity.

The Three Levels of Functioning

The Functional Fifth Chakra

Our ability to edit and translate our inner world is sufficient for creating quite harmonious relationships in our lives. Others can understand what we try to convey. We have the ability to express our needs and wants clearly. Our personality is somewhere in the middle, between the introverted and the extroverted, maybe with a little bias toward one of the two. Mostly, we demonstrate a satisfactory level of self-control: feedback from our environment tells us that we usually know when we should keep silent and when we should say something, and that our habit of criticism and gossip is not too destructive. We even demonstrate an ability to transcend our fears of communication (such as stage fright) and our demand for justice (such as in intimate relationships) in order to attain real interactions. We can express very warm and soothing words directly from our hearts, and we almost never repress them. Of course, from time to time we do suffer from outbursts of an imbalanced expression (tears or rage), but we can quite easily come back to ourselves.

The Balanced Fifth Chakra

We have reached a state in which we have freed ourselves from the compulsive need for self-expression. We can actually use our voice as a tool, and we can stop using it as a manipulative power for our own agendas. We don't need to 'sell' our truth, and we can speak directly and honestly. We take full responsibility for our own needs, and we externalize them only in harmonious ways. This makes our expression extremely non-violent: on the one hand, we use our voice mainly when we are actually *needed*, and on the other hand, we are able to express our own unique voice, without forcing our voice onto others. Most of the time we are silent. We use our voice either when we are asked to, or when it can be used for creative, constructive aims or for further mutual development. Essentially, we have a feeling of transparency, as if there is only a thin line between the inner world and the outer world. We express a natural spontaneity, an effortless flow of sharing, and our voice is sweet and calm. We possess an impressive ability to translate ideas and abstract feelings, an ability which can be beautifully expressed through the various arts and even leadership. Although we mostly convey ourselves harmoniously, when there is an important collision between our authentic voice and the environment, we are willing to express unpopular ideas and, at the same time, accept the fact that we might not be heard as we would like to be.

The Awakened Fifth Chakra

Here the voice becomes the mere servant of the universal, transpersonal, and objective truths. The voice no longer serves our 'uniqueness,' and we do not possess the egoic need to be heard—it is the voice of truth itself, and it is the truth's will to spread and manifest itself in the world, that drives the transparent personality. We will mostly be drawn toward silence, and if there weren't an outer need to receive the higher truth, we would immediately go into silence forever. We simply give our voice to truth, and that truth is, in essence, the transcendence of the inner and the outer worlds, which means that it is beyond the ordinary state of the relationship-oriented fifth chakra. Here we find the expression of unity consciousness, an expression that takes place for the sake of humanity as a whole. Even when one expresses himself through the arts, that form of communication will only serve humanity, never self-fulfillment. Since the whole purpose of the throat chakra is to give form to that which is inner and abstract, in its awakened state, it will fulfill its complete potential, since the highest truth is also the most abstract one; externalizing it actually bridges the most distant heavens and the earth.

> ## Polar Emotions
>
> Suffocation / spontaneity, need to be heard / listening,
> separation from environment / transparency.

Type of Trauma

Simply put, traumas of the fifth chakra are traumas of communication, and they always stem from times in which expressing ourselves ended badly. This can include moments in which we were vulnerable enough to express a deep and genuine need but were harshly rejected, times in which we voiced our opinion and were disregarded or even mocked, or situations in which our inner truth was scorned and we paid a high price for it (such as a punishment or some great loss). There are also times in which we may have faced a grave injustice, been wrongly judged and couldn't represent our own version of the truth. This could have happened in front of a judge, a journalist, a crowd or even our parents when we were adolescents.

The inevitable conclusion of this kind of trauma will be: 'It is dangerous to express myself and to expose my inner world and opinions.' Naturally, this conclusion can lead us to several patterns of behavior, such as conformity to what others seem to want to hear, great suffocation or deep suppression of our needs, which can become manifest as a stammer, stage fright or reticence.

Type of Personality

The fifth chakra personality type is extremely extroverted and possesses a tremendous capacity to influence, inspire, magnetize and enrapture crowds. Clear examples of this personality type are speakers and lecturers, teachers and politicians, prophets and channelers, and charismatic leaders and rhetoricans. This category also includes entertainers and stage personalities, salesmen and lawyers, copywriters and even some of the more outgoing publicists and writers.

This personality type can change the world by the power of speech or any other kind of self-expression. (Some fifth chakra musicians can influence many generations by the power of their unique voice expressing itself through singing or playing.) Being present at a lecture or performance of a fifth chakra personality can make one want to change one's life and immediately leave everything behind to follow the new idea. This is the personality that possesses the highest ability to present clear, lucid and convincing ideas and arguments. Quite often the fifth chakra personality combines with a sixth chakra quality to create revolutionary leadership in many fields.

Since the fifth chakra personality type holds a great ability to 'translate,' it is also very talented in bridging different and even opposing worlds. So, all kinds of negotiators and mediators are fifth chakra talents, along with those who are capable of translating difficult ideas from their own field to a mass level understanding, like speakers who bridge between spirituality and science, or those who write popular science for the sake of the simple man.

Of course, possessing such power of influence holds within it a great danger: the fifth chakra personality can be either idealist or cunning, and even when it is the idealist type, it can be extremely forceful in its effort to implant its own ideas and visions. It can adapt very sophisticated forms of speech, which manipulate the listener into doing things that he or she usually doesn't tend to do. This can reach an art level of near-hypnosis. Naturally, only high moral values can restrain the tremendous influence of this personality.

In the Ayurvedic system, this personality type is regarded as a pitta type, which means it has the power of fire.

In its extreme imbalanced expression this personality type can suffer from chattering, a total lack of listening skills and, as mentioned, argumentative, manipulative and forceful tendencies.

Famous Fifth Chakra Expressions

Solon, Muhammad, Beethoven:
prophetic, visionary, inspiring and magnetizing.

Male and Female Energy

The male aspect of the fifth chakra is its power of influence and leadership through speech and other forms of expression. It is also found in the ability to stand up for our beliefs, worldviews and inner truths, and the willingness to expose them and to pay a high price for being unpopular. So, it is both about expressing our authentic individuality and using our voice to magnetize and impact our surroundings.

The female aspect of the fifth chakra allows higher truths to voice themselves through us. We become, then, just like a musical instrument, which 'someone else' plays. A higher truth can be anything that goes beyond our egoic interests: from fighting for whales and dolphins to expressing the truth of spiritual enlightenment. Whatever it may be, it is a higher force that we feel moves through us, takes form through us and demands attention.

Type of Happiness

For the fifth chakra, happiness is the natural flow of expression of what, for us, is the innermost truth. This can be, for example, an expression through various arts, when we give form to abstract feelings and are actually heard and accepted by others.

Another powerful form of happiness is having the ability to guide others and transmit to them our accumulated knowledge and wisdom. The growing ability to guide and lead others can be quite intoxicating since it is, in a way, seeding them with our own innermost truths—when others agree to take them in, it is a subtle form of birth-giving.

Life's Meaning and Purpose

Life is perceived as a field (sometimes, as a battlefield) of numerous unique voices and inner truths, which struggle to be heard, seen and accepted. Life's purpose is to become who we are, manifest our inner vision and be seen among the crowds. Creating an impact through our unique voice is a crucial part of being alive. Love is an expression of my innermost self in totality, while I let the other, or others, 'sing their song' too. Death can be transcended if we successfully leave behind our unique voice and message, which might prove to be 'eternal.' God is realized through loyalty to one's true voice and through the revelation of authentic uniqueness—the uniqueness of the 'soul' is God's will and God's imprint in us; obeying God is voicing the truth.

Ages of Development of the Fifth Chakra

The fifth chakra develops from the age of twenty-eight to the age of thirty-five. After we have learned, through the fourth chakra, how to commit and devote ourselves, how to take part in service of the world and how to come out of ourselves for the sake of something greater, it is time for us to look for our own unique voice and to define what our innermost truths actually are. It is time to connect with our dormant potential of participation (what one can call our 'mission') and to contemplate ways in which we can actually make a difference.

Usually at this stage we have accumulated enough experience, knowledge and wisdom. Even if we have already completed our studies and begun to work, this is the most natural time to ponder what our own unique contribution to the field of service in which we engage can be. This is a seven year period, in which the fifth chakra is actually expected to bring out something of its own; some skill or ability that others don't possess or some idea or perspective which can be considered 'ours.'

Individuality, which was first solidified as an inner sense of independent power in our adolescence (third chakra), now rests on the more selfless foundation of the fourth chakra, and must take its second leap through the fifth chakra: toward a unique voice and a unique contribution.

Psychosomatic Disturbances

Since the throat is simultaneously the only entrance in the body through which vital ingredients can be assimilated, *and* the gateway through which the innermost self expresses itself outwardly (vocal cords and mouth), psychosomatic disturbances include disruptions in both directions.

By understanding the throat as the borderline between the inner world and the outer world, we can determine whether our throat problem is connected with *letting something in* or with *letting something out*. Thyroid imbalances, swollen thyroids or tonsils, chronic inflammations, and infections of the tonsils are quite often examples of a difficulty in letting something in, while stammers and other speech impediments, such as hoarseness, loss of voice, chronic coughs and mouth ailments are more associated with problems of self-expression (either over the top self-expression or limited self-expression).

Collective Imprints

The most powerful collective imprints of the throat chakra are those of perpetual oppression and persecution of people who dare to express different and unique worldviews and beliefs—from minorities to radical thinkers. By sticking out from the herd they subject themselves to hatred, penalty and violence. Quite often throughout history there was one worldview that suppressed all others, and that worldview was the only one allowed to speak out in public, so other voices were forced to go underground and seek alternative routes of expression.

This is why, in our days of Western society, the right for free speech has become so important: we are all bruised from the long and harsh silencing of the past. Nowadays we witness the very opposite of this silencing: an influx of contradictory worldviews and perspectives. The most important thing is to make our unique voices heard, and the freedom to rise up and speak for or against something is being sanctified. Supported by post-modern democracy and technology, such cellular phones and social networks, the voice of the individual has become the focus of attention.

More than that, the pursuit of 'self-fulfillment,' in the context of the unique potential that hides within each and every one of us, has become increasingly important. The notion that everyone possesses some sort of individual destiny and special role in the world drives many to look for their own 'unique voice.'

Evolution of the World

The first signs of the individuated fifth chakra, at mass level, appeared in the humanistic approach of the Renaissance—an approach which separated from religious worldviews in order to attach prime importance to humans rather than divine, supernatural matters. This approach gave way to the Western emphasis on self-expression and inner truth.

The greatest revolution, however, was the individual psychology of Freud, which brought man's inner world to the forefront and established that as the truth that can set man free. This approach, in many respects, revealed and *created* inner depths in the human psyche. Of course, this individual psychology was only one part of a tremendous revolution, through which the individual separated himself from collective truths (all 'isms') in order to find and define his own inner truth. Democracy was and is the greatest support for the individualist movement: by allowing free speech to all citizens alike, the pluralistic self-expression of 'my truth' became a natural habit in human civilization.

Common Interactions with other Chakras

The second and the fifth chakras combine to create artistic expression. The second chakra evokes the creative urge, while the fifth chakra translates it into outer manifestation. One can say that the fifth chakra is the final passageway for any creative urges.

When the third chakra is paired with the fifth chakra, it is a very powerful combination. Together, they create individuality. Without the third chakra, there can be no sense of individual power and no integration of self; without the fifth chakra, there can be no expression of selfhood and no manifestation of the will to act. Together, they create a wonderful flow of will and fulfillment, authentic individuality and authentic expression. All great individuals who have changed the world possessed a strong third and fifth chakra combination. However, it is not a coincidence that the fourth chakra sits between these two chakras—one might imagine that there could be a direct flow between the third and the fifth chakra but the heart chakra is actually essential for the smooth flow between them. The heart chakra harmonizes and soothes the expression of individuality on its way out to the world through the warmth of emotion, intimacy, love and communion.

The combination of the fourth and the fifth chakras supports our ability to express emotions. Tears, either of joy or sadness, are a very tangible example of this interaction.

As a bridge between the fourth and the sixth chakra, the fifth chakra actually allows a balanced blend between emotion and intellect.

There is an extremely important connection between the fifth and sixth chakras. Together, they give structured forms to abstract ideas and visions, and the mouth is the meeting point of their final expression. The sixth chakra unfolds creative possibilities, while the fifth chakra supports the translation of abstract thoughts and visions into practical forms.

The fourth, fifth and sixth chakras combine to fulfill our unique mission in the world. The fourth brings about the urge to serve, the sixth realizes the nature of this mission, and the fifth translates it into practical action.

In the Process of *Kundalini*

In the process of *kundalini*, the fifth chakra functions as a bottleneck, separating the four lower chakras, which are, essentially, the human psyche, and the two higher chakras, which are the abode of the spirit.

When the *kundalini* flows upwards, it collects the physical and psychological energies, aspiring to 'translate' them into a more refined, spiritual energy through the great translator—the throat chakra. The moment these grosser energies are translated and transmuted successfully, they flow powerfully into the sixth and seventh chakras, enriching and empowering their spiritual levels of functioning.

Recommended Practices

The introverted personality will benefit a lot from practices that support a better flow of expression for their needs and wants. These practices can include: associative writing, which can free stagnated self-expression; cathartic speech in dynamic meditations and therapies; intentionally speaking our minds in front of people with whom we usually sink into silence; singing, chanting, and even healing through laughter, which can also clear the voice and open it up, and clearing traumas of a fifth chakra nature, which is essential.

The most important practice for the introverted personality is paying attention to the feeling of suffocation in the throat: What is its message, and what does it have to convey? These should be the guiding questions. The answer to these questions can come in many forms, first and foremost through spiritual therapy.

On a more practical level, the introverted personality must play a little with more outgoing roles and duties in life; leading and guiding others and, from time to time, putting oneself in center-stage situations. Releasing one's thoughts through print or on the internet can also be beneficial in this context.

For the extroverted personality, practices for limiting the process of speech and bringing awareness to it are essential: from right speech (no gossip, no criticism, no unnecessary sharing) to silence retreats (especially in nature), which can reflect back to us our inability to edit ourselves. Even observing one day of silence every week can be extremely beneficial—actually, even observing one hour of silence every day can be great! Occasionally limiting the number of phone calls, SMS texts and social-network interactions is important too. The freedom of speech is wonderful, but it is not necessary to express everything just because we can.

When we speak, we can play with our known paths of communication: we can focus on listening, we can speak only when asked something or when we are clearly needed, or we can speak only when there is something essential to say, something that can benefit both sides of the discussion.

Whenever we feel a tremendous urge to speak our minds—to complain, to demand to be heard, to make clear what our needs are, and generally, to create a conflict—it is essential to examine our demands in a meditative state, through mind-inquiry or silent meditation. We should express only that which has survived the cleansing power of silent withdrawal.

The Sixth Chakra:
The Search for Wisdom

Location and General Orientation

The sixth chakra is located in the space between the eyebrows in the lower forehead. It governs the hypothalamus and the pituitary gland, the brainstem, the small brain, the two hemispheres and, most importantly, the neo-cortex. Naturally, this makes the sixth chakra the 'headquarters' of the entire subtle endocrine system (which is, as mentioned earlier, the chakra system).

The hypothalamus links the nervous system to the endocrine system via the pituitary gland. We can speculate that, correspondingly, the sixth chakra links the *nadis* system to the chakras, and therefore controls and regulates all conscious and unconscious activities in our subtle anatomy. Being the equivalent of the human brain, this is the 'mother' of all other chakras, the one that guides the entire flow and gives it direction.

Being directly linked to the neo-cortex, which is the abode of conscious thinking, it is also the center of mental perception: comprehension, data processing and interpretation (unlike the sensory perception of the third chakra and the emotional perception of the fourth chakra). In humans, the mental realm governs all other layers of being, so the sixth chakra is, in fact, the discriminating authority, which selects from all data presented to it by the other chakras.

It also negotiates between the right and left hemispheres, and has the power to unite their different activities—linear reasoning in the left hemisphere and holistic reasoning in the right hemisphere—into more wholesome activities. This is an important possibility, as far as spiritual evolution is concerned, and it will be discussed further in the section titled 'In the *kundalini* process.'

The sixth chakra is also connected with the eyes and the seeing mechanism, which implies that it is in charge of seeing into realms of existence that are subtler than the visible world of phenomena, and thus deciphering the mysteries of these invisible realms. In addition, it governs the ears and the hearing mechanism, which implies receptivity toward subtler messages and transmissions and the ability to translate them into understandable signals for the brain. In this context, the sixth chakra is not only the 'inner eye' or 'third eye', as it is traditionally and popularly regarded, but it is also the 'inner ear' or 'third ear'.

Basic Psychological Themes

The sixth chakra is the choosing faculty: it is the one that determines what is 'true' and what is 'false', what is good to identify with and what is wrong and must be banished from the territory of the self, what is significant and calls for attention and what is insignificant, and may be neglected. It is the inner eye, which observes and selects—whatever it approves of is translated into its current terminology and stored within the memory cells for reuse. Just like a torch of attention, it enlightens one thought or emotion (or one piece of information from the outer world) in every single moment, and determines, according to the sixth chakra's level of development, whether it deserves attention and identification. This is a highly important role, since whatever this chakra considers to be 'real' and 'true', the self then takes in and merges with; in a way, we become what the sixth chakra perceives as real.

This role of order-making completely depends on the quality of thought and the level of intellectual and spiritual intelligence in the body. That is why the basic struggle of the sixth chakra is its effort to reach and maintain a state of *clarity*, order, reason and truth. This task can be quite challenging at times: at every given moment this chakra must identify the reality of ideas and experiences; it has to balance between sensory, emotional, intellectual and rational contradictory 'truths', and it has to integrate the stimulants and impressions of the other six chakras, which means negotiating between all inner forces and 'voices'.

How can this chakra know for sure what is real and what is false—especially when something that seems true and relevant at a certain point in time, is found to be untrue and irrelevant when one meets with a different situation at another time. For example, how can we tell when it is best to insist on our individual and separated will (third chakra) or when it is best to give something up for the sake of loving and caring for others (fourth chakra)? How can we tell if it's time to listen to our logic or to our intuition? And how can we tell which of the impressions emitted constantly by the chakras—patterns, dreams, thoughts, emotions and psychosomatic disturbances—are most worthy of our attention? Indeed, the mission to coordinate intelligently between all the different parts of our being can be taxing!

More than that, the mission doesn't end in choosing what is real. The sixth chakra also has to *interpret* whatever it perceives, which means giving it a meaning, context and purpose, again, according to the chakra's understanding of 'reality' and 'truth'. This demands an ability to integrate the subjective world and the objective world, a growing conceptual and contextual development, in an increasing capacity for abstraction, and an ability to understand and interpret these things in a systematic, ordered and logical way—in general, increasing levels of *complexity*.

Understanding this complex role (and we do understand it through our sixth chakra!) can make us realize that, in many respects, this is the most important chakra. After all, one can live happily with a damaged body, and one can live with wounded emotions as long as the mind is clear and balanced. First and foremost, our 'mind' must be in order, otherwise the supervisor of the entire system is gone—and anything can happen when the supervisor is gone.

This brings us to the understanding that the general issue for the sixth chakra is clarity versus confusion, and, on the other side of it, a domineering mind (cold rationality) versus a willingness to listen.

The first aspect of an imbalanced sixth chakra is confusion. Confusion can be defined as the inability of this chakra to play its destined role in the chakra system, that is, to 'rule' the other six chakras and to give them one unified direction. It is as if the master is gone, so the body-mind complex becomes a battlefield of many contradictory voices and possibilities.

In actuality, the restless stream of contradictory thoughts which accompany almost everyone, are nothing but impressions of the first to fifth (and also seventh) chakras that are translated into a fake logical thinking. Confusingly, we may regard them as sensible thoughts, but, really, they are only emissions of irrational impressions, which our *real thought* should face. Our real thought, or intelligent attention and listening, is supposed to listen to it all, interpret their meaning and determine what is real and what is false, what requires attention and what has no importance whatsoever.

When this intelligent listening does not exist, our attention will be swayed by every insignificant inner voice. In the absence of an organizing and responsible intelligence, we will be doomed to suffer from a constant mental turmoil, which leads inevitably to mood swings and unreliable patterns of behavior. We have to keep in mind that each chakra is a whole and complete worldview, with its own set of values and feelings, so when each chakra expresses itself as an independent entity, it will naturally oppose all other chakras' worldviews and values. This will lead to a constant inner argument (that is why thoughts almost always appear in contradictory pairs of opposites). The great mystic Gurdjieff described this common disorder as having many I's in one body-mind complex with each 'I' trying to overcome all others. In this sense, we are not one unified and holistic being, but rather many fragmented selves.

In the absence of a directing center, every fleeting fear, urge or desire might take the throne for brief glory. One will not be able to reject the unnecessary, and will be unable to locate and pay attention to that which is truly significant and 'true'. Every thought, or every emotion pretending to be a thought, can destabilize the entire structure of being and arouse doubts in everything that seems to be reality. Subjective experience will overcome all objective knowledge and experience. Dreams will become a battlefield of the chakras' unconstrained energies. Some level of attention disorder will gradually appear.

This conflict will increase whenever we are called to make a decision, which are in fact the moments in which we are demanded to determine what is real and significant for us and what is not. When we are heavily pressured by people and situations to be clear and one-minded, we have to face the true state of our sixth chakra. Trying to be decisive when our vision is completely blurred by fears, desires, expectations and deep-buried traumas, can be a cause of great irritation. Since we are totally lacking in inner guidance, we will desperately cling to the 'pros' and 'cons' of our hardly functioning logical thinking.

Sometimes the filtering powers of the sixth chakra might weaken even more, and this can lead to a confusion crisis. Our entire logical mind will be threatened by new and earth-shaking data, by environmental pressures or simply by an overflow of chakra disputes. It will not be possible for us, then, to define what is real and what is false, so the very structures of our perception will become dangerously loose. Of course, this can reach borderline states, which sometimes call for psychiatric aid.

So, confusion is basically the sixth chakra reflecting conflicts between the other six chakras. We have to remember the other side of confusion, which is the lack of development in this chakra. If this chakra is not exposed to higher levels of intelligence, it will not be stimulated enough to develop the capacities required for mastery. When it is out of contact with higher levels of intelligence—rational-logical, intellectual, philosophical and spiritual—the sixth chakra is extremely susceptible to this imbalance of constant confusion.

The polar aspect of the imbalanced sixth chakra is the absolute dominion of logic and intellect. Ideally, the sixth chakra is an intelligent, or wakeful, attention (or intelligent wakefullness), but when it is out of balance it tends to judge everything through the eyes of cold rational and conceptual thinking. In this case, higher thinking will not be an organizing and negotiating wakeful intelligence, but rather a tyrant that forcefully suppresses the other six chakras.

This means that everything will be judged from a conceptual point of view. There will be less living and more thinking about living. The sixth chakra will withdraw into reactive and automatic patterns of behavior. It will not allow any level of healthy confusion—which means blocking the entrance of new data and knowledge—but rather, it will cling to the known and familiar. Rigidity and dogmatism will master all impressions and interpretations.

Unavoidably, cold rational thinking leads to an extremely judgmental and critical mind, as well as an extremely opinionated mind. We don't have the ability to see things in simpler ways, beyond our rigid observations. Everything in the objective world should appear the way our thoughts imagine it should appear. Also, everything in our subjective world should behave the way we think it should, and if it doesn't, we will brutally suppress and avoid it.

We are then detached from feelings and sensations, urges and instincts. We estrange our bodies, as if they are some bad company that might irrationalize and destabilize our line of behavior. Through dogmatic thinking we slowly but surely minimize the flow of our life force.

Of course, both aspects can appear in one single person. In fact, rigid thinking might lead to unexpected turmoil from the confusion created when things don't happen as they 'should' or when sudden pressure undermines our patterns of logic; too much confusion might lead one to desperately cling to rational thinking.

The root-causes of these two imbalances are also quite similar: traumas of the first chakra, which make us cling to safe, conceptualized thinking; collective consciousness, which supports rational thinking and tends to suppress and neglect the other six chakras, and the basic tendency of the brain to seek predicted patterns of survival and safety.

Psychological Reactions of the Imbalanced Sixth Chakra

The first aspect of the imbalanced sixth chakra, which is confused thought, creates disordered vision and a general inability to cling to one solid truth. Being unable to separate oneself from the stream of thought, and silently and intelligently observe it all, makes it quite impossible for us to trace the false portions of thought (irrational impressions pretending to be rational thinking) and the true portions of thought—the intelligent, higher parts which can integrate and connect the other six chakras into a unified being. Without the ability to observe and discern, one becomes, in every moment, whatever his thought stream presents to his mind's eye.

This leads to a distorted process of filtering outer information and knowledge, a lack of conceptual coherency, a wrong and unsystematic interpretation of events and inner and outer messages, an inability to produce wisdom out of life's experiences, and a periodical loosening of all reality structures (in other words, a mental breakdown). Only the power of true intelligence can create mental stability and coherency, and without mental stability the entire personality is completely fragmented, and thus unable to properly process and use data or wisdom. So, confused thought will wrongly judge situations and experiences, and these conclusions will turn into false imprints, which will inhibit the accuracy of responses and actions.

It is important to understand that the confused sixth chakra has a major influence on the output of the fifth chakra. Confused thoughts lead to confused decision-making, contradictory and unreliable behavior and uncontrolled externalization of inauthentic parts of oneself (while wrongly judging that they are totally authentic).

When a confused thought tries to act, it will not be able to manifest itself coherently. In the morning the confused thought will stick to one idea, and in the evening it will change its mind; today it will passionately defend one course of action, and tomorrow it will deny it. This is what happens when we are one with our stream of thought. From time to time, in order to overcome this confusion, we might strongly stick to rigid conceptual thinking, but even this cannot last for too long, since it is only an irrational impression in disguise, which can easily be replaced by a totally different portion of ourselves.

In the absence of a higher organized thought process, there can be an overflow of emotion—we will give tremendous importance to fleeting emotions and sensations. After all, we are an easy prey for the lower chakras' imbalances. Also, our concentration will be very weak, since we are easily swayed by anything that is noisy and stimulating, with no regard whatsoever to the level of truthfulness in it. This is where the various expressions of attention disorder manifest. Furthermore, we will be extremely indecisive, and try, as much as we can, to prolong the process of decision-making, forever pondering the 'pros' and 'cons' of decisions, with no ability to complete the process and make a final conclusion.

Confused thought will manifest as a very hesitant personality, which is easily influenced by both inner and outer impressions. It creates a weak mind, which has no center, no strong opinions and worldviews, and no systematic course of action. This can lead one to depend on stronger minds, looking for the help of Gurus and other authoritative guides, and it can also lead to a life that has no direction or solid sense of purpose. This weak mind requires an outside agency to tell it what is real and what is false, but systematically following this external truth will be almost impossible—the moment doubts and fears from the lower chakras capture the mind's attention, it is helpless to overcome them and to obey one voice.

The other aspect of the imbalanced sixth chakra, which is the domineering mind, turns the brain and process of thought into a sort of 'closed system.' This means that thought continuously reinforces its known and familiar structures, while forcefully pushing away everything that might negate or destabilize these structures. While confused thought is incapable of producing wisdom out of experiences because of its distorted interpretation, the domineering mind is incapable of doing so because it imagines it already knows everything.

This is an extremely arrogant mind. It takes pride in its ability to logically and rationally discern everything; it idolizes scientific thinking and elevates analytical values, but it is unaware of the fact that this ability is hindered both by unconscious impulses and by a limited, unevolving and stagnant logic. This kind of mind believes that it has reached the pinnacle of evolution, while in reality it is doomed to degeneration—no mind can ever evolve without higher stimulants that provoke and shake its structures.

This is the mind that says 'I already know,' and thus cannot flow anymore. When this mode of thinking occurs in the spiritual mind, there develops what we may call the 'spiritual ego.' It resists learning, although it may have a mistaken self-image of being a great learner. In reality it is conceptual, rigid, reactive and proud. It possesses 'memory-boxes' in which information and knowledge are stored, and it compares any new data to this previous knowledge, very elegantly pushing away the new and affirming only that which suits its past conclusions. It highly regards information—quotes, impressive data and cold facts—and confuses information with true knowledge. There is no ability to distinguish between important, transformative and liberating wisdom, and the meaningless storage of information.

True knowledge stems only from a direct and vulnerable communion with life's experiences —actually letting life shape us. True knowledge also comes from encountering higher wisdom, manifested in wise books and wise persons. The domineering mind is incapable of being penetrated by outer experiences and wisdom. It is, by its very nature, a male energy that has no balancing opposite. It aspires to conquer knowledge and to declare that it possesses complete knowledge. It is deeply disconnected from the body and feelings, and coldly analyzes feelings and sensations as if observing them from afar. It always tries to control life through ideas (how life should be and how life shouldn't be). It is completely inflexible when meeting real life.

When encountering a higher knowledge it will proudly block the knowledge out and say 'oh, yes, I know that.' Inquiries into truth are always made through comparison to stored memory and never through the shock or surprise of insight and revelation. There is no room for mystery—life is perceived logically, it is not a vast unknown—and therefore there is no room for a sudden insight. There will be a general inclination toward independence, being free from all 'authorities' and external 'truths,' but this independence, in regard to this kind of mind, is really just an ongoing state of stagnation and degeneration.

The domineering mind suppresses the other six chakras for the sake of an uninterrupted self-image. It has a set display window, and it can never allow confusion to shake this self-image. It ignores the fact that there is indeed a healthy confusion caused by the entrance of new information, which can lead the mind toward further complexity.

This kind of mind is extremely possessive of the one and only truth, so it is also very inattentive, very critical and very judgmental when communicating with others. It is convinced that the choices it makes in life are the best ones—a model to all—and that its choices are also very rational and logical. The truth is that, due to its high level of suppression, most of its unconscious motivations are really irrational impressions that abuse the higher capacity of thought in order to be rationalized and justified.

Solutions for the Imbalanced Sixth Chakra

The key solution for the sixth chakra lies in the realization that one's current level of thought is limited and inevitably engenders confusion or control issues. Therefore, only the transcendence of thought can ever bring about clarity and intelligence. The search for clarity is often wrongly directed toward the realm of thought; alternatively, by giving up this direction, and by understanding that *there is no clarity in thought*, a new state of openness, true listening and insight will reveal itself.

Sincerely inquiring into the structure of thought can gradually clear both the confused and the domineering mind. We will soon see that these two polar mindsets stem from the same root, the ignorance of relying on thought as the source of wisdom. Thought is not wisdom; it can only be a tool of wisdom, because wisdom lies beyond the boundaries of thought. A tool is only a tool, and thought is nothing more than a means of memory-storage in the brain.

Thought is the vehicle through which information and knowledge is accumulated in the brain. This is a servant's work, certainly not a master's work! Thought is memory and time, and therefore, it is always doomed to be fragmented and relative. The holistic nowness of truth and wisdom can never be captured by thought, and when thought tries to capture it, it stops the ongoing movement of the mind toward further realms of revelation.

When we begin to realize the limitations of thought, a new aspiration will be ignited within us: the aspiration to put thought into order by creating a superior level of intelligence to which thought will have to submit. This is the beginning of the journey toward a genuine spiritual authority, which culminates in the awakening of the sixth chakra.

Both confused thought and arrogant thought will benefit from developing the ability to disassociate one's attention from one's stream of thought. In fact, this practice is the only one that can ever bring the sixth chakra into balance. Usually this is thought of as the preliminary stage of meditation. Silence of the mind is possible only when one can disregard the content of thought in its entirety. Practices of observation are essential here, whether they are practices of active observation, such as inquiry into the structure of thought, or passive and meditative observation, which merely listens to this structure or even simply ignores its content (what traditionally is called 'an equal vision').

We must understand that we forgot the greatest power we posses, as the vehicle of self-awareness: we hold the power of attention. Ideally, our attention should be separated from all observable objects. For most of us, our attention is lost in the stream of thought, and we simply have to pick it up. Learning to separate our attention from observable objects helps us realize that we actually hold the power to give specific significance to one thought or another. This realization is the beginning of self-mastery, which is the role of the sixth chakra.

The more this process of disassociation takes place, the more we are capable of possessing deep silence in the mind. True silence is not the absence of thought, but really a new state of the brain and the mind, in which holistic and receptive listening opens up. This state gives way to a new level of mental functioning, which is non-linear and is not the direct result of memory accumulation—it still uses memory, but it does not rely on it for revelation. We can call this new level 'insight,' the sudden appearance of a complete and wise understanding through the holistic and aligned state of the brain and the mind.

When this transcendent spiritual authority solidifies as the higher level of our mind, a more complex hierarchy of thought evolves within us. The first level is the one we should slowly discard: this is false thought, formed by unconscious and untreated impressions. The second level is the functional one, which stores useful information. The third level stores knowledge that we have verified through experience and insight. The fourth level stores creative thinking. Beyond all four levels there is the pure mind, which uses the other four as vehicles, yet identifies with none. Logic then becomes a wonderful tool for systematic and coherent *expression*, but we never forget the liberating truth that logic is not who we are, so it cannot become the center of our minds.

Besides practices of observation and silence, there are more pathways through which we must develop the higher intelligence of the sixth chakra. Nowadays, there are great mind-techniques and forms of meditation, that can systematically lead us toward states beyond thought. In addition higher contemplation is a tremendous practice—it means dwelling in transpersonal wisdom and the great questions of life, which transcend our self-interest. By doing so, we shift our focus from ordinary thought to a much broader—and eventually more liberating—context.

Part and parcel of developing higher intelligence is being able to trace knowledge that can actually transform and liberate us, as opposed to knowledge that has no transforming effect on us. The more attracted we are to liberating wisdom, the more it 'comes' to us. We must remember that storing knowledge within our brain cells can evoke some sense of having great intellectual possessions, but in reality, if it doesn't free us, it burdens us.

To develop and balance the sixth chakra we have to aspire toward an objective and absolute truth. Objective and absolute truth is the higher authority we seek; it is an intelligence by which we should measure all other relative truths and thoughts within and without. When we acquire some level of contact with objective truth, through meditative practices and higher wisdom, it serves as a reflector of illusions of thoughts and feelings. Thoughts and feelings will then easily reveal their impermanent nature, and we can handle them with a greater level of discrimination.

We must keep in mind that there is really no end to the development of intelligence. The more we inquire, remain open and aspire to higher wisdom, the more complex we become. Complexity is not complication—on the contrary, it means that our mind is able to hold more components with less contradiction; so really, complexity is a higher state of simplicity!

When we realize, as the American philosopher Ken Wilber stated so beautifully, that the complete understanding of today will become a part of the complete understanding of tomorrow, we embark on an ecstatic journey that has no end. Yes, the goal is complete understanding, but since the mind's perception is fragmented by its very nature, we soon realize that ecstasy lies in the ongoing *process* of inquiry and revelation. Throughout this ongoing process, the structures of our thought continually collapse and are re-organized, since there are always new components to include and new perspectives that broaden our insight.

For this process, we must be willing to humbly get in touch with a higher knowledge. Being independent does not mean closing oneself of from others, but, first and foremost, being free from our own previous forms of thinking. There are great teachings that can confront our brain with its own limitations, and we must become vulnerably exposed to them. This does not mean that we shouldn't come to our own conclusions, but the initial stages of encounters with genius teachings demand a completely surrendered state of receptivity, like an open womb. As a by-product, these teachings inspire us to develop better logical and systematic structures of thought, and help our minds get used to thinking on great matters and aspiring to attain objective knowledge. We will soon realize that profound humbleness is far more joyful than the proud and repeated quoting of ourselves.

In general, a balanced sixth chakra consists of two central and complementary opposites: the first is the masculine energy, which is an objective, highly discriminative and authoritative wisdom, and the second is the feminine energy, which is totally receptive and willing to be penetrated by a higher wisdom. Both must be simultaneously cultivated. The imbalance of confusion is corrected primarily through the masculine part—a disassociation from thought and the attainment of higher knowledge. The imbalance of the controlling mind is corrected more through the feminine part—becoming increasingly receptive to the unknown, clearing space by letting go of memories, and practicing true listening.

Also, for both kinds of imbalances it is essential to understand that the more we balance the other six chakras—clearing away all sorts of unconscious impressions—the more our mind becomes mentally clear, since the mind, in its current state, is merely a reflector of untreated impressions, which are waiting for a higher spiritual authority that can untie them all.

Other practices for balancing the arrogant mind are: keeping our relative opinions in proportion and letting go of our idea of how things should be. The arrogant mind must agree to go through periods of healthy confusion, in which new components and perspectives shake up its safe structures of thought. In these periods, the mind must listen without judgment and allow clarity to rise out of the ashes of the no-longer-validated thoughts. One last crucial practice is what we can call 'living with a question.' The power of a question, held within the mind without one rushing to cathartically resolve it, is immense: it teaches us to love the presence of questions as a fertilizing force, and to realize even more deeply that insight doesn't stem from the brain, but really is the natural, effortless result of true silence. Silence is a state of wakeful, vibrating and holistic receptivity; a question is a sign of the mind's willingness to receive wisdom, and insight is born from the union of silence and a question.

The Three Levels of Functioning

The Functioning Sixth Chakra

We have a good measure of rationality, which enables us to control and restrain all irrational structures within us. We have a good level of logic and reasonable thinking. When we need our thoughts for decision-making and processes of understanding, they are coherent and can maintain lucidity. It is possible for us to give coherent interpretations of our experiences, both inner and outer, and we can mentally translate and digest them. Our perception of reality is consistent, and if our inner experience contradicts objective reality, we can let go of our subjective experience. When needed, we are capable of disassociating ourselves from our thoughts. We are quite ready to receive new information and knowledge, and we do not block it with arrogance and reactivity. We can assimilate complex knowledge, and, in general, we are able to listen to other perspectives and worldviews. Our level of concentration is good; we can maintain focus as long as it is needed. We still suffer from a restless stream of thought, and we do get caught, from time to time, in the fake rationality of untreated impressions, but still, we are able to demonstrate a good level of consistency and reliability.

The Balanced Sixth Chakra

We continuously realize that we are not defined by thought. We do this by developing our ability to listen to the entire world of thought, without identification or judgment, as if we were an equal-visioned researcher. This enables us to avoid the automatic responses of memory-based thinking, to holistically listen to everything that happens and to observe what is, without the interference of mental interpretation. Our brain simply listens, and there is a lot of flexibility in our responses, choices and actions. We develop a higher spiritual authority, which transcends rational thinking and uses logic, but doesn't identify with it. There is a new master of spiritual intelligence, and the other six chakras have to align with its knowledge and worldview. Indeed, all impressions in the other six chakras go through a process of cleansing in the light of this new mastery, and as a consequence, the brain becomes clearer with the disposal of each untreated impression. The inner eye opens to get in touch with a subtler view and understanding of reality. We have a deep understanding that objective truth is not to be revealed in the visible world, since the visible world is a realm of impermanence. We have a great attraction toward the transforming and liberating knowledge of the absolute and transpersonal truth of life, as revealed in scriptures and higher wisdom. Everything in life is measured by this absolute worldview; impermanence is an illusion, since reality, by its very nature, is permanent. There is a very broad context to life—the context of the evolution of consciousness—and the purpose of life is seen only in this broader context. The inner Guru awakens within us as a result of this worldview, and dominates all processes of decision-making and evaluation. Subtle spiritual powers appear, such as spiritual vision and intuitive understanding.

The awakened sixth chakra

The barrier that separated the individual brain from the cosmic brain is shattered, and the individual brain is flooded with the higher intelligence that created the universe. From then on, the brain functions as a part of the whole, ecstatically united with divine intelligence and wisdom. The brain ceases to have an independent existence, and serves as a mere receptor of higher knowledge. It is as if the brain becomes a mediator, which constantly translates the inconceivable into conceivable mental forms and structures. Since it is now open to infinite intelligence, it can never retain immobility and is forever evolving, trying to 'catch up' with the divine's total perception. This brain becomes increasingly more complex, with unique interconnections that enable it to have divine perception. It reveals the order and laws of creation, while essentially remaining completely still and empty. It is no longer memory-based, and cosmic energy continuously flows within it, stimulating the pituitary and the pineal glands. This is a merging brain; when it inquires into something, it moves toward the truth by abolishing all divisions between subject and object, investigator and investigation. It experiences itself as one with the cosmos, and its worldview is made up of the broadest existential context of the universe itself. There is an uninterrupted recognition of the permanent, objective and absolute truth, beyond and beneath all phenomena. This brain moves freely in all directions and through all dimensions, from the most earthly to the most spiritual. While the most spiritual dimension encompasses everything, the brain can be extremely flexible in life's experiences, and it can be fully responsive, with no trace of rigidity in thought.

Polar Emotions

Confusion / clarity, mental noise / silence, irrationality / discrimination.

Type of Trauma

A mental trauma occurs whenever our perception of reality is destabilized to the extent that we no longer know what is real and what is false, and whenever we fall into a state of what seems to be dangerous confusion. This can happen, for example, when a strong-held conviction—such as a belief or worldview—shatters in the face of a new reality (or a new revelation of reality). We could hold strong religious views, which shake when reality invades; we could go through a powerful hallucinogenic drug experience, which destabilizes our perception of reality and forcefully exposes us to subtler dimensions; we could meditate until a new terrifying depth is revealed, which leaves us with the feeling that everything we thought was real is actually an illusion. Sometimes we hold strong convictions about life or people around us—about how things should be—and events prove us wrong. Other times, we may go through long periods of confusion, not knowing where to go or what to do, and this can seem dangerous and earth-shaking.

Sometimes we may go through periods of mania or even megalomania, in which we touch the frontiers of true madness—experiencing a total disruption of the mental interpretation of reality. These times prove to us that we cannot properly control our minds, so it is dangerous to destabilize, even to the slightest degree, our rationality and self-control.

This kind of mental trauma can lead us to this polarized conclusion: 'it is dangerous to know, and it is dangerous not to know'—which means that when you think you know something, it can be harshly taken away from you, and when you know nothing, you are totally lost and vulnerable. When we conclude that it is dangerous to know, it can lead us to nihilism, cynicism and the irrational rejection of all ideas, reducing us to automatic thinkers with no higher values whatsoever; in addition, it can lead to extreme hesitation and procrastination in decision-making or taking a stand. On the other hand, when we conclude that it is dangerous not to know, it can lead us to over-conceptualization, to the extent that we deny reality; we will simply stick to our belief system, even when everything has changed around us.

Type of Personality

The sixth chakra personality type is best represented by the philosopher: the introverted thinker, who observes life from afar, and watches everything carefully and silently in order to decode the mysteries of life and death. This personality type is characterized by its almost tormenting ambition to attain perfect wisdom, wisdom that encompasses the entire universe. Sometimes this aspiration is defined as the search for the 'theory of everything.' (It is no coincidence that both physicist Stephen Hawking and philosopher Ken Wilber, two typical sixth chakra expressions, often use this phrase in the context of their own ambition to decode cosmic mystery.) This kind of person seeks to understand, as Einstein put it, 'how God thinks,' delving into the universal brain of the creator. They are driven by the feeling that there is a total truth, which awaits them somewhere in the corners of the universe, and if they strive hard enough, they will find the key. In a more religious and mystical sense, this is their way of merging with the divine—through the brain's aspiration to perceive the unperceivable.

The sixth chakra personality type always observes and tries to realize out of observation inner and hidden structures. Structure means perfect order, and perfect order, at least in their eyes, is God. They like mapping everything, creating hierarchies of knowledge, and finding patterns—mathematical or logical. Philosophers, mystical seers and thinkers, scientists, researchers and inventors are included in this category: from Socrates to Einstein. In the Ayurvedic system, they are a vata-pitta mix: a combination of the air element (rising high above) and the fire element (tremendous creative urge).

Because of their strong introverted and observant tendencies, they are very inclined to loose balance and forget all about the real world. They quite readily disconnect from bodily and earthly life, so, in their imbalanced state, they exchange life for ideas and become nothing but a thinking head with no structure to hold it. They might also become extremely rigid—seeing everything in life through their maps and observations, and becoming obsessed with their *interpretation of life*. They could definitely benefit from grabbing a shovel and digging up real ground from time to time, rather than obsessively digging in their minds!

Famous Sixth Chakra Expressions

Socrates, Nietzsche: brilliant, logical and arrogant observers.

Male and Female Energies

The male energy of the sixth chakra is the power of discernment: being able to clearly distinguish, through fierce inquiry, between real and illusory, true and false, high and low. This kind of energy is extremely hierarchical (in its imbalanced state it is also extremely judgmental and arrogant). Another aspect of the male energy is the mental authority that governs all thoughts, emotions and sensations, and directs them.

The female energy of the sixth chakra is the state of holistic and receptive listening, in which the brain lets go of control and humbly contacts that which lies beyond its own frontiers, wishing to be penetrated by true insight. All higher knowledge can only be received by the brain, and can never be created through the power of our memory-based thinking. Another aspect of the female energy is equanimity, a pure observation that judges nothing and accepts what is.

Type of Happiness

Happiness in the sixth chakra is best symbolized by the ecstatic exclamation: "Eureka!" This is the exclamation of newfound discovery, such as realizing some hidden mystery or decoding the brain of God. The sixth chakra experiences happiness whenever we unveil a fragment of the divine plan or clearly see subtle structures of perfect order.

On a more common level, it is also experienced whenever we go into intense contemplation or a process of ecstatic philosophical inquiry, while holding within our minds the greatest questions of life. The brain then transcends its survival mode and enjoys the bliss of its own higher functioning.

Life's Meaning and Purpose

Life is the expression of divine intelligence. By communicating with this intelligence, we can understand life and realize our union with it. The purpose of life is to decode the intelligent order behind all phenomena, and we can do that through logic and mathematics, because perfect reason underlies everything. The whole universe is made up of structures and patterns. Love is the love of wisdom (this is also the meaning of the term 'philosophy'); Death is just another mystery to unveil by means of wise inquiry or investigation, and God is the tremendous flow of creative intelligence that has given rise to this universe.

Ages of Development of the Sixth Chakra

This chakra reaches its peak development between the age of thirty-five and the age of forty-two. This is the third layer of our chakra development in adult life. After we have realized that life is about extending ourselves and committing to higher purposes (fourth chakra), and after we have seriously considered the question 'what exactly is my own unique contribution to this world?' (fifth chakra), it is high time to integrate the accumulated wisdom of all of our human experiences. It is time to gather our deeper knowledge and to solidly define our worldview and perspective. Until this age, we may have wavered from time to time, being swayed by other people's perspectives and the general worldview of our environment, but now we are called to solidify our own conclusions about everything in life.

Our brain is ready for this task. In many respects the brain, in this seven years period, is at its peak of intelligent activity, so this is our chance to create a reservoir of the highest knowledge we have ever encountered. If our knowledge is extremely limited, after the age of forty-two—when our brain becomes more fixed and rigid—we might loose the chance to become 'wise and old.' So, this is the best time to stop and contemplate life, and also to be stimulated by whatever we perceive to be a higher knowledge.

Psychosomatic Disturbances

Psychosomatic disorders in the sixth chakra include, first and foremost, all types of headaches, from tension headaches to migraines, which tend to stem, among other reasons, from mental imbalances, such as stressful over-thinking.

Secondly, disorders in the sixth chakra can create different levels of mental borderline states, sometimes to the extent of causing psychiatric disruptions. When the sixth chakra is in a fragile state, it can lead to an increasing inability to tell the difference between reality and illusion. This is where anxiety, illusions, and split and fragmented realities enter into the picture. In general, all personality disorders may appear in this context. The person might experience themself as more than one entity, or they might feel as if other, or even alien, entities reside within them—this can be a mild experience, or a totally disturbed ongoing state. Nightmares, and even hallucinations while daydreaming, can accompany the anxious and irritated sixth chakra.

Also included in this category of mental imbalances are all levels of attention disorders. Depression and mood swings, which sometimes call for the aid of selective serotonin reuptake inhibitors (SSRI), are linked to brain imbalances.

The sixth chakra imbalances can also affect the eyes and the visual system. Being regarded for centuries as 'the inner eye' or 'the third eye,' the metaphor is quite clear: it is all about the ability to 'see' things as they really are. Psychosomatic disturbances can also revolve around ear disorders, such as disruptions in the hearing process, pains and infections, which subtly imply an inability to be receptive to messages and transmissions.

The process of deterioration in the brain—memory deterioration, dementia, Alzheimer and so on—is also connected to the sixth chakra. Prevention calls for the support of both practices for the brain's ongoing enhancement and the intake of herbal supplements.

Herbal supplements can also support the sixth chakra personality types who strain their brains continuously, to the extent that it faces the danger of a breakdown. In general, mental debility from over-straining one's brain is a source of headaches, migraines and mental imbalances.

Collective Imprints

First and foremost, the collective sixth chakra is ingrained with the fear of absolute truths. Absolute truths have proved to be extremely destructive. Not only did they literally crush the lower chakras of humanity through the brutal dominion of higher 'values' and ideologies, but they also led us to countless disasters, such as wars and cruel regimes. All 'isms'—dogmatic thinking, morals, religious rigidity and great ideologies—have brought about tremendous sorrow and chaos.

Growing distrust in absolute truths gave rise to the postmodern era, which is extremely pluralistic and considers all perspectives to be relative by their very nature. There is no higher and lower, all hierarchical distinctions are abolished in the face of the postmodern liberation. Of course, this brings about great freedom and tolerance, but we also have to consider nihilism and cynicism, which create an inability to revolutionize and awaken new world movements.

On the other hand, there was a rise of rational thinking and 'cold' scientific logic, which was necessary in order for us to rid ourselves of superstitions and illogical beliefs. But everything comes with a price, and this take over of rational thinking also crushed the other chakras of humanity. Along with superstitions, we have too often lost contact with our spirit, our intuition, the illogical dimensions of life, the direct feeling of living in a body, our animalistic instincts and a large portion of the simple joy of living. In a way, the dominion of rational thinking has detached us from the rest of our body, leaving us with only our head. We abide in the restless stream of thought, while the irrational worldviews of the other six chakras are forcefully repressed.

Evolution of the World

The sixth chakra first evolved through great ancient doctrines, such as the Vedas in the east and Kabala in the west. These vast teachings developed very complex systems, which 'organized' all reality, from the most divine to the most mundane, into perfect structures. Astrology, medicine, mathematics and other forms of intuitive science, which stemmed from these teachings, expressed the divine order in all things.

A tremendous leap for the sixth chakra took place in ancient Greece, where great philosophers and scientists alike gave rise to the careful, logical observation of reality. In this context, logic was the greatest breakthrough of the collective sixth chakra, and slowly but surely it worked its way through the entanglements of religion, until it untied itself completely from all the bondage of superstition.

This was the peak of evolution for the sixth chakra in humanity: at first only a few individuals dared to detach themselves from the superstitions and the unexamined presuppositions of religion, but eventually the scientific brain severed all contact with the religious brain, aspiring to see things as they are and to freely investigate uncharted territories. Nowadays it is natural for us to think that all claims for truth have to be examined through the lenses of logic and systematical proof; truth ceased to be something we strongly believe in, and became something that can be proved through repeated experience and careful inspection.

Common Interactions with Other Chakras

The first chakra and sixth chakra intersect in traumas that destabilize the way we perceive the world, like when things that seemed real to us no longer make sense or when there is a major shake-up in the structures of reality.

The combination of the second and the sixth chakras is essential for the translation of creative impulses into organized and systematic mental structures (of course, the eventual outcome of this combination of impulse and structure will be expressed through the fifth chakra).

The third and the sixth chakras create a powerful combination of self-control and self-mastery. While the third chakra supplies self-control over the urges, impulses and instincts of the two lower chakras, the sixth chakra adds a layer of mastery over all thought and emotion. These two chakras are also responsible, in the process of spiritual awakening, for the rise of spiritual powers (siddhis)—the third awakens powers that result from self-control, and the sixth awakens subtler powers of perception.

The fourth chakra and sixth chakra together create the wisdom of the heart: an extraordinary unification of emotion and intelligence. This is where compassion and wisdom are one and the same; they are one movement of insight and action. Love is then intelligence in action and vice versa.

The fifth and sixth chakras combine in the process of editing and translation. Together they 'decide' what should be externalized and how it should be externalized. They also translate ideas and visions and determine the best ways to manifest them.

The sixth and seventh chakras intersect in the process of merging into the divine truth. The seventh chakra allows the direct experience of truth, while the sixth understands it and utilizes it for right discrimination between illusion and reality. Consequently, it gives meaning and context to the inconceivable apperception of the seventh chakra.

In The Process of *Kundalini*

The sixth chakra is traditionally considered to be the third Granthi (knot). The third Granthi either blocks or enables the final flood of the pranic stream upwards, toward the seventh chakra. When this knot opens up, on the verge of final liberation, the individual *prana* and the universal *prana* can merge, and thus shutter the barrier that separates us from infinite reality.

This is the last chakra to be fully awakened before complete Enlightenment. In it, the final individual merging takes place: while all through the chakras' journey the two streams of *ida* (feminine) and *pingala* (masculine) only intersected, here they actually realize their union and together create one 'I AM', one integrated and harmonious being that can finally transcend into the unknowable realm of the seventh chakra. Here, the 'I AM' prepares for its great leap into the infinite ocean of pure consciousness.

The sixth chakra is the last and subtlest form of duality, represented by the two hemispheres of the brain. Transcending this subtle duality means going beyond the perceived (since the sixth chakra is the layer of perception) to that which is unperceivable.

Recommended Practices

The single most important practice for the sixth chakra is the detached observation of the stream of thought, feeling and sensation. Disassociating one's attention from that stream creates the gateway to freedom, deep balance and spiritual transformation. Also the practice of equanimity—seeing everything that takes place in life simply as it is, without attaching any dramatic interpretation— develops a balance in the sixth chakra. Although this is highly important for everyone, this is an essential practice for those with an imbalance of confused thought.

All practices for the development of concentration and focus, such as mantras or other practices for putting one's attention on one point, are also very important.

Mind-techniques that help the brain transcend thought are very useful. Techniques that enable the brain to reach continuous Alpha or Theta waves can be useful too. Psychoanalysis and all other forms of fierce inquiry into understanding the structures of thought can also benefit us. Dream-solving can help us organize unconscious impressions and decode their confused messages.

Any kind of transpersonal contemplation will help the brain to free itself from the constraints of the too-personalized and limited context of human living. Contemplating the great questions of life, while also learning to hold important questions in our mind, is a wonderful way to evolve.

Reading challenging scriptures and encountering supreme teachings can be very beneficial. When these types of teachings are a little above our present understanding, they create a healthy evolutionary pressure on our brains. This can also humble the cunning brain. The writings of the 20th century philosopher Jiddu Krishnamurti, a typical sixth chakra personality, can be a tremendous awakening for the sixth chakra.

If we are a sixth chakra personality type, or if we become this type in specific situations when we over-strain our brains (spiritual aspirants also over-strain the brain and the nervous system), it is important to balance long periods of tense thinking with some level of pleasure and rest. More bodily experiences and physical activities can relax the brain. There are also supplements for the brain, which can be taken under the supervision of natural health practitioners. Good examples are AFA, DHA, vitamin B-12, 5-HTP, Reishi Mushroom, Korean Ginseng, Bee pollen, Magnesium and phosphatidylserine.

The Seventh Chakra:
The Search For God

Location and General Orientation

The seventh chakra is located in the vertex of the head, like a skullcap. Unlike the other six chakras, it is not connected to major physical organs, but it seems to energetically connect with the medial longitudinal fissure (the deep groove that separates the two hemispheres of the vertebrate brain) and the pineal gland.

While the two hemispheres can be considered the last dual expressions in the human body, the deep groove that separates them is like the uniting and transcendent element. It actually takes us beyond all separation. In the yogic tradition, this groove is called the 'Brahma Randhra'—the void between the hemispheres—and it is not only where the mystical integration of the right and left side of the brain takes place, but also where the union between the separated self and the cosmic consciousness occurs. The innermost channel within the central column, which is called the 'Brahma *nadi*', goes right through the top of the skull; when fully awake, it leads a highly refined flow of *prana* to the 'Brahma Randhra'. By doing so, it simultaneously unifies the hemispheres and literally pierces the energetic layer of the vertex in order to create a 'hole' through which cosmic *prana* can freely flow downwards into the body.

The pineal gland, which is located in the center of the brain between the two hemispheres, seems to be the ruler of the psyche itself, and theoretically can be thought of as the master gland. This gland controls the modulation of waking and sleeping patterns, and therefore, seems to be in charge of the different states of consciousness itself. It has been theorized by Gabriel Cousens (M.D.) that the pineal gland affects all the glands of the body as a master regulator, and as such, we can further speculate that this gland serves as an antenna for the subtlest layers of the universe—a mediator between the cosmos and the individual consciousness. Scientifically speaking, this gland is quite mysterious apart from its known role as the regulator of waking and sleeping patterns and melatonin secretion (although, interestingly enough, one research study found higher than average melatonin concentrations in advanced meditators).

In the chakra map, the seventh chakra is considered to be the seat of the spirit. While the first to third chakras are the seat of sensations, the fourth chakra is the abode of emotions, and the sixth is the center of the mind or thought, this chakra possesses the most abstract properties. It is very often called the 'crown chakra,' and this is both due to its transcendental ruling over all other chakras and due to the way it is directly experienced: as a golden-white light crown or a skullcap that majestically covers the vertex.

Both experientially and traditionally this chakra is thought of as the center from which the 'soul' or 'consciousness' leaves the body in deep meditation or in death. This also supports the general definition of this chakra as the barrier between the cosmic and the individual.

Basic Psychological Issues

The seventh chakra controls the borders between the self and the universe—between the separated and unique self-consciousness and the consciousness of the universe as a whole. Essentially, this separation enables the evolution of each unique person; it gives shape to the increasingly growing inner world of each person, with specific worldviews, perspectives, interpretations, thoughts and feelings. This distinction between 'me' and the rest of the world gives rise to the evolving 'I' and makes the process of personal evolution possible.

On the other hand, every 'I'—every separated self—inevitably possesses an increasing tendency for self-preservation. This tendency causes us to place disproportionate emphasis on the reality of the self, especially given the fact that this is clearly an impermanent kind of reality. Slowly but surely we confine ourselves to this limiting relative reality. We observe everything through the eyes of our separated self, and our entire relationship with life is dominated by the wants and needs of this tiny grain of consciousness. Naturally we fear death or deny it, and in a way we begin to think of our personal self as the true, unbroken continuum of reality. We build high walls around our inner world of experience in order to separate us and protect us from the self-nullification that the vastness of the cosmos constantly reminds us of.

In the imbalanced state of the seventh chakra, our most basic sense is one of limitation and contraction. It is as if our consciousness is glued to this one impermanent organism that is locked up in time and space, and we can never break free from those very clear barriers. In fact, this is the subtlest form of suffering, and although it takes a highly mature mind to consciously recognize this form of suffering, we all experience it in one way or another: it hides within every contracted feeling and thought and the very sense of having limitations. Sometimes, in moments of vulnerable frustration, we exclaim, "I am tired of myself," or, "I cannot stand myself any longer." In these moments, we get in touch with the confining measures of our own selves.

Even if we unconsciously recognize these sorrowful limitations, there is still an even stronger unconscious fear: the fear of loosing oneself in the vastness of the universe. One could even say that thought is, in some respects, the mechanism that strives to overshadow the emptiness that surrounds us all and to create the illusion of a permanent self-existence. As Descartes so accurately phrased, "I think—therefore I am." This implies, in our context, that as long as we think, we can preserve our sense of self-existence.

It seems that this fear is deeper than the fear of loosing our body and the fear of physical death. In a way, the 'I' can imagine that, even after loosing the body, it will still remain—perhaps reincarnated or moved to another, even better world. So, thought imagines that it can actually go on forever, be it as a soul or an ever-existing ego. So, the death of the self—the complete end of our own psyche—is much more intimidating and, in fact, incomprehensible; it means loosing our psychological barriers and becoming fully saturated in the deep ocean of the cosmos, becoming unknown even to ourselves.

No matter how much our thoughts try to alter this horrifying fact, the universe is almost a complete mystery. Yes, we can decode some tiny percentage of this mystery by deciphering some of its physical laws, but the deeper layers of the cosmos will probably never be revealed. They are not 'unknown,' which implies that one day they can become known, but rather unknowable, which means that, by their very nature, they cannot be known. How and why has this universe come into being? Even if we follow the scientific trail of the big bang, it is not the true origin of the universe, but only, perhaps, the starting point of the unfolding of the universe. What was before that? If we answer 'God,' then what is this God really? Saying that God is the creator of all is like saying that the artist can only be known through his creations, and never as a subject or a being in itself.

The tremendous unknowable nature of the universe encompasses us in all directions. In deep sleep the world disappears, and we loose all cognition. No one really knows what death is and what lies beyond it, if anything. One thing is certain: our existence as a separated self is impermanent, which means that it is not an eternal reality. Knowing that, whether consciously or unconsciously, gives us something to fear, since beyond the frontiers of the self there lies the great mystery of nothingness.

The reality of nothingness is an eternal truth. 'Nothingness' might be a somewhat misleading word. When using it, I do not mean an empty and hollow space, but rather a reality that is totally undivided and that contains nothing but itself; being indivisible, there is only one 'that,' which includes the 'me' that recognizes this fact. This means that, in this reality, there is nothing to observe and nothing to know. Essentially, this is a revelation that goes way beyond ecstasy, but for the imbalanced seventh chakra it seems like a disaster, because there is no room for the separated self in this celebration. Whatever doesn't accommodate the self seems, to the imbalanced seventh chakra, like a form of death after which there is only a barren void.

As mentioned earlier, the imbalanced seventh chakra simultaneously experiences the two poles of imbalance inherent to the sense of separation: the pain of contraction and the fear of loosing one's own self. Again, the fear of loosing one's self is greater, since it is better to suffer than to lose the reassuring knowledge that we are a somebody who owns a name, a shape and a consistent character.

This fear has at least four levels. There is, of course, the basic fear of the dissolution of the self in the face of the vastness of the universe. It is like a drop of the ocean that separates from the waves for an instant and then fears to go back and to dissolve into the oneness. Along with the self, we might loose all of our dreams and longings, our past and our future, and the very sense of being... As liberating as this may sound, it is a dreadful possibility for the memory-based thinking that gives shape to our illusory self.

The deeper we get into meditation, the more we realize that this fear has its own subtleties: we fear emptiness, we fear loneliness, we fear the loss of the mythological God and we fear madness.

Whenever we go into deep meditation, we risk ourselves by getting closer and closer to nothingness. It means reaching a space devoid of all knowledge and objects of knowledge. It even means, when we go really deeply, reaching a space devoid of the knower—us. It's like snorkeling in the depths of the ocean and suddenly entering an endless darkness, where there is no ground to stand on and nothing to hold on to. Getting in touch with emptiness, and more than that, feeling its peculiar and powerful attraction, can be frightening, and sometimes it can even make us withdraw from all meditative activities.

Another aspect of fear that arises from deep meditation is the realization that we will slowly transcend the level of perception in which relationships are possible. In the higher levels of perception there is no duality, and this implies that there is nothing and no one to relate to. We slowly reach a state of aloneness, in which only the universal 'I' exists. In a way, it means being alone in the universe, *as* the universe. In the indivisible reality there are no two states of being, so when we merge into it, we merge into pure and absolute aloneness.

Aloneness sounds, to the separated self, like loneliness. It cannot tell the difference between the two, and one of the things that most frightens the self is loneliness. That is why people surround themselves with constant noise from within and from without. One cannot disconnect from motion and sound, because one always has to relate to something or to somebody. So, it is very understandable that profound meditation seems like a dangerous thing. Also ingrained in the no-relationship state is the loss of emotions, and since so many of us define our experiences through emotional content, this states seems cruel, cold, lifeless and inhuman.

One more aspect of fear that reveals itself in deep meditation concerns the loss of the mythological God. Considering the two former layers of fear, this is quite inevitable: when we reach the state of emptiness and aloneness, the mythological God—a creator that is clearly separated from his creation—simply cannot exist. We realize that God is not a 'who' but rather a 'that', and that communion with God is not through a relationship but rather through union and absorption. Thousands of years of constant conditioning are effective enough to make us fear this true meditative revelation. The theological implications are far too radical for many of us.

This kind of revelation also makes us fear that we might go mad, or 'loose our minds' so to speak, or at lease become completely detached, disconnected and ungrounded. Intuitively we recognize the meditative experience as one which tickles the edges of sanity, and since we don't trust ourselves—we don't feel we possess a strong enough psychological foundation—it seems to simply be too risky.

Because of this multi-layered fear, we shy away from profound meditation, allowing ourselves to only enjoy the circumference of a radical breakthrough—meditating just enough to release the constant tension of being a somebody.

Psychological Reactions of the Imbalanced Seventh Chakra

The first type of psychological reaction in the imbalanced seventh chakra is common to almost all men and women on this planet: it is the development of the clinging self, which holds on with all its might to the limited and short-lived experience of the personal 'I.' The clinging self does everything in its power to banish death from reality, since death represents the impermanent existence of personal drama. The best way to banish death from reality is through total denial. For the more vulnerable clinging self, death creeps in, filling the mind with horror and despair.

In cases of denial or fear, there is a great struggle to hold on to the seemingly uninterrupted continuum of personal drama. One acts as if there is no death at the end of the road, as if the road will go on forever. The habit of holding on to possessions is the clearest expression of this illusion: we don't want to lose our 'things', because by collecting them we can define ourselves more strongly. If we do lose them, in many respects we lose ourselves. Of course death underlies every moment in life, and therefore we have already lost everything—these types of possessions were not actually ours in the first place.

The clinging self will do anything to strengthen its sense of separateness. In fact, many of our actions and responses in life stem from this drive. The most important thing for this clinging self is self-definition—identity. By creating and supporting its individual identity in thousands of ways, it feels structured and safe. Defining a limit to oneself, like 'here is me and this is where I end and the other begins' can make one feel extremely safe. Psychologically, we are driven to make our borders more and more concrete and clear, and becoming more and more of a unique 'me' seems, to us, like a tremendous purpose in life. We sanctify the unique individuated self, and the more determined and reactive it is, the more evolved and integrated it appears. Thus, being a 'man' or a 'woman,' a 'homosexual' or a 'heterosexual,' an 'Israeli' or a 'Palestinian,' or a 'Christian' or a 'Muslim,' becomes more than perspective: it becomes who we are, in spite of the fact that that we cannot hold on to our impermanent identity in death. In death we all become nothing.

While death is the greatest friend of a balanced seventh chakra on its way to full awakening, for the imbalanced seventh chakra it is a myth that all rational minds must elegantly discard. The greatest means for the denial of death is attachment. One must attach, as much as possible, not only to self-identity, but also to people and all other objects. The clinging self holds on to objects first and foremost, because they support self-preservation. This is why the clinging personality has to constantly occupy its mind with objects. This preoccupation with the self becomes the driving force behind out thoughts, and this is the deepest cause of our endless stream of thought. Slowly but surely we become so restless, from within and from without, that we cannot keep silent for a single moment. We always have to be doing something from without, and if there is an external pause, we will keep doing things from within. Of course, very quickly we reach a state in which closing our eyes and going within our minds, or even simply relaxing our edgy nerves, seems like a frightening task. Many unconsciously dread the moments of darkness we experience before sinking into deep sleep; the darkness of the nothingness seems unbearable, and many cannot go to sleep without thinking for hours until complete exhaustion takes over.

Personal drama has to be cultivated to the extent that every small detail in it seems amazingly important. Our personal story is the center of the universe, and it has to take all of our energy. We must also draw the attention of others to it.

But we are not fools: deep within us the agitation of contraction and limitation makes us desperately seek out a state of no-limitation. Since we don't want to look for this freedom in our own consciousness— the questioning of our own structures is dangerous—we seek objects and experiences that can briefly bestow upon us the feeling of limitlessness. This is how strong addictions and powerful distractions come into being. Brief orgasms from sex and masturbation, drugs of all types, risky adventures and the enhancement of our sense of personal power can give us short-lived relief from the pain of the contracted self.

We have collectively created very sharp and narrow definitions of sanity, so we all react very strongly to anything that might endanger and shake these definitions. The unconscious collective agreement is that whatever destabilizes the 'rational' self should be condemned. This, of course, includes everything that carries the deep fragrance of the mystery of life. That is why profound meditation challenges our conditioning: it brings to life many powers and forces that lie hidden within us, and which come directly from both the unknowable and the unknown. Meditation puts us on a journey outside the realms of the self.

True meditation is dangerous for the clinging self. True spirituality can lead us to the threshold of insanity. Thus we avoid it, or we engage in superficial and dual spirituality, which maintains the boundaries of the self and only gives us a small level of relief from our constant turmoil. This kind of spirituality is highly conceptual, and it is no coincidence that it promises the clinging self its own eternity, be it through reincarnation or the other, better, world. This form of spirituality also maintains the duality of the believer and the external God through prayer, devotion and obedience to the law.

When in meditation, the lower six chakras help protect us from real meditation, efficiently bringing us back to 'ourselves.' We avoid getting in touch with the mystery of life through serious inquiry and contemplation. We believe that no important questions should be asked, because it is better and safer to stick to the known. That is why our science allows mostly materialistic investigation, while vehemently denying all the subtler layers of the universe.

There is yet another, totally different, type of psychological reaction to the imbalanced seventh chakra. Although quite rare, this reaction is found in meditative people. These people are inclined to escape to the other pole of imbalance: they fear life, with all its earthly challenges, and they find it 'easy' to stay unattached and free from all earthly commitments. Supported by an imbalanced first chakra, they cling only to the spiritual realm of self-dissolution, abandoning all obligation to face their psychological layers of existence. They proudly proclaim that life has no meaning and no purpose but the liberation from earthly bounds, and that we are here only so we can free ourselves and escape to the subtler realms of self-annihilation.

For these people, the Eastern principle of liberation from all incarnation seems very appealing. Unknowingly, they use spirituality as a refuge from challenges and meditation as an ultimate relief. In closing their eyes, they go back to the womb, acting as if the purpose of life is to regress to the primordial state of existence.

These people tend to demonstrate a tendency toward airiness and remoteness. They can be very ungrounded, and engaging in spirituality only worsens this tendency. It is as if skipping to the higher chakras is extremely easy for them, but at the same time, they have no 'legs.' They have no lower and animalistic tendencies, no feeling of aliveness and none of the much needed desire for life.

Solutions for the Imbalanced Seventh Chakra

The key solution for the imbalanced seventh chakra lies in understanding that true and profound happiness can be realized only by breaking through the limitations of the self. Confusingly, we search for happiness within the limitations of the separated self, trying to extract the nectar of happiness from enhanced experiences and possessions, but in reality, the very sense of separation *is* limitation, and limitation *is* suffering.

Happiness is ignorantly sought after as another sort of accomplishment for the personal self. This happiness, even when found for brief moments, is quickly nullified by its very complementary opposite, pain. Unlike this sort of happiness, true and profound happiness transcends the opposites of joy and pain. That is why the better term for happiness is 'bliss', which is supreme or sublime happiness (in the yogic tradition it is called 'Ananda'). This is a state of uninterrupted happiness, and it is to be located in the deeper layers of consciousness, beyond the grasp of the separated self, with all its wants and needs. Basically, it is bliss because it is a genuine state of limitlessness, and the lack of limitations *is* bliss.

The seventh chakra teaches us that by losing our boundaries we reach the happiest state possible. When this chakra fully blossoms, it maintains the transparent outlines of the personality, and at the same time, becomes wide open, enabling the total blending of the personal and the transpersonal, the cosmic and the unique. In this blending, there is an ever-growing sense of oneness with the divine, and along with this increasing sense, there comes intoxicating happiness and total relaxation. Very quickly we will loose all interest in the fake no-limitation state that life's experiences offer us and move our focus to an endless expansion toward infinity.

When there is balance in the seventh chakra we experience spiritual maturity, which arises out of countless spiritual experiences and revelations. On the one hand, we become weary of the egoic spectrum of experiences, which constantly fail to bring about the happiness they promise, and on the other hand, we get more and more in touch with the amazing bliss of limitlessness in our consciousness. This teaches us to connect happiness with this state of limitlessness alone, and we cease to foolishly follow egoic dreams and promises. We realize in our innermost layers of consciousness that the ecstasy of limitlessness can be everlasting only in the realm of the spirit, so we shift our energy from draining and disappointing external experiences, and we begin to put our energy and love into the process of expanding our consciousness.

That being said, this doesn't mean that we should obsessively try to attain as many spiritual experiences as possible. That would mean reverting back to the tendency of the egoic self to accumulate as much as possible in order to possess sublime happiness. We will quickly learn that all experiences that occur in the field of the personal self are limited by their very nature, and even powerful spiritual experiences are nothing but echoes of the great absolute reality. So, we will embark on a journey of transformation, in which experiences of bliss are only meant to encourage us. The true destination of this journey of transformation will be the final and complete shattering of the borders of the self.

The deeper we get in the transformative journey, the more our newfound insight—that suffering is separation and happiness is to become inseparable—is reaffirmed. Affirmations come in many forms: through direct spiritual experiences, through deep insight, through spiritual teachings and teachers, and so on. These affirmations help us grow our confidence and dissipate all our doubt and fear.

Slowly but surely we will realize that whenever we boldly go into deep meditation, we can see fear just as it is: as a momentary fraction of thought. This fraction of thought must not get in the way of our sacred path. We can clearly see that these doubts and fears are only remnants of the conditioned thoughts of the clinging self. Once we get past it, we will discover that this fear of self-dissolution managed to trick us. The only thing our fear has protected us from is the greatest happiness possible. Self-dissolution is the happiest state possible, and in this state we can laughingly see that our real fear should have been that we would stay where we were, forever limited and painfully separated.

The more our *prana* flows upwards through the central column, the more blissful we become. This constant movement upwards creates bliss, while holding on to our earthly bounds, moving downwards so to speak, creates sorrow. Whenever the pranic flow bursts through our seventh chakra, we expand toward infinity and experience the death of the separated self. Gradually death becomes our greatest companion, and physical death seems to us like the ultimate orgasmic expansion—the ultimate breakthrough of our known limitations.

It is important to understand that the more we flow and expand upwards, the more we lose our attachments and desires. They drop like leaves in the autumn: effortlessly and unconsciously. When we are filled with bliss, we do not feel thirst or hunger anymore; it is as if the divine nectar has quenched our soul's thirst. For example, you won't long for physical orgasms once you can fully enjoy the orgasmic expansion of consciousness. This is particularly important, because we shouldn't struggle with attachments or desires; we should continuously flow upwards in the context of a true transformative process.

I have now presented the key solution for the clinging self: a deep, penetrating understanding of the true nature of happiness, which stems only from ongoing, direct and transformative engagement, such as meditation or spiritual contemplation. Balance in the seventh chakra can only take place when our innermost layer of consciousness awakens and realizes the lost link in its search for happiness.

There are yet two more specific paths of balance. One is for those who tend to be more earthly and fearful of transformation, and one is for those who tend to demonstrate an imbalanced tendency of escapism.

For those who face intense fear in the seventh chakra, it is highly advised to embark on a more gradual transformational journey. Of course, they also have to consciously agree to engage in a deep transformational process, through profound meditation and contemplation. Nonetheless, they don't have to go all the way in the process at once. One can joyfully, yet seriously, go through a gradual and more controlled process of transformation, which takes into consideration the immaturity of the brain and the nervous system, the physical and the subtle. Going all the way might 'burn' us, so it's sometimes better to accept the limitations of our body and mind and to slowly assimilate the light of the divine self. Since even the slightest piece of the divine greatly increases our appetite, we will soon discover that we are able to take in more and more and that we really want to go deeper into our transformative process.

It is also important to take it slowly because we have to mature and settle in a state that is beyond feelings and relationships, and is even—to the horror of the believer's mind—beyond an external God. Sometimes this state is pretty hard to digest, and only the increasing levels of bliss soothe these deep shocks.

If fear dominates our relationship with the spiritual dimension of life, a deep intellectual understanding of genuine spirituality is very important. The intellect must be fully involved in this process, because when our sixth chakra is spiritually intelligent, it can act as a solid foundation whenever we embark on a journey toward new territories of the unknown.

It is highly advised to choose an experienced master or a solid system that bestows confidence and trust on us. Having an expert or a knowledgeable tradition on our side enables us to walk into the unknown infinity in the light of accurate wisdom which can save us from traps and guide us even further along. An expert can also serve as a model of someone who has gone all the way and is now absolutely calm in the groundless fields; the expert's relaxed and fearless position will easily untie our own fears and doubts.

Lastly, we must awaken the seventh chakra, while at the same time creating foundations and balance in our six lower chakras—most importantly, the first and the third chakras. Only when there is a strong foundation in the lower chakras can we feel truly safe, since with this foundation alone can we feel firmly rooted in the earthly dimension. It is like having a base from which we can travel and to which we can comfortably return, filled with new knowledge and adventurous experiences.

For the escapists, it is also strongly advised to work on balancing the lower chakras, but for a different reason. As long as the escapists 'fly high' in the spiritual dimensions with no stable ground to stand on or to come back to, their flight will deceivingly serve as a means to escape the challenges of life. Escapists are not very fond of life; life is a dangerous and demanding place, while meditation is liberating and soothing. However, bliss shouldn't be an escape, especially when considering the fact that as long as we do not resolve our relationship with life, we will never be able to stabilize our transformation, no matter how 'spiritually high' we are.

We should keep in mind that true spirituality can be developed only on the basis of a positive life experience. One should love life, and out of this love, one can transcend life lightheartedly. So, for those who are inclined to flying high, it is important to remember that sometimes this 'fearless' approach stems from a deeper unconscious fear!

It is essential to take care of our livelihood and basic needs for survival. A functional first chakra can enable us to truly relax in meditation. It is also essential to solve psychological patterns, since meditation must not turn into merely an efficient way to running away from pain. All human dimensions are important to regard, to heal and to fully experience, and when we avoid them, it is due to a deep-hidden pain that we are desperately trying to avoid.

The escapists should avoid their tendency to exaggerate their spiritual ambition. In the escapist, the air element might increase to a dangerous level of ungrounded detachment. They should also avoid radical approaches, although radical approaches will be most appealing to them because of their imbalanced tendencies. A more stabilized and balanced approach, supported by wise tradition, and structured and 'limited' forms of spiritual practice will best suit this kind of person.

The Three Levels of Functioning

The Functional Seventh Chakra

We move slowly but steadily through the spiritual journey. We are filled with appreciation for enlightened masters and traditions, and yet we are not seriously interested in actually transforming ourselves. Intellectually we understand, and even agree, that the separated self is an illusion, and we also recognize that God is not an external phenomenon, but our spiritual practice is not radical enough for us to realize it in the depths of our being. This does not mean that we cannot get in touch with states of emptiness during profound meditation—we can even meditate without excessive fear and without losing the ability to come back to the ground afterwards. We are also able to retreat in silence and deep meditation for days. At the same time, we take care not to cross the boundaries too much, and in a way, we use the spiritual dimension to balance our minds and our life. Our egoic experience still fascinates us very much, and we feel that there is a lot to experience before we can discard the physical world and move into unknown realms. We carry earthly desires, which are the strongest drives within us, and we balance them with frequent experience of meditative bliss.

The Balanced Seventh Chakra

We are spiritually mature human beings. The first indication of this maturity is our ability to feel and clearly recognize that the contracted self *is* suffering and the expanded consciousness *is* bliss. This recognition totally overcomes our fear of self-dissolution, and our spiritual longing to lose all barriers is no longer limited by fear and doubt. The evolution of consciousness is our focal point, and spiritual masters are our role models. We experience an uninterrupted attraction to merging with the divine. We know through our hearts and minds, and out of our countless direct experiences, that God is not a somebody or a something, but rather a state of consciousness. In meditation, we are capable of entering into very deep meditative states, and for long periods of time we are saturated in the divine light of Samadhi (self-absorption). Our seventh chakra continuously opens up to receive cosmic energy. We love being alone and leaving the whole world behind—this is not because we dislike life, but because we are totally attracted to self-absorption. We no longer depend on feelings to define ourselves. Our experience of individuality is very refined, as if our 'I AM' is transparent and nearly non-existent. Our earthly desires steadily diminish. Death seems like an ecstatic dissolution or expansion. In fact, in this balanced state of the seventh chakra, the only thing that keeps us separated from the divine is our inability to conduct enough light through our nervous system, both physical and subtle.

The Awakened Seventh Chakra

For this level, the borders of the seventh chakra have completely shattered and cosmic energy can freely flow into the individual subtle anatomy. The separation between the personal and the cosmic disappears, and they blend into a new being that is simultaneously human and divine. There is an actual loss of the feeling of having borders in the vertex, and one feels headless, as if cosmic energy broke open one's skull. It is just like the Taoist saying: "The sage has no mind of his own." The central column merges into infinity above the head, through the transpersonal eighth chakra. The seventh chakra opens up just like a fountain, and at the same time, it becomes an empty vessel that limitlessly accepts cosmic energy. We effortlessly and ceaselessly conduct divine light through our physical and subtle nervous systems. We do not get complete answers explaining the greatest mysteries of life and beyond, but we realize that merging with these mysteries is the ultimate answer. The divine self takes the place of the personal self, and from then on the universe uses the remnants of the separated self (the transparent personality) for its own creative needs and urges. The personality becomes functional and not a force in itself. Attachments and desires are no longer great challenges, and they are certainly not sources of struggle. Death is no longer a possibility because only the eternal IS. The spiritual journey is complete with the happy realization that there is no one to merge with anything since the seeking subject and the sought object are one and the same. There is undifferentiated oneness, accompanied by an almost constant inner recognition that 'I am That.'

Polar emotions

Fear of emptiness / bliss, attachment / liberation, separation / oneness.

Type of Trauma

Spiritual traumas occur whenever we prematurely experience a loss of our self-boundaries, and whenever we directly touch the spiritual truth but are unable to assimilate it, making our well-organized worldviews collapse. This could happen during meditation or in any other setting of spiritual revelation during which we could stumble upon emptiness and groundless space (for religious believers this might lead to a religious crisis). This could also happen while experimenting with psychedelic drugs and psychoactive plants, when our brain and subtle anatomy become vulnerable to either illusory or real dimensions. Sometimes a premature encounter with a spiritual master (or with a false spiritual teacher, who leads us to the verge of breakdown) can also destabilize us. A spiritual trauma can also take place when we have an unexpected spiritual awakening or a *kundalini* crisis in which the spiritual force moves in twisted directions throughout the *nadis* because of psychological or physical disturbances. Sometimes the clash between spiritual revelation, an immature brain and psychology can lead one to some sort of 'madness,' such as various forms of mania or megalomania. A trauma can take place when individuals who aspire to become quickly enlightened begin to experiment with practices that create *prana* imbalances; they become totally confused and ungrounded and thus avoid spiritual practices from then on. One last possible spiritual trauma occurs when one has a near-death experience.

The general conclusion reached through this kind of trauma is: 'It is dangerous to open up completely.' We become very distrusting toward the spiritual dimension of life and its 'representatives'—spiritual masters and esoteric traditions. We develop a deep fear of meditative experience and do our best to constantly ground ourselves. Sometimes we reject spirituality and move to the other extreme, of 'simple living,' that is living 'like everyone else.' We fight our spiritual and airy tendencies and fear feelings of detachment. We create a very solid definition of sanity, since we fear going insane. We become strongly attached to logical thinking. For some, it may take years to realize that spirituality doesn't have to be destabilizing and that there are very balanced teachings and teachers in this world; others will never return to spiritual practices.

Type of Personality

This rare personality type can be best represented by the image of the Yogi. It is totally devoted to the state of self-dissolution and absorption in divine light. This is where we find the renunciates ('Sadhus' in the yogic tradition), who effortlessly demonstrate a lack of interest in the world of time and space. These people tend to shy away from all external engagements and withdraw into caves, forests or monasteries. They are very inclined to observe long periods of silence or even total silence, and they are also drawn to very long periods of meditation and fasting. Their sole interest in life is in the purity of the state of no-self, and even when they attract many devotees, they are still mostly immersed in this state, coming out of it only in rare moments when they help enable others to get closer to it.

In a lesser form, we can also find here those who are mostly interested in meditation and who find it quite hard to respond to life's challenges because of a simple lack of interest. In the face of western life challenges, these people might demonstrate an imbalanced remoteness from the world, a general feeling of not belonging to the world and a disassociation from the body. Many times, these people find themselves totally unsupported by the western collective consciousness. They are torn between monastic life and mundane engagements, including family life. In the Ayurvedic tradition, these people are Vata expressions: airy, ungrounded and spiritual. They will always prefer hovering in meditation to feeling the actual ground beneath their feet.

> ## Famous Seventh Chakra Expressions
> Gautama the Buddha, Ramana Maharishi:
> blissful, absorbed in Nirvana and silent.

Male and Female Energies

The male aspect of the seventh chakra is the total mastery of both the psyche and the body. It is the highest authority; the spirit which, when awakened, becomes one's supreme identity, worldview and reality. Once awakened, all other knowledge and perspectives are measured by its own knowledge and perspective. The absolute non-dual nature of reality becomes the worldview that overpowers all others.

The female aspect of the seventh chakra is becoming a completely empty vessel into which the divine pours itself. We open up without any resistance in order to receive the divine light, and we are in fact penetrated by the presence of the spirit. We transform into almost-perfect conductors of divine light, knowledge, compassion and creative urges.

Type of Happiness

Happiness, in this chakra, is the ultimate bliss of self-absorption, which is to be found in deep states of Samadhi—when we expand our consciousness to the extent that we lose all boundaries and all limitations. The upward flow of the *kundalini*, which unties all earthly bondage and takes us to the inner heavens, is happiness in action. Attaining final liberation or enlightenment is complete happiness, which can transcend both happiness and pain. Enlightenment is the end of our illusory search for happiness in the world of objects.

Life's Meaning and Purpose

Life is nothing but the play of God, an eternal game of hide-and-seek, which is won through the spiritual revelation of the always liberated state of nothingness. On a higher level, even that cannot be said, since here and now there is only 'That,' and the world doesn't exist at all. This realization is the sharp knife that skillfully cuts through all illusion. There is absolutely no meaning or purpose in life, except for spiritual liberation and enlightenment. We are here only to 'undo'; in a way, we are meant to simply regress to the perfect state that existed before creation. There is nothing to do, nowhere to go; spiritual paths and spiritual destinations are mere traps, hindering this stainless realization. There is no reincarnation, since the soul doesn't exist; nothing can be separated from the divine. Love is the radiance emanating from the non-dual state. It is an effortless radiation that dispassionately touches everything. Death is a cosmic joke; there is no death in the eternal being. God is not something to believe in, because God is the only thing there is. One's job is simply to surrender to this fact and to merge into the one and only being.

Ages of Development of the Seventh Chakra

There is no line of natural psychological development that inevitably leads to this chakra, so we cannot define the period of time that most supports the seventh chakra's evolution. If there was a natural line of this kind, then it would begin between the age of forty-two and the age of forty-nine. Ideally, it would be natural that, after all commitments for society have been fulfilled (chakras four and five) and after individual knowledge and wisdom have been integrated (sixth chakra), there would be a growing tendency to go within and to realize God or the spirit. The more one grows, the more one can shed earthly obligations and feel confident enough to open up to the realization of life's deepest secrets and mysteries.

In more spiritually supportive communities, such as the Vedic ashram system, at the age of fifty people are encouraged to move to the Vanaprastha ('gone to the forest') period of life. The age of fifty marks the completion of all obligations as a householder, and the beginning of one's full devotion to divine realization (moksha). It is the starting point of the transition from material life to spiritual life: the spiritual aspirant retires and lives as a hermit after partially giving up material desires.

Psychosomatic Disturbances

Psychosomatic disturbances in the seventh chakra mainly revolve around a loss of balance in the different states of consciousness: from sleeping disorders (insomnia, for example) to the ramifications of the loss of consciousness (for example, traumatic anesthetization and cerebral concussion). We should remember that the pineal gland, which is connected to the seventh chakra, controls the wake/sleep modulation (through its melatonin production), so whenever the basic states of consciousness are disturbed, it can lead to either short-term or long-term diseases.

Any kind of disruption in the ordinary perception of wakefulness is connected to the seventh chakra. This can include the long-term influence of psychoactive plants and psychedelic drugs, as well as simpler disturbances, such as vertigo. There are also psychiatric imbalances related to this chakra; mania, as one example, is often followed by a sense of energy flowing through a wide open vertex.

There is also a vast range of *kundalini* imbalances that quite often involve a too-open seventh chakra. These imbalances can cause strong feelings of disconnection, disorientation, and hypersensitivity, along with the very ungrounded feeling that one has no safe and defined boundaries. Basically, every strong spiritual experience can leave its momentary mark on the exhausted body, brain and nervous system, but sometimes psychological or physical blockages can lead to energetic and psychosomatic breakdowns.

Collective Imprints

The most powerful collective imprint in the seventh chakra is the image of the external and mythological God, as constructed by religion. This objectification of God, which gave rise to the complex relationship between Him and the believer, has imprinted in the human brain a strong line, separating the Creator from the created. Of course, the countless stories of creation from all over the world strongly support this concept. The other pole of this imprint is the atheist approach, which negates the creator and leaves us only with creation itself (a self-creating universe). These two poles are a great hindrance to our effort to transcend both creator and creation and to finally realize that there is only 'That.'

Following this concept of an external God, there is the belief in the need for a religious or a spiritual mediator (a priest, a rabbi or a guru) who will negotiate between the believer and the external God. A mediator translates our prayers into a divine language, which God can understand, and simultaneously translates divine language into humanly understandable messages. This is another blockage on our path to divine communion, since the dormant seventh chakra is a direct communicator with the universal light.

There is a great resistance to transformative spirituality in all forms of society, particularly in Western society. Psychology and psychiatry outline very clearly the borders of sanity, so according to them, the depths of our transformative spirituality might be considered, in some respects, insane. Our science is quite atheistic and materialistic, so it does not recognize the subtle layers of consciousness that are implied by the esoteric teachings. Renounciates are considered to be freaks in secu-lar, money-oriented and family-based societies. Of course, the central religions that support the dual notion of God and his mediators, negate the radical idea of merging with a non-dual God. This means that being a true spiritual aspirant of the non-dual teaching goes against all western cultural structures.

Evolution of the World

The collective seventh chakra was developed in the esoteric teachings and transformative sects of every great religion, including Yoga, Tantra, Sufism, Kabala, Zen and Mahayana (two extensions of Buddhism), the Essenes, the Pytagorians and more. These sects separated from the religious crowd in order to devote themselves to radical transformative practices of self-dissolution and union with the divine. Enormous beings, such as Gautama the Buddha and Jesus, have paved the path to direct transcendence and self-liberation. That is why they were considered, in the eyes of institutionalized religions of their own time, to be dangerous. 'Be a light unto yourself,' the great guidance of the Buddha, remains to this day as a milestone in the development of the collective seventh chakra.

However, the greatest leap in the development of the collective seventh chakra took place in the 20th century, when the Eastern world of spiritual enlightenment, especially the various Yogic lineages, sent its excellent representatives to the West. They spread the notion of an autonomous spirituality, a spirituality that takes place as a direct, inner revelation, which does not look up to the heavens but rather turns its eye inward, which does not believe but rather aspires to merge, which encour-ages all people to cultivate their own communication with the divine, and which has teachers who merely point us toward our own inner light. Great speakers, such as Jiddu Krishnamurti and Osho, delivered powerful messages regarding the negation of religion and the external God. These messages were excitedly accepted by many, especially the hippie subculture. As a result, the notion of the inner God now seems obvious to every New-Age believer.

Common Interactions with Other Chakras

The first and the seventh chakras combine in two kinds of traumas: the spiri-tual trauma (which is described in detail in the section 'Type of trauma') and the sometimes-unconscious trauma of the escapists. Escapists tend to express interest in transformative spirituality for the wrong reasons: they would like to find a way out of living, and they want to leave their physical bodies. This is a very subtle form of suicide. Self-dissolution simply seems like an appealing notion to their eyes, but really, they are motivated by conscious and unconscious traumas that drive them to flee from the challenges of life.

The connection between the second and the seventh chakra is highly important. While both chakras deal with the desire for limitlessness, the second chakra looks for this state in extreme and exciting experiences, and the seventh chakra seeks it in the spiritual realm, which is beyond all feelings and experiences. Looking for a state of limitlessness in experiences is a major cause for the development of desire. The seventh chakra can powerfully calm down the desires of the second chakra by actually offering it deep fulfillment and redemption found in the spirit. It is in the power of the seventh chakra to transmute and alchemize any urge or experience in the second chakra into a state of pure merging (essentially, this is the core of the Tantric teachings). At the same time, we must not forget that the second chakra is the source of the merging impulse—the drive toward ecstasy that can be found through self-forgetfulness—so the seventh chakra also depends on the second as a source of primordial urge and energy.

The third, sixth and seventh chakras intersect in the process of self-development. The third chakra turns us into a master who can control all urges and desires; the sixth goes further, and develops us into a self beyond all thoughts and feelings, and the seventh chakra allows us to develop total mastery over the psyche and the body, and eventually, over the entire subtle anatomy.

The fourth and the seventh chakras combine to create a simultaneously dual and non-dual relationship with the divine. The heart keeps the flame of devotion and love alive, while the seventh chakra dominates it with its revelation that there is no form of relationship possible at all.

The sixth chakra powerfully intersects with the seventh chakra. When combined, the seventh brings about the direct revelation of the formless 'One,' and the sixth translates this revelation into a tool of discrimination between reality and illusion. The sixth also translates this abstraction into the actual meaning and purpose of life itself.

In the Process of *Kundalini*

Undoubtedly, the seventh chakra is the most important center in the process of *kundalini*. After the spiritual aspirant has managed to break through the three *granthis* (uniting the three lower chakras, awakening the heart and opening the 'third eye' of the sixth chakra), he is ready to take the final leap toward the non-dual state of the seventh chakra. This is like succeeding in overcoming the force of gravity—the earthly energy of the body and the psyche will actually change course, because they will be completely magnetized toward the heavens. There is now one last step to be taken, a groundless step into the formless space of the seventh chakra.

In the sixth chakra there is yet a very transparent 'I AM,' a sense of self-existence that separates one from the whole. This refined duality is transcended in the seventh chakra. Traditionally, moving beyond the sixth chakra is believed to require the aid of a skillful master or a powerful act of heavenly grace. However, this leap can also be understood as a final culmination of great momentum, in which we completely defeat the force of gravitation.

The moment we take the leap, it is as if a separated tiny drop of water has returned to the ocean. The great paradox is that there is no feeling of gain or victory, since we are merging with the only reality that ever existed. In many respects, nothing happened; only the illusion of separation has been shattered.

Recommended Practices

The balancing and awakening of the seventh chakra demands engagement in transformative spirituality (which is the direct experience of dissolution into oneness). Deep meditation, silent retreats, fasting retreats, and initiations and radiation of energy from spiritual masters are all beneficial practices in this context. We should keep in mind that there is a clear distinction between ordinary spirituality and transformative spirituality: the later aims at the loss of all self-boundaries in order to realize the ultimate truth of no-separation. Naturally, some practices support it more than others. For example, focusing our mind on self-inquiry—deeply inquiring 'Who am I?' or contemplating the mystery of the self—is a very direct approach, and thus can be regarded as transformative.

Both the clinging self and the escapist self will greatly benefit from the balanced structures of stable transformative traditions. This does not negate the fact that we all must walk on this path alone; there are just many traps that traditional knowledge can easily trace and remove, and there is also a great traditional understanding of the nature of the final goal for everyone, so one can hardly ever get stuck.

Both personalities will also benefit from a profound intellectual understanding of spiritual transformation. It is not enough to meditate; we need the sixth chakra on our side in order to accurately translate the meaning of meditation's abstract expansion of consciousness. Without the aid of the sixth chakra, the bridge between the seventh chakra and life itself can never be created.

Both personalities can correct their imbalanced expressions by choosing more moderate and gradual processes, which take into consideration the present state of their immature nervous system and the conditioned brain. While engaging in transformative practices, it is essential to untie impressions in the lower chakras and to respond to life challenges that are presented to us by our lower chakras. We must keep in mind that only a well-established and balanced self can ever irreversibly merge with the Godhead.

It is best if both personalities don't forcefully push away desires and attachments. Self-discipline is good, but we must not forget that we need joy and pleasure in the second chakra. Instead of battling strong desires, one should move more and more into the light of the self; by doing so, attachments will gradually and effortlessly fade away.

More specifically for the escapists, it is important not to get swept away by certain tendencies, such as over-ambition, ungrounded living, radical experimentation and disinterest in material matters (such as livelihood).

Summary:
The Seven Wisdoms of Life

As the title of this book suggests, understanding the different lessons of the seven chakras also means to understand the seven lessons of life as a whole. We don't need to guess what the core teachings in our life are—they are presented to us perfectly and fully in the seven layers of our psyche. Each one of us has to go through these seven lessons, and only by passing through them can we ever realize the complete phenomenon of life. The more we go through these passages, the more our wisdom grows, and we can then become the embodiment of a realized life.

Just like bees, we are meant to fly around from one flower to another, extracting the finest wisdom from each of them. After we complete this journey through the seven 'flowers,' we are loaded with life's riches, and filled with the kind of wisdom that only the direct and fullest experience of life can ever engender. This means that the seven chakras are also, in fact, the seven lessons in the school of life.

Every chakra is like an entire world of identity, perspective, experience, urges, feelings, sensations and, of course, insights. In the initial stages of our encounter with its wisdom and teachings, it seems to offer a tremendous range of confusing possibilities and polarities, but the more we get to know it, the more we are able to overcome all distractions and to focus on its main teaching. This is the precious time of extraction, during which we are prepared to complete the teaching of the chakra and to release its essential wisdom. Once released, the chakra becomes fully awakened, or spiritualized, and partakes in the general awakening of the body-mind complex as a whole. When all seven chakras fully release their deepest wisdom, there are no more core lessons for the individual mind; in many respects, one has graduated from the school of life and can be considered a liberated human being. This does not mean that the chakras completely cease to purify and evolve, but rather that their prime lessons have been learned; from then on, the remaining lessons are quite peripheral and very refined.

In general, there are four main ways to extract wisdom from each and every chakra.

The first is by a means of purification. Purification is a therapeutic process, during which both body and mind are cleansed of psychological impressions and memories. These impressions appear in the chakras as *vrittis*—personality tendencies that reflect our deepest subconscious. Each chakra carries its own positive and negative *vrittis*. The positive ones support the chakra's balanced activity, while the negative ones distort its balanced functioning and hinder its ability to fully awaken. By clearing away the central negative *vrittis*, the chakra can progressively release its dormant potential.

The second is, of course, through right choices and actions in life itself. In most cases, it is almost impossible to fully learn and to become wise without actually engaging with life. This, of course, demands a quite painful process of trial and error. Sometimes it is clear that we have to act in a way that totally opposes our personality-tendencies, while in other cases, we must express ourselves just the way we are. Sometimes we have to take risks and experiment with uncontrollable situations, and sometimes we must do just the opposite. This is not a safe and clear territory, and nothing, not even the safety net of moral codes, can tell us exactly how we should act in order to complete a certain chakra lesson. This requires very attentive listening; we must listen to our journey as it appears *moment to moment*, since no past conclusions can help us determine precisely how to respond to new challenges.

The third way to extract wisdom from the chakras is through spiritual practices. Spiritual practices significantly reduce our need for psychological purification and for direct experiences in life. They help awaken the spiritual qualities in every chakra, and thus release direct *inner* wisdom. Spiritual practices evolve and expand our self-identity, increase our *prana* intake, purify the *nadis* and awaken dormant capacities in the chakras. In this way, we become wise without having to actually go through *all* of life's mistakes.

The fourth and last way is through higher wisdom. Higher wisdom, which can be found in the words of enlightened beings and holy scriptures, can equip us with ancient insights that will minimize our need for direct experience and direct us toward the highway of complete liberation.

Essentially, each and every awakened chakra releases extracts of wisdom, which are made up of a combination of psychological purification, right actions, spiritual practices and higher wisdom. In a way, all four make an inseparable string of wisdom.

Although clearly mentioned throughout this book, here are the seven teachings of life, as reflected in the seven chakras. Viewing them together, as a complete journey, can provide an enlightening insight into life as a complete phenomenon.

- Life isn't meant to be safe, stable and unchangeable—*You* are meant to be your own sanctuary. It is in *your* power and in *your* hands to create an inner world of rock-like stability.

- Our joy in living does not depend on powerful experiences or peaks of pleasure, and it shouldn't diminish when pain and disappointment come in the form of external experiences. The joy of living is the non-causal state of an ever creative and complete spirit.

- Power is not about outer force and control, but rather the power of self-presence and genuine self-control. By attaining complete self-control and realizing a truly integrated self, we will no longer seek an outer expression of power, and we will use power only when it is truly needed.

- True love stems from an unbroken *wholeness*, never from *neediness*, and it is fulfilled not through what we *receive*, but rather through what we *give*.

- Use your voice only when it will clearly serve mutual growth and development and support the greater good. Express yourself only for service—only when it leads to constructive ends.

- Only the transcendence of thought can ever bring about clarity and intelligence. *There is no clarity in thought.* In the still mind, a new state of openness, true listening and insight reveals itself.

- True and profound happiness can only be realized with the breakthrough of the limitations of the self. Bliss, uninterrupted happiness, can be located only in the deeper layers of consciousness, beyond the grasp of the separated self's wants and needs.

There are two ways to perceive the journey along the chakra system. The first way, which I have just discussed, is linear and progressive, while the other way is multidimensional and simultaneous. Both ways are true and relevant.

The first way is based on the idea that no higher chakra can ever fully stabilize and awaken without the solid foundation of its lower chakras. This idea holds the understanding of the nature of genuine evolution. Just like a tree, which has to have solid roots in order to develop a strong trunk and to eventually open its treetop to the infinite sky, and just like a building, which must be built upon firm foundations, the human consciousness needs stability in order to grow: it has to develop, brick by brick, in order to move higher and higher without the danger of ever falling back. Although, in actuality, the evolution of the chakras is not strictly linear and very often there is some level of balancing and awakening occurring in higher chakras, in spite of our 'lower' evolutionary stage, in terms of *stages of development*, it is completely linear—only when we complete the fundamental lesson of a lower chakra, can we fully move to the fundamental lesson of the next one. The reason for that is simple: the lesson of the higher chakra is always more complex, and inevitably demands the awakened insight of the previous chakra.

Only after we create a planetary and spiritual foundation (first chakra), can we ever gain enough confidence and stability to allow ourselves to powerfully, totally and boldly experience life (second chakra). By contacting the powerful and intense energies of the life force, we slowly learn how to handle them, harness their power, restrain them, and direct their power toward worthy aspirations (third chakra). On the solid foundation of a stable and powerful self, we are able to gradually learn to shape our aspirations in the spirit of love and service (fourth chakra). Acquiring the ability to love, we can properly express aspirations for the greater good (fifth chakra). On the basis of the accumulated qualities from the five lower chakras (stability, joy, power, love and creative expression), we develop wisdom and clear perceptions of the meaning and purpose of life (sixth chakra). This wisdom finally leads us to the search and the realization of the ultimate purpose of life (seventh chakra).

When a chakra stabilizes in a state of awakening, it releases a higher sense of awareness, which was stored within it, into the mind, thus adding a new layer of wisdom and awareness to the mind. This is not merely a transcendence of the previous layer of awareness, but rather an *inclusive transcendence*. This means that we are not simply moving higher and higher, forgetting all about our previous attainments—on the contrary, we are developing more and more complex structures of consciousness.

The second way to perceive and understand the journey along the chakras is as a process that is multidimensional and simultaneous. This understanding does not negate the first perception, but, in fact, teaches us of the final purpose of its linear, brick by brick evolutionary journey. As whole human beings, we are not destined to simply transcend the lower chakras and abide only in the seventh chakra. We have to go through the full linear journey in order to awaken the entire spectrum of chakras and all of the layers of the psyche. However, once awakened, there is free movement between the chakras, which actually enables us to have seven perspectives, worldviews and experiences of life. We are destined to embody these seven perspectives simultaneously, and freely use them in the different dimensions and challenges of life.

In this way, the chakra system reveals itself not only as an evolutionary line, but also as a holistic and total model of life and consciousness. This model equips us with seven types of happiness, which are all meant to be fully experienced, and with seven types of love, which, when intertwined, provide us with the full experience of human love. There is no need to choose or prefer one type of love to another. Biological love (first and second chakras) is a wonderful experience, especially when it is enveloped in the astonishing compassion of the universal heart (fourth chakra). Artistic expression (second and fifth chakras) is ecstatic and holy, especially when it is immersed in the divine urge to create (sixth chakra).

This means that the chakra system teaches us how to become fully realized human beings not only in the transcendental context, but also in the context of our complete potential. With the help of these seven layers, we will never miss even one single bit of the great possibilities of life on this earth. Living fully does not mean choosing one perspective, but rather celebrating our multidimensional range of perspectives. This range of perspectives reveals our unique human destiny, which is to embrace and unite heaven and earth, and to have deep earthly roots while still spreading our wings toward sublime heights. This can be thought of as the eighth lesson of life!

As long as our seven chakras are not all fully stabilized and awakened, we will find ourselves every so often identifying with one specific chakra. We will perceive everything through the lenses of this chakra since it is the center of our current teachings and lessons. This 'entrapment' in one layer is, in fact, natural and unavoidable. Actually, once we understand the teachings of each chakra, we will be able to trace anyone's perspectives, convictions and reactions back to the corresponding learning stage of the chakras. When we reach the sixth chakra, after stabilizing the five lower chakras, we will begin to integrate them all into one holistic, multidimensional perspective. In the seventh chakra, we will finally unite all of the perspectives into a super-perspective, creating the transpersonal eighth chakra. The eighth chakra will absorb all seven chakras into one unified line of consciousness. Then, the seven chakras become seven tools of expression within one free being. This being is able to live life the way it is meant to be, like a colorful and magnificent rainbow.

Appendix 1:
The Journey of *Kundalini* Along the Chakras

In this additional chapter, I will discuss in detail the dynamics that bring about transformations in the chakra system. There is no real difference between discussing the somewhat abstract notion of spiritual transformation (enlightenment or liberation) and discussing the awakening process of all seven chakras—spiritual transformation *is* this very process of awakening. In other words, the awakened seven chakras are the anatomy of enlightenment.

Understanding the awakening of the chakras equips us with an overwhelmingly clear map of the different stages that lead to the culmination of spiritual transformation and final liberation.

Before we go into the actual dynamics, we must get to know the two facets of our subtle being better: our anatomy and our physiology.

Basic Subtle Anatomy

The chakras constitute a central part of the subtle anatomy, but another major part is the *nadi* system. Both the chakras and the *nadi* system are essential for understanding the dynamics of liberation. There is a third important part of the anatomy known as *Koshas*—different layers of consciousness and subtle bodies—but they will be mostly ignored in this chapter in order to better focus on the chakra system.

The seven chakras are glands of the subtle anatomy. Just like physical glands, they are organs that process, produce and secrete substances, but unlike physical glands, the substances produced here are mental, emotional, energetic and spiritual. When the chakras are highly energized by cosmic *prana*, these raw materials can be transmuted into more and more refined states of consciousness. The chakras can actually alchemize any given state of mind, raising it to a higher level of awareness.

The *nadis* make up the nervous system of the subtle anatomy. They are hollow channels that are very similar not only to the nerves, but also to blood vessels and the lymphatic system. The many thousands of branches of this nervous system actually intersect at seven major points—which are, not surprisingly, the seven chakras. The *nadis* ('streams') function as conductors, which allow subtle energies to pass throughout the entire body, both energetic and physical, including through the brain, nerves, endocrine system, organs, skeleton and cells. The *nadis* interact with the physical nervous system, and are aided in their mission by the chakras' ability to translate subtle energy into material energy and material energy into subtle energy.

There are fourteen major *nadis*, while three of them are particularly relevant and directly connected to the seven chakras: these are the *sushumna*, the *pingala* and the *ida*.

The *sushumna* is the central *nadi*, which makes it the central energy channel. It is, in fact, the equivalent of the vertebral column; it even follows the same line (although the *sushumna* is straight and crosses the center of the body). The *sushumna* starts at the base of the spine and ends at the crown chakra, where it branches out into two new routes—one which passes through the sixth chakra before it reaches the Brahma Randhra (the gap between the two hemispheres), and one which passes through the back of the skull before it reaches the Brahma Randhra. The *sushumna* itself consists of three separate layers of *nadis*: the outer layer is the *sushumna*, the middle is the vajra and the inner is the chitra or citrini. During the process of liberation, the citrini *nadi*, the core of *sushumna*, transmutes into the extraordinarily important Brahma *nadi*, the column of light. The Brahma *nadi* leads directly to the Brahama Randhra, and, in a way, is the equivalent of the spinal cord.

The *sushumna* is the central supplier of *prana* to the chakras and all other energetic organs. It is the *nadi* that allows the rise of the *kundalini* (the spiritualizing force) and it is the *nadi* responsible for the absorption of cosmic *prana* through the crown chakra.

In the *sushumna* there are three *granthis* (knots), which function as gateways for *prana* rising. They either block or enable the flow of *prana* throughout the *sushumna*, thus playing an important role in the awakening process. The first granthi is in the area of the first chakra, the second is in the area of the heart and the third is in the area of the sixth chakra.

The other two central *nadis*, the *pingala* and the *ida*, are intertwined and wrap around the *sushumna nadi*, intersecting at the first six chakras. Both start below the first chakra and end in the sixth chakra, and because of their coiled shape (which resembles the structure of the DNA double helix), they have traditionally been perceived as two intertwined snakes. Just like the *sushumna nadi*, both the *pingala* and *ida* originate in the kanda region beneath the first chakra, and this point is called the *yukta triveni*—which means the coming together of three streams.

The *pingala* starts on the right, beneath the first chakra, and ends on the right side of the sixth chakra. Traditionally it is connected with the sun. It is responsible for masculine energy and psychology. For the more physiological aspect, it is responsible for physical movement and activity, vitality, power, mental efficiency and constructive actions. Energetically, it has a heating effect. For the psychological aspect, it is responsible for motivation, ambition, willpower, wisdom and the desire for deeper spiritual knowledge. It gives shape to the right half of each chakra, and therefore determines the balance or imbalance of the masculine aspects of each chakra. When the *pingala* is unbalanced, it will be expressed through the chakras as anger, righteousness, criticism, over-ambition and self-centeredness.

The *Ida* starts on the left, beneath the first chakra, and ends on the left side of the sixth chakra. Traditionally, it is connected to the moon. It is responsible for feminine energy and psychology. For the physiological aspect, it is responsible for the parasympathetic nervous system, and it also has a cooling effect; it conducts mental and pranic energy, can calm the mind, and can tone down material impulses. For the psychological aspect, it expresses passivity and withdrawal and is connected to soul-like qualities, such as caring, love, devotion, intuition, inspiration and emotion. It gives shape to the left half of each chakra, and therefore determines the balance or imbalance of the feminine aspects of each chakra. When the *Ida* is unbalanced it will be expressed through the chakras as remoteness, a lack of grounding, a lack of emotional and intuitive balance, possessiveness, dependency, insomnia, fear and nightmares, vulnerability, a loss of healthy self-limitations, psychological and sensual hyper-sensitivity, weakness and exhaustion.

Both *pingala* and *ida* play a major part in the awakening process of the chakras, supporting the rise of the *prana* throughout the *sushumna*, and awakening the dormant spiritual potential of each chakra.

Basic Subtle Physiology

There are four important forces in our subtle physiology: *kundalini, ojas, tejas* and *prana*. All four forces originate in the kanda region below the first chakra, which is also the origin of the *nadi* system. This region holds the life-force for both the body and the psyche. This is the basic life-force in its undivided, wholesome form; it is a spark of the universal or cosmic life-force.

Classically, this wholesome life-force is called *shakti kundalini*, and is usually thought of as being 'coiled like a serpent' in three and a half coils. In 'Yoga Vasistha' it is said that the shakti *kundalini* resides within a *nadi* called antravestika. This *nadi* is the source of one hundred other *nadis*, and it is connected to all the subtle pathways, from the first chakra to the crown chakra; all *nadis* are connected to it. It is the seed of all awareness and consciousness. It is also said that this energy is the primordial power in all beings, and the catalyst of all other forces in the body and psyche.

The shakti *kundalini* has two aspects. The more mundane aspects are responsible for supplying the vital energy force that runs all the daily and ordinary functions of the body and the psyche, while the dormant aspects are made up of potential energy, which patiently waits to spring upward for the sake of higher levels of consciousness. This spiritual aspect of the shakti *kundalini* also holds an inherent merging impulse, which aspires to go upwards and to unite with the greater cosmic life-force (or cosmic *kundalini*)—to unite the drop with the ocean.

The vital life force lies beneath the first chakra in its wholesome, undivided state, but when it leaves its abode and moves along the body, it branches off into three different forces: *prana*, *ojas* and *tejas*. These three forces interact to create life in the body and psyche.

Prana can be considered the basic vital life force. Basically, *prana* fills the entire universe with the subtle breath of life, not only the individual body. It is the subtle energy of air and ether, and can be thought of as the oxygen of the subtle anatomy—the life energy that sustains the body and mind. *Prana* is the guiding energy behind psycho-physiological functions and the coordination of breath, the senses and the mind. It is also the driving force behind deeper spiritual states of consciousness. *Tejas* is the inner fire, and is deeply connected to the fire aspect of the spiritual *kundalini*. Physiologically speaking, it is the inner radiance and intelligence of the body, but on a subtler level, it also energizes and governs higher perceptual capacities. *Ojas* is the subtle energy of water and earth. It is the stored-up energetic life force of the body, the primal vigor. It is responsible for physical, sexual, mental and spiritual endurance.

Our physical and subtle foundation and balance depend on the strength of *ojas*. *Tejas* is the heat and light energy of *ojas*. *Prana* is the energy that radiates from *ojas* after *tejas* sets it on fire. *Prana* is the energy behind all psycho-physiological functions. We need to 'burn' *ojas* to create *prana* in precisely the way one burns logs in order to create fire. The *prana* is the result of the burning *ojas*—and it is necessary for the vitality of the various psycho-physiological functions.

The cosmic *kundalini* continually descends, in its pure form, through the crown chakra, energizing the sixth and the seventh chakras directly. From there, it moves down the body to energize the other chakras. In this process, it interfaces with the shakti *kundalini*, which is rising from its source just below the first chakra. However, by the time the cosmic *kundalini* reaches the stored energetic center of the shakti *kundalini*, there is not enough combined energy to ignite the stored spiritual aspects of the shakti *kundalini*. At the same time, a certain amount of the shakti *kundalini* is always moving up the spinal cord, fulfilling its function as the prime life force of the body, and will eventually reach the brain. Both cosmic *kundalini* and shakti *kundalini* are waiting for a moment of combustion, in which they will unite, and thus spiritualize the entire body-mind complex.

Now that I have presented the different participants in the process of transformation—on the one hand, the anatomy of *nadis* and chakras, and on the other hand, the physiology of the *kundalini*, *ojas*, *tejas* and *prana*—we can take a deeper look at the dynamics of the awakening process.

The Process of Awakening

There are four major stages in the transformational process of awakening:

Initial Kundalini Awakenings

This stage can sometimes last for a whole lifetime. In this stage, there are many minor 'combustions' of union between the cosmic *kundalini* and the shakti *kundalini*. The combustions result from a temporary alignment between all of the chakras, a sudden *kundalini* flow or an increase of *prana*—all of which can occur through meditation, inspiration from nature, contemplation, the presence of a spiritual teacher or a spiritual community, and so on. These moments of union can be quite short (a few seconds or minutes) or quite long (a few hours, days or even weeks). Nevertheless, they dissipate in time, leaving us with the imprints of heart based knowledge and spiritual wisdom and longing. In these initial awakenings, the dormant spiritual aspect of the shakti *kundalini* awakens, causing a pranic surge upwards in the *sushumna*. *Tejas*, the internal fire, burns some *ojas*, causing a spread of spiritual heat throughout the *nadis* (mainly the three central *nadis*). The fourth, sixth and seventh chakras are highly stimulated by this pranic surge, and so they absorb much more of it. This then leads them to momentarily release new levels of their potential heightened awareness. These awakenings are more like cosmic invitations, which wake us up to the possibility of a stabilized, uninterrupted universal consciousness. However, without consistent spiritual longing, self-motivation and effort, purification of the chakras and intense spiritual practices, it is almost impossible to turn this cosmic invitation into an actual evolution.

An Irreversible Awakening

At a certain point, the cosmic *kundalini* manages to reach downwards with power and intensity, and at the same time, the spiritual shakti *kundalini* manages to reach upwards with power and intensity. This evokes a 'magnetic' attraction between the two, which is capable of drawing them naturally toward one another. From then on, a whole new process takes place, in which the cosmic *kundalini* continuously fills the *nadis* and chakras, and the shakti *kundalini* ceaselessly and effortlessly moves upwards, in pranic surges, through the *sushumna*, *pingala* and *ida nadis*.

The Process of the Awakened Kundalini

This is the inevitable outcome of an irreversible awakening. At this stage, the dormant spiritual *kundalini* awakens, and has enough momentum to keep moving upwards, through the *sushumna*, and to never go back to sleep. The *kundalini* continuously 'shoots' pranic surges upwards, energizing the *sushumna*, *pingala* and *ida nadis*. This pranic flow energizes the chakras, and as a result, they absorb more cosmic energy and release more of their heightened awareness and capacity. However, the chakras also release their hidden *vrittis*, unconscious impressions, in order to clear away all disturbances of the pranic flow. Simultaneously, all *nadis* begin to release any blockages to the flow to the surface; the greater the flow, the greater the awareness of the resistance to the flow. The pranic flow is like a persistent river, which will flow at all costs and overcome all floodgates. The *kundalini* first focuses on the first granthi, which resides in the area of the first chakra. This means that hidden issues of the first chakra appear first; after the floodgate of the first granthi is removed, the *kundalini*, overcoming the great gravitational force of the first chakra, is much freer in its journey upwards. Whenever a chakra becomes awakened, there is a great leap in one's level of awareness and in one's ability to spiritually endure. Because *ojas* is being continuously burned by the internal fire, *tejas*, more and more *prana* is being released, which leads to powerful spiritual revelations and a corresponding demand for purification. This process lasts at least two years (for the most advanced yogis), but for most aspirants it will take seven, ten, twelve or even twenty-one years. Sometimes it is impossible for someone to complete in a lifetime.

Liberation (Or Pranic Union)

After the pranic flow of *kundalini* has sufficiently energized the *sushumna*, *pingala* and *ida*, and after the first six chakras have completed their major processes of awakening, the *sushumna* and the shakti *kundalini* are magnetized completely upwards, and are inevitably attracted to the cosmic *prana*. Now they aspire to break through all divisions and barriers between the individual life-force and the wholesome, universal life-force. With the power of this attraction and the tremendous pull of the cosmic force, the life-force can finally move to the crown chakra, thus creating an opening in the crown, through which cosmic energy can freely pour. All duality between the two kinds of *prana* and the two kinds of *kundalini* will then dissolve, and the aspirant will merge into the united consciousness, in which his or her own identity merges with the cosmic wholeness.

Let's proceed now into a more detailed description of this process, and examine what exactly takes place in the chakras during each one of the four stages of awakening.

The Awakening Chakras

The seven chakras are continuously working: absorbing pranic energy and translating it into material energy, connecting the different layers of body, mind and spirit, releasing psychological and psychosomatic imprints and accumulating new ones, gradually opening in the process of learning the seven wisdoms of life, and more. As long as the *kundalini* has not awakened sufficiently, we can only aspire to develop functional chakras—the ideal of balancing and spiritualizing the chakras is far from our reach until the spiritualizing force, the dormant spiritual *kundalini*, becomes active and conscious. It is only in the power of the *kundalini* to integrate the seven chakras into one unified and whole being; until then, we are inevitably fragmented and divided within ourselves into seven contradictory pieces of being.

Once awakened, the spiritual *kundalini* begins its sacred task of turning us into spiritual light-beings. It would be insufficient to simply ignite the three most spiritually potent chakras—the fourth, the sixth and the seventh—since every solid building needs foundations and every proud tree needs strong roots. So, the awakened *kundalini* works simultaneously at awakening the tremendous potential of the three higher chakras (through spiritual revelations and powerful energy boosts), and at purifying and 'building' the three lower chakras.

The three lower chakras are amazingly important to the process of awakening. They are also the most challenging task for the *kundalini*, because as long as they are unbalanced, the gravitational force in the subtle anatomy and the psyche will always pull us back to our ordinary earthly consciousness. Overcoming the gravitational force can shift our basic inclination forever—we will no longer be an aspiring seeker who has to push upwards, but rather an effortless wholesome wave of energy with a natural attraction toward the divine.

The three lower chakras always put our spiritual aspirations and strength to the test. Whenever our spiritual ego boosts us with the conviction that we are superior and evolved human beings, one financial storm, sexual desire, or societal pressure can and will immediately bring up untreated unconscious impressions, thus drowning us in confused and flawed reactions. Until we have managed to create a solid spiritual being, which can withstand all earthly pressures and circumstances, we will have to endure a painful fall after every spiritual peak: one moment we will be immersed in Samadhi, and the next we will once again become obsessed with personal drama.

In the detailed description of the awakening of the first three chakras, we learned that the *kundalini* supports the gradual development of an inner self that does not depend on externals. This inner self is stable (first chakra), joyful (second chakra) and powerful (third chakra). It draws its sense of stability, joy and power not from external phenomena, but rather from the rich and solid inner life of the spirit. This inner self can live in the world without the impending danger of loosing its spiritual foundations. It can totally and fully engage in the world, and at the same time, remain untouched and uncorrupted, since its sense of belonging is inward-oriented.

Clearing and balancing the first three chakras will also guarantee that we do not have unconscious impure motives that drive us toward spirituality and transformation. We are not mere escapists, who try to avoid life and drown their troubles and pain in fake Samadhi—we are mature human beings, who relate to life freely, and who are interested in transcendence simply because every grown up tree must turn his treetop toward the infinite sky. Of course, when we develop this level of maturity, there is no danger of becoming unbalanced in our spiritual journey—it's like having a solid vessel, which can withstand the powerful and occasionally overwhelming energies of spiritual awakening.

The union of the three lower chakras creates an inner self that is totally independent of time and space. This greatly helps us to preserve our spiritually expanded consciousness for longer periods of time during our waking hours.

Throughout the continuous process of vertical *kundalini* flow, major blockages in the *sushumna, pingala* and *ida* appear ever more strongly. These major blockages must be fully released in order to give way to the flow.

The first kind of blockage is, of course, the unconscious impressions of imbalanced chakras, which appear as fixed personality tendencies. Whenever the pranic surges energize one or more chakras, these tendencies reveal the unconscious impressions that formed them in the first place. This is a thing to remember: the more a chakra is stimulated and energized by *prana*, the more it releases its specific layer of subconscious thought to the surface of our body and mind. Quite often, the psychological lesson that surfaces includes an interaction between at least two chakras, and this results in what we can regard as the periodical chakra map: a present map of chakra interactions, which will change once we complete the current chakra's lesson. Lessons are very often the outcomes of external pressures that bring forth relevant hidden psychological impressions—and the *kundalini* uses these external pressures to clear away blockages in its journey upwards.

We must keep in mind that the *kundalini* does not aspire to clear away all psychological and psychosomatic blockages and disturbances, just the major chakra blockages that hinder its direct vertical flow. These major blockages always have something to do with the seven lessons of life, which are the essentials of human spiritual evolution.

Blockages in the chakras are divided into two main categories: the masculine type and the feminine type. Every chakra consists of two halves, the right half connects with the right *nadi*, the *pingala*, and the left half connects with the left *nadi*, the *ida*. Each one of us has either masculine imbalances or feminine imbalances in one or more of our chakras—sometimes we have one major tendency, which means we have, in general, more *pingala* or *ida* oriented imbalances. Those who are addicted to control, sex, power, ambition, anger, detachment, independence, leadership, intellect and ego, are naturally more *pingala*-oriented in their imbalances. Those who are addicted to worries and anxieties, guilt and shame, weakness and dependence, emotional attachments, shyness and withdrawal, and those who are used to surrendering to others' views and influences and habitually submitting themselves to external powers or authorities, are naturally more *ida*-oriented in their imbalances.

Correspondingly, by clearing these masculine and feminine imbalances, we move away from the extremities of the *pingala* and *ida*. Gradually, these two *nadis* align with the central column, the *sushumna*, which unifies the two halves of male and female energies into one holistic flow. Instead of attracting too much *prana* toward their own separated streams, the *pingala* and *ida* begin to support the major pranic flow, thus promoting the unification of the male and female basic duality. Slowly but surely the *pingala* and the *ida* start influencing the awakening of the higher spiritual aspects of the masculine and feminine halves of the chakras, which then unite into one paradoxical enlightened expression and action.

The second kind of blockage is caused by the already-discussed three *granthis*, or knots, which are basically meant to prevent a dangerous overflow of pranic energy. An overflow might endanger and destabilize the tender *nadis*, physical nervous system and brain. So basically, *granthis* are guards that are destined to keep the subtle balance. They only allow the full flow of energy when the spiritual *kundalini* has completed its full awakening process for certain fragments in the *sushumna*, *pingala* and *ida*. When the three lower chakras become unified as one string of awakened awareness, a more powerful surge of energy is allowed upwards, since we have become much more capable of enduring large amounts of *prana*—here the principle of strong roots is reaffirmed. When the heart chakra fully blossoms, the second knot opens up and there is a leap in our evolution. When the sixth chakra awakens, the third knot opens up, and we are ready to complete the journey through the chakras, which is essentially the journey toward the realization of life itself.

After the unification of the three lower chakras, the journey of the *kundalini* along the higher four chakras becomes significantly easier. The law of the chakras is that when the lower chakras stabilize, the higher four respond with a gradual alignment.

The higher four chakras (especially the fourth, the sixth and the seventh) evoke tremendous spiritual energies and transmute consciousness during their awakening process. They strongly develop and expand the subtler koshas (layers of consciousness), and they create radiation, which actually forms our light-being.

The fourth chakra is the center—or the 'heart'—of the *kundalini* process. It is just between the awakening of our earthly dimensions and the awakening of our heavenly dimensions. It is even divided within itself between the lower heart chakra and the higher heart chakra (located in the area of the thymus gland). When the heart chakra opens fully, our sense of identity expands. While the self of the awakened three lower chakras is an inner being, who is free from time and space, the self of the awakened fourth chakra is unified with everything. This self has no boundaries, and it is immersed in the consciousness of oneness. Jesus beautifully expressed the awakening of the heart in *The Gospel of Thomas* when he declared, "Split a piece of wood; I am there. Lift up a stone, and you will find me there."

The fourth chakra, in its awakening, clears the way for an upper pranic surge and engenders the transcendental self. Just like the three lower chakras, the fifth, sixth and seventh chakras are destined to form a whole unit of consciousness.

When the upper pranic surge approaches the sixth chakra, the *pingala* and *ida* combine into one awareness that transcends the duality between male and female energies. The central column, the *sushumna*, awakens and is strongly felt, and it also becomes visible to the aspirant's inner eye. The Brahma *nadi*, which is the thin, light *nadi* that is enveloped in the two layers of the *sushumna*, conducts refined spiritual *prana* into the Brahma Randhra—the gap between the two hemispheres that is connected to the seventh chakra—and in doing so, it takes the yogi beyond time, space and existence and leads him into an uninterrupted union with the cosmic *prana*.

When there is a sufficient pranic flow in the Brahma *nadi*, it pierces the center of the skull and creates a cosmic union. All seven chakras become one unit of consciousness, and they will never again be activated as fragmented and divided layers of the psyche. The different chakras and the *sushumna* become fully saturated in the ocean of cosmic *prana*, and the cosmic *prana* flows into the subtle anatomy of the yogi in ever greater waves. The symbol of the caduceus becomes alive within us.

The chakras form one awakened unit of consciousness and their different levels of awareness are actually transcended, shifting the focus into the eighth chakra. The eighth chakra is above the head and is completely transpersonal by its very nature. The eighth chakra is both all-inclusive and beyond all levels of consciousness. It is a clear conductor of the infinite light of the divine, and only uses the seven chakras as tools of expression and manifestation.

This is the power of the spiritual *kundalini*, which is the most important subtle force for the spiritual evolution of mankind. The spiritual *kundalini* is the unifying force that drives all dualities toward their potential final union, wholeness, harmony and fulfillment, and eventually turns them into one eternal being. The spiritual *kundalini* unifies the *pingala* and the *ida*, the *tejas*, *ojas* and *prana*, the individual *prana* and the cosmic *prana*, the seven chakras, the shakti *kundalini* and the cosmic *kundalini*, earth and heaven, matter and spirit, and the self and God. In this process of unification, the *kundalini* finally reveals the highest purpose of the chakras, which is to serve as a sublime evolutionary structure that enables material organisms to channel the awareness of divinity.

Appendix 2:
Questionnaires for Self-Evaluation

1. Chakra Personality Type Evaluation

Introduction

The teaching of the chakras tells us that each one of us has, at the core of our personality, one major chakra that shapes our most fundamental worldview, our set of values, our attractions and repulsions, our professional inclinations and our behavioral expressions and reactions. In the section titled 'chakra personality type,' which appears in each chakra's presentation, you can find a brief description of the basic outline of the specific chakra's personality type.

It is very important to understand that our chakra personality type has nothing to do with our level of balance or imbalance in any specific chakra. Rather, a chakra personality type is determined by our inherent tendencies and attractions, our longings and aspirations, our basic psychological and energetic structures, our natural worldview, our set of values and our gut-feelings regarding the meaning of life. So, even if we have an intense imbalance in a specific chakra that leads us to pay more attention to a specific layer of our psyche and life, it does not hint at all at our personality orientation.

There is no one higher or superior chakra personality type, so please don't try to manipulate the results of this questionnaire. Each personality type plays an immense and necessary role on this planet, and once a personality type blossoms and radiates its unique gifts, the magnitude of its influence can be extraordinary: Confucius and Moses were amazing expressions of the first chakra, while Einstein embodied the sixth and Gautama the Buddha, the seventh. Who can really say which person was more important and essential for the evolution of mankind?

In a very gross estimation, 40% of the human population possess a first chakra personality type. This high percentage makes a lot of sense, since first chakra personalities are the builders of the world—those who lay out the foundations, structures and orders. Following this high percentage are the third chakra personalities, which make up about 25%. These types of people have energetic minds and bodies and they drive the world toward further achievements, goals and destinations. 15%

of the population are the fourth chakra personality type. They are the people who express the power of emotion and love (among them are activists, social reformers, and those who run world movements for change, religious movements of sacrifice and devotion and so on). 7% of the population are a fifth chakra personality type. They are leaders, teachers, speakers and charismatic guides of all kinds. Another 7% includes the second chakra personality type: artists, adventurers and world-explorers. 5% are the sixth chakra personality type—the philosophers, contemplative scientists, inventors and 'wise ones'—and only 1% of the human population are a seventh chakra personality type. They are natural-born renouncers and great meditators.

Along with this central chakra personality type, we possess a secondary chakra personality type. This secondary chakra can be seen as the means through which we realize our major chakra's personality.

For example, if my central chakra is the sixth chakra, which implies that I am a philosopher, a scientist or some sort of developer of ideas, my central tendency can be aided by the fifth chakra, which enables me to accurately and lucidly express my philosophical visions to the world. This combination usually characterizes philosophers or scientists who are destined to bring very clear and structured teachings into the world, teachings that will help change the lives of many.

We can easily deduce that 42 chakra personality types exist in the world, since each chakra has six possible secondary chakras.

At the same time we must remember that eventually, after the full awakening of the seven chakras and their unification into one holistic unit, one will become, in many respects, an all-inclusive 'eighth chakra personality type.' This trans-personality type, which resides in the eighth chakra (beyond the vertex), includes all seven worldviews, types of happiness and awakened capacities, and yet it is also a totally transcendent state of being—the whole is greater than the sum of its parts.

This transcendent, transpersonal personality type is simultaneously a developmental stage beyond any 'I AM' (and therefore beyond all definitions of mere personality) and a free expression of the seven different wisdoms. It is also more than that, since the liberated personality still embodies one dominant chakra and one secondary chakra. These two chakras combine in the radiant manifestation of their unique aspects of divinity. As the seven chakras represent seven aspects of the divine, every person is destined to manifest one central aspect of divinity and one secondary aspect of divinity, and the eighth personality type can successfully and elegantly demonstrate that to the world.

The following questionnaire will enable you to determine your central personality type along with your secondary personality type. This is done very easily, by calculating the points you accumulate when answering the statements accurately and honestly. When you answer, remember: *choose 1 if the saying perfectly relates to you, 2 if it matches your personality fairly well, 3 if the saying doesn't match your personality very much, and 4 if it doesn't match at all.*

If you accumulated 5-7 points in one chakra it is probably your central chakra. 7-9 points usually indicates that you located your secondary chakra. Chakras in which you accumulated more than 10 points should be quite far from your fundamental personality. However, do not get attached to these numbers—instead, simply check which chakra gave you *the least amount of points*, and that one will be the closest to you; then check to see which chakra had the second lowest number of points and this will be your secondary chakra.

For example, if this is my result:

First chakra—15 points;
Second chakra—20 points;
Third chakra—12 points;
Fourth chakra—6 points;
Fifth chakra—7 points;
Sixth chakra—11 points;
Seventh chakra—12 points,

it means that my central chakra is the fourth chakra, and my secondary chakra is the fifth chakra. This result, by the way, usually suits people who are destined to profound expressions of love, service, intimacy, oneness and compassion. The visibility of their heart expressions can be a great model for others.

It is possible, in rare cases, to get an equal result for two chakras. This implies that we have to go through a more detailed and thorough examination to determine our central personality type. If the results stand firm, then we are among one of the rare cases in which one person embodies a balanced combination of two personality types where both are fundamental to our personality type and necessary to each other's fulfillment.

It is not in the scope of this book to present the vast implications of realizing our chakra personality type. After you complete the questionnaire, you are advised to examine the following sections of this book about your central chakra and secondary chakra: 'Type of personality,' 'Type of happiness' and 'Life's meaning and purpose.' All of these sections give us a hint of the specified personality's worldview. You are also advised to examine the section on 'Psychosomatic disturbances,' as it is possible that you are prone to these specific disturbances. Lastly, the 'Recommended practices' may be more suitable for you than practices designed for other chakras (although these practices must be combined with intense practices for your most imbalanced chakras).

Other topics that do not appear in this book are, for example, the recommended way of living (including food, herbs and other kinds of physical nourishment), the unique challenges and obstacles, the unique life practices, the best spiritual practices and spiritual paths, the most suitable professions and careers and even the best romantic matches. The more we know about our chakra, the more useful it becomes to know our own uniqueness as reflected through the amazing chakra map.

First chakra

1. The nuclear family gives me a strong sense of security and stability, and I cannot actually imagine myself without it. The best thing in the world is to come back, at the end of each day, to the family nest.

   1 2 3 4

2. Laws, moral codes and societal or religious order give me a strong sense of inner order and relaxation. I feel good when everyone obeys the law and follows moral codes. The world feels right when it functions with the correct structures and with orderly behavior.

   1 2 3 4

3. I could easily and happily manage the same stable routines and the same life structures for the rest of my life—including the fixed hours and the fixed cycles of activity and rest. Basically, I prefer the life that I am familiar with, and I am not inclined toward intense and radical adventures that might disrupt this familiar life. I also like dealing with the small details of life, and I'm quite patient when doing that.

   1 2 3 4

4. I feel a deep and fundamental connection to my parents and my entire family lineage, to my land and my country, and to the tradition and the mentality into which I was born (or to any one of them in particular).

   1 2 3 4

5. I am capable of working for long periods of time (at least for two or three years) at an unexciting job, as long as the general conditions are good and there is a generous and stable income.

   1 2 3 4

Second chakra

1. Sex is a divine experience for me. It is among the greatest peak experiences of life. Sexual experiences are, in a way, my gateway to spiritual elevation and even transcendence.

   1 2 3 4

2. I love exciting and thrilling experiences. I love going on surprising adventures, and even being on the verge of real danger. I love the sensation of 'adrenalin' in my body.

   1 2 3 4

3. I can't spend even one day without experiencing some sort of intense pleasure, or a sensual and stimulating experience (such as a powerful sexual orgasm, dancing, hiking, nude-swimming, unrestrained humor, intense laughter, mischievousness, unruly behavior, wildness of any kind or even 'law-breaking').

   1 2 3 4

4. I experience life through powerful sensations. Life, for me, is a sensual and even erotic realm, and I feel like devouring every sensual opportunity in sight.

   1 2 3 4

5. There are many social taboos that I would like to break and many 'forbidden fruits' that I would like to taste in my lifetime—and I definitely intend on doing so!

   1 2 3 4

Third chakra

1. I love the feeling of achievement I get from conquering goals. For me, to be alive and to breathe means to constantly set goals before my eyes; whenever I reach a goal, I go for a new, more ambitious and advanced destination. I love the feeling of reaching a goal and then targeting another.

   1 2 3 4

2. I am a strong and opinionated individual. I have very well defined ideas and worldviews. I firmly stand for my beliefs, and I will not let anyone convince me otherwise or make me give up my beliefs.

   1 2 3 4

3. I have a tremendous amount of energy, and so am able to follow missions that I strongly trust and believe in, I'm capable of persevering and enduring, even when my body becomes tired. When following these missions, my self-discipline will never allow me to give in to weakness

and exhaustion. I usually end my work-days with a strong sense of intensity and achievement. I could go on and on, into the night if no one stopped me.

1 2 3 4

4. I believe that a man is measured by what he does and by his marked achievements—by what he leaves behind him at the end of his life.

1 2 3 4

5. I have a strong feeling that everything depends on me and lies completely on my shoulders. For this reason, I like to centralize power and tasks and organize them all by myself.

1 2 3 4

Fourth chakra

1. Emotions and relationships are the central theme in my daily thoughts.

1 2 3 4

2. In my mind, love—the experience of love and the realization of love— is the meaning and purpose of life; it is the supreme value and the highest destination.

1 2 3 4

3. Without the fulfillment of a deep romantic love, I will feel that my life lacks logic and meaning. The union between another and me gives meaning to everything.

1 2 3 4

4. The peak moments of my life were times when I shared profound intimacy and emotional vulnerability with other people, animals or God.

1 2 3 4

5. In my mind, love is the power that can save the world and change it for the better. Deep healing through love is the only real thing that this world needs.

1 2 3 4

Fifth chakra

1. From my direct experience and from other people's feedback I have learned that, when I talk to people, I magnetize, enrapture and influ-

ence them very strongly. It seems that I possess a high capacity to convince and influence those around me.

1 2 3 4

2. I can easily explain and interpret complex ideas in a very accessible and effective way. It seems that I can help others understand things that don't belong to their ordinary field of knowledge.

1 2 3 4

3. I excel in manifesting and materializing ideas and initiatives. There is a long list of ideas and initiatives that I have managed to realize and fulfill. I also have many plans in my mind that are waiting to be fulfilled in the future.

1 2 3 4

4. For me, the most important thing in the world is to succeed in voicing the truths I believe in. I am hoping to influence others in this way. I have a tremendous urge to express myself clearly and powerfully. It is like an engine that ceaselessly works and roars inside of me.

1 2 3 4

5. It is clear to me that I am capable of leading people toward the fulfillment of ideas that I believe in. It seems like the most natural thing for me is to guide and teach others.

1 2 3 4

Sixth chakra

1. Understanding how things work and why they work this way is my deepest urge in life. The central themes in my thoughts are universal questions, which are all motivated by my urge to decipher the laws behind the universe.

1 2 3 4

2. The most admirable role models in my mind are philosophers, inventors, researchers and other people who have managed to penetrate the mysteries of the universe through their wisdom and their inquiring minds. I follow in their foot-steps by trying to develop insight into the nature of the universe.

1 2 3 4

3. The things that give me the highest ecstasy are brilliant mental structures, perfect and wholesome ideas, wise models and ladders of development and sublime mental orders that accurately copy the subtle harmonies of the cosmos.

   1 2 3 4

4. Ever since I can remember, there was something in me that remained uninvolved, observing the world and humans as if from afar, and inquiring into their customs and habits. Quite often, this impersonal, detached and sometimes even arrogant observation seems stronger than life itself.

   1 2 3 4

5. Whenever a strong emotion appears inside of me, I am not interested in experiencing and feeling it, but I am interested in investigating it, as if I am a scientist observing a phenomenon in my lab. I passionately examine its more universal aspects, its dynamics and the general, impersonal insight that is concealed within it.

   1 2 3 4

Seventh chakra

1. Without any difficulty or doubt I could renounce the world and move into a cave for full-time meditation or join some spiritual order for the rest of my life. When abandoning the world I wouldn't feel any desire to return and fulfill missed opportunities.

   1 2 3 4

2. The subtle melting down of personal barriers is, for me, the supreme type of fulfillment and, in fact, the only type of fulfillment. Everything else is completely secondary and pales in significance.

   1 2 3 4

3. Observation of silence, fasts, solitude, retreats and very long meditation practices are very natural for me, and I tend to practice them quite often.

   1 2 3 4

4. Sexuality, romantic partnerships, family, self-fulfillment, advancement in life and achievements of any kind trouble my thoughts very little, if at all.

   1 2 3 4

5. The heavenly and spiritual realms are my true home, and I feel that, in a way, I did not originate from this earth. I carry the feeling with me daily that I actually abide in realms that are very far from the visible world, and that I'm only a guest in the material dimension.

   1   2   3   4

2. Chakra Imbalance Evaluation

Introduction

Basically, this entire book is a detailed and comprehensive description of psychological imbalances in the seven chakras, and the purpose of writing it was to encourage the reader toward a wholesome introspection of his or her psyche and life. That being said, this chakra imbalance evaluation can help you focus on your more central and essential imbalances.

No questionnaire can ever spare you from the challenge of being honest and real. Try to be truthful as you are facing the questions; examine your behavior and actions, rather than your self-image and what you would like to think of yourself. Try to imagine what others would have said about you—sometimes we get direct and consistent feedback that we choose to reject.

The recommended way to answer this questionnaire is to first fill it out by yourself in quiet and relaxed surroundings, and then to fill it out again with someone who knows you very well—someone who loves you and, at the same time, is capable of seeing your shortcomings. Some of us tend to be too stringent with ourselves, so in that case, the views of the other person might soften the results a bit. The advantage of another's view lies in the fact that other people can see us from the outside, as we are manifest through our behaviors and actions, while we tend to see ourselves from the inside, through our protective and sometimes self-denying self-image.

When you contemplate the truthfulness and relatedness of a certain saying, try to look back at your patterns of behavior as they have manifested in the last five years of your life.

You will notice that some chakras have five questions and some have six or seven questions. This does not alter the calculation at the end, and is actually intended to provide elaboration for the chakras that seem to require a more thorough estimation of their level of imbalance.

When you calculate the final results in each chakra, check how many a's and b's you accumulated. The a's and b's indicate a high or satisfactory level of balance. If you accumulated more c's and d's in a chakra, it means there is some level of imbalance or even an extreme imbalance in that chakra. Chakras with two c's or d's have some level of imbalance, while chakras which have three or more c's or d's have a high level of imbalance.

When you locate highly imbalanced chakras, it is advised that you re-read the relevant chapters. Always start with the lowest chakras, as higher chakras tend to automatically and naturally align with the balancing process of the lower chakras (but not vice versa!).

You can then create your current chakra map of imbalances, which will reveal your current developmental challenge. By balancing the imbalanced chakras, you are actually responding to your present stage of development. After sufficiently clearing this chakra map, you will realize that the map has changed and that you are facing a new and subtler level of challenge and development. That's why it is highly advised to fill out this questionnaire twice a year, every six months, in order to clarify the true developmental challenges ahead.

It is important to note that there are also more temporary chakra maps, which appear as a result of changing life pressures. One event can engender an entire set of chakra interactions, which subside soon afterwards. The following questionnaire doesn't, and cannot, cover these transient aspects, but rather brings up the more deep-rooted and fundamental tendencies of imbalance.

First chakra

1. How would you describe your ability to maintain a good and continuous livelihood, a stable job, healthy routine patterns and a solid family foundation or other interpersonal relationships?

   a. Very high.

   b. Quite satisfactory.

   c. Quite problematic.

   d. Low.

2. Describe your emotional solidity and balance in the face of crises and dramatic endings, such as separation from loved ones, divorce, dismissal from a job and death?

   a. I'm usually calm and practical.

   b. I'm distressed but can overcome it quite easily.

   c. I'm very emotional and worried.

   d. I tend to collapse into depression and anxiety.

3. Rate the level of your daily mental worry and concern. How many worries and concerns do you have throughout the day—such as 'What might happen with this or that? How will I get through this or that? How can I manage to make sure that things that should happen will happen, and how can I avoid the pain of the things that shouldn't happen?'

   a. Very few.

   b. Not very many.

   c. Many.

   d. A lot, worried almost all the time.

4. Describe your attitude and feelings toward your own physical death.

   a. I see it as a liberating and beautiful event.

   b. I feel calm and trusting.

   c. I never think about it.

   d. I have anxiety when I think of my own death.

5. Choose the most accurate description of your life experience.

   a. The world is manageable, challenges are easy to handle and pain is a healthy part of the flow.

   b. The world is tiresome, life is demanding and pain is something to get through.

   c. The world is harsh and painful, challenges are frightening and pain is overwhelming.

   d. The world is cruel and dangerous, life is extremely hard and pain is excruciating.

6. Describe your attitude toward food.

   a. Food is nourishing, but I don't really need it—I simply eat a little, only what is essential for my health.

   b. Food is something that I think about and crave.

   c. Food is my source of strength. I am afraid to be hungry, and I eat more than I need.

   d. Food is my comfort in life and also a source of happiness and fulfillment.

7. Describe your reaction when you go through intense physical pain, such as a disease, a sudden injury, or even a visit to the dentist's office.

   a. I am quiet and do not complain at all. I show no sign of misery and never shirk from any kind of physical suffering.

   b. I complain a little and flinch a little.

   c. I complain quite a lot, feel miserable and fear these situations very much.

   d. I find these situations unbearable.

Second chakra

1. Rate the level of your obsession, addiction and neediness regarding food (over-indulgence, sweets, junk foods) *or* sex (pornography, masturbation, ejaculation and orgasm). Please also include in this rating your obsessive and addictive thoughts.

   a. Very low.

   b. Moderate.

   c. High.

   d. Extremely high.

2. Rate your joy of living—is it low (morning depression, wanting to stay in bed, fatigue, dullness and a general 'turned off' feeling) or high (excitement for life, love of life and a ceaseless drive to live and experiment)?

   a. Very high.

   b. Moderate.

   c. Low.

   d. Very low.

3. Rate your life-force energy—is it low (chronic fatigue, weakness, dragging yourself from one place to another) or high (bubbling energy and an abundant sense of vigor)?

   a. Very high.

   b. Moderate.

   c. Low.

   d. Very low.

4. Rate your creative urge—is it low (no creative urge, no new ideas and creative initiatives) or high (inexhaustible creative urges, endless new ideas and initiatives)?

   a. Very high.

   b. Moderate.

   c. Low.

   d. Very low.

5. Try to imagine: if there were no good and bad, no should and shouldn't, and no laws or social limitations, how different would your life have been?

   a. Exactly the same.

   b. Different in some ways.

   c. Quite different.

   d. Very different.

6. Rate your sexual appetite.

   a. It is there, but awakens only in response to natural and healthy sexual situations.

   b. It can be out of balance sometimes: either going too low or going too high.

   c. It is too high / it is too low.

   d. It is extremely high / It is extremely low.

Third chakra

1. Rate the level of your daily anger—is it very low (almost absent both in thoughts and in behavior) or very high (outbursts of all-consuming rage)?

   a. Very low.

   b. Moderate.

   c. High.

   d. Very high.

2. How much can you see of yourself in these two characteristics: a tendency to over-do things and to be over-achieving, always having to do something and reach some goal; a tendency to feel incapable of doing anything, to lack self-discipline and to have very little willpower and perseverance.

   a. These two characteristics are very far from me.

   b. I can see myself a little in one of these two.

   c. I can see myself a lot in one of these two.

   d. One of these characteristics is just how I feel and behave.

3. How much can you see of yourself in these two characteristics: I'm easily and powerfully affected by any passing emotion, such as fear, worry or desire; I ignore my feelings—I have no time for them.

   a. These two characteristics are very far from me.

   b. I can see myself a little in one of these two.

   c. I can see myself a lot in one of these two.

   d. One of these characteristics is just how I feel and behave.

4. How much of yourself can you see in these two characteristics: I'm easily influenced and persuaded by strong people with strong minds, and I'm intim*ida*ted by powerful authorities; I'm so convinced of my belief system that nobody can ever influence me or change my mind.

   a. These two characteristics are very far from me.

   b. I can see myself a little in one of these two.

   c. I can see myself a lot in one of these two.

   d. One of these characteristics is just how I feel and behave.

5. How much can you see of yourself in these two characteristics: I am extremely critical, judgmental, domineering and impatient with other people; I am really concerned about what others think of me, and I do my best to conform to their good judgment.

   a. These two characteristics are very far from me.

   b. I can see myself a little in one of these two.

   c. I can see myself a lot in one of these two.

   d. One of these characteristics is just how I feel and behave.

6. How much can you see of yourself in these two characteristics: I feel that my life is totally out of my hands and that I'm unable to choose and shape my own destiny; I feel that life is in my hands, that it is totally in my control and it is my responsibility to shape my destiny.

   a. These two characteristics are very far from me.

   b. I can see myself a little in one of these two.

   c. I can see myself a lot in one of these two.

   d. One of these characteristics is just how I feel and behave.

Fourth chakra

1. How easy is it for you to maintain a lasting, stable and deep romantic relationship in the face of the challenging and demanding crises that sometimes accompany it?

   a. Very easy and natural.

   b. Quite easy, although sometimes it requires overcoming my tendencies.

   c. Quite problematic.

   d. Quite impossible.

2. How do you feel in moments of profound and vulnerable intimacy, when it seems like you can be seen completely by the other and that you can see the other completely?

   a. Wonderful! I am waiting for these kinds of moments!

   b. It feels right, although a bit uncomfortable.

   c. It is awkward and embarrassing for me.

   d. It is terrible! I want to run away.

3. Rate the degree of your self-contentment—how deeply complete do you feel? Do you feel that you don't need the other's love and appreciation, or do you feel that you always need affirmations that you are loved and appreciated from those around you? Do you share love without demands or with many frustrated expectations?

   a. I'm highly content and carry no expectations.

   b. I'm quite independent, but I do have demands and expectations.

   c. I strongly feel that I need love and appreciation from those around me.

   d. I feel totally dependent and am filled with expectations.

4. What happens when someone abandons you or 'betrays' your trust in any way?

   a. I understand their point of view and let them be.

   b. I am slightly disappointed but can easily move on.

   c. I feel offended and sorrowful.

   d. I am deeply hurt, lonesome and shaken to the core.

5. How easy is it for you to serve others abundantly, without thinking of yourself and your own needs?

   a. Very easy!

   b. Natural, but I'm sometimes divided within myself.

   c. It takes effort.

   d. Extremely hard and unnatural.

Fifth chakra

1. Estimate your ability to manifest and realize creative urges, initiatives and ideas. How easily can you follow the process of manifestation without doubts, fears, hesitation or procrastination?

   a. It is the most natural and enjoyable thing for me.

   b. It is troublesome, but it happens in a quite satisfactory manner.

   c. It is difficult and I often fail.

   d. I almost always fail. I mostly give up before the process even begins.

2. How much can you see of yourself in these two characteristics: I'm a chatty person who likes to gossip, and I very often tend to ceaselessly speak without paying too much attention to other's needs; I'm a quiet person who finds it very hard to speak out, so I often simply withdraw into a protective bunker.

   a. These two characteristics are very far from me.

   b. I can see myself a little in one of these two.

   c. I can see myself a lot in one of these two.

   d. One of these characteristics is just how I feel and behave.

3. How capable are you of voicing unpopular opinions and points of view? Are you usually capable of saying them, even when they endanger your status and popularity, or do you often avoid it in the effort to maintain harmony and status?

   a. I write or say unpopular things when I feel I have to.

   b. I say unpopular things, though with some degree of hesitation and fear.

   c. I rarely say unpopular things.

   d. I'll always avoid it as much as I can.

4. How much of your real self is known to the world? Is your true self fully presented to the outside world, or is there a division between what people see in your display window and who you actually are (what you feel and what you know deep inside).

   a. My true self is completely visible.

   b. I am mostly visible to the world.

   c. Perhaps fifty percent of my real self is visible.

   d. The division is very strong between my real self and my perceived self.

5. How easily and clearly can you express your inner ideas, feelings and experiences to others?

    a. I am extremely clear and precise, and everyone can understand me.

    b. I am a bit foggy and confused in my transmission, though mostly understandable.

    c. Often people don't understand what I'm trying to convey, and both sides become quite frustrated.

    d. It's extremely hard for me to convey my inner thoughts to others.

Sixth chakra

1. Rate the level of your daily mental activity. Do you possess a silent, still and calm mind, or are your thoughts swirling around, restless, contradictory and in a constant inner quarrel?

    a. My mind is still, relaxed and uninterrupted.

    b. I mostly possess a quiet and relaxed mind.

    c. My mind is active and often distorted.

    d. My mind is always working, 24 hours a day, and there's always some level of tension and restlessness.

2. How easily can you sit for an hour of uninterrupted silent meditation?

    a. Very easily and happily!

    b. Quite easily and comfortably.

    c. It is difficult and demanding.

    d. It is impossible.

3. How easily and clearly can you focus on one thing for a long time—for example, at work or while listening to a lecture?

    a. I'm totally focused. Nothing can disturb me.

    b. I can focus, but I can also go astray from time to time.

    c. Focusing is hard for me, and I need to take many breaks.

    d. Focusing is almost impossible.

4. Describe the process of your decision-making. How easily can you tell what's right and what's wrong? How do you tend to handle this process in general?

    a. I listen attentively and with a quiet mind when making a decision, and the answer comes of its own accord.

    b. Decision-making takes some effort and thought, but I'm quite clear and decisive.

    c. Decision-making is stressful and demanding.

    d. Decision-making often leads to a stressful breakdown.

5. How easily can you fathom complex philosophical ideas that are clearly beyond your present capacity of understanding? How do you approach a higher level of complexity?

    a. I'm extremely attracted to higher wisdom and joyfully delve in it.

    b. I feel interested, and I can grasp the idea after some effort.

    c. It doesn't attract me, and it's demanding.

    d. I usually avoid complexity.

Seventh chakra

1. How attracted are you to the idea of reaching broader and limitless states of consciousness?

    a. Extremely attracted. My attraction is fearless, powerful and easily fulfilled.

    b. Quite attracted, though a bit ambivalent.

    c. I have very little attraction toward these things.

    d. Not attracted at all.

2. Describe your connection to God (the source of all-life).

    a. God is my real inner self, into which I totally merge. God is my own unlimited consciousness, which is to be revealed through intense meditation.

    b. I feel a tremendous love for God. I am devoted to God and I surrender to God.

    c. I believe in God and trust Him totally.

    d. Only the material realm exists. God is a superstition.

3. Rate your level of affinity with this sentence: 'The meditative state is the only bliss one can ever realize and fulfill.'

   a. This is my sentence!

   b. Quite accurate for me, though there are also other kinds of happiness that I can think of.

   c. There is some truth in it, though very partial.

   d. There is no truth in this sentence as far as I'm concerned.

4. In meditation, how easy is it for you, to leave the whole world behind, including all thought forms, and to dissolve your ordinary self?

   a. It happens in less than a second.

   b. It happens, but it takes some settling in.

   c. It only happens in special occasions and unique circumstances.

   d. It never happens.

5. What do you think of enlightened masters and teachers of enlightenment?

   a. They are external representations of my one true self. I easily merge with their inner being.

   b. They are a tremendous inspiration and a great source of wisdom.

   c. They are interesting, thought-provoking and challenging to the mind.

   d. I have no interest in them.

6. Rate the fulfillment of your meditative drive. How much do you actually practice serious meditation?

   a. The meditative practice is an integral and highly active part of my daily life.

   b. My involvement with actual meditative practices can fluctuate from time to time, but usually it is very high.

   c. I meditate sometimes, but I usually don't possess the required self-discipline.

   d. I seldom meditate.

Bibliography

Barbara Brennan, *Hands of Light: A guide to healing through the human energy field*, Bantam Books, 1988.

Gabriel Cousens, *Spiritual Nutrition*, North Atlantic Books Berkeley, California, 2005.

Cyndi Dale, *The Subtle Body: An encyclopedia of your energetic anatomy*, Sounds True, 2009.

Colin Griffith, *The New Materia Medica: Key remedies for the future of homeopathy*, Watkins Publishing, London, 2007.

Patricia Mercier, *The Chakra Bible*, Octopus publishing group, 2009.

Swami Venkatesanada, *Vasishta's Yoga*, State University of New York Press, 1993.

Other Books by MSI Press

A Believer-in-Waiting's First Encounters with God

Blest Atheist

El Poder de lo Transpersonal

Forget the Goal, the Journey Counts...71 Jobs Later

The Gospel of Damascus

Joshuanism

Losing My Voice and Finding Another

Mommy Posioned Our House Guest

Publishing for Smarties

Road to Damascus

The Rise & Fall of Muslim Civil Society

Syrian Folktales

The Marriage Whisperer

Understanding the People Around You: An Introduction to Socionics

When You're Shoved from the Right, Look to the Left: Metaphors of Islamic Humanism

Widow A Survival Guide for the First Year

Shai Tubali